Music in Video Ga

In recent years, video gaming has taken its place alongside film and television as one of the dominant forms of media; indeed, in terms of sales and mass consumption, video gaming has begun to overtake its older, and less interactive, media progenitors. One of the most important—and most ignored—aspects of video gaming is the (often ubiquitous) music. From its earliest days as little more than a series of monophonic outbursts to its current-day scores that can rival major symphonic film scores, video game music has gone through its own particular set of stylistic and functional metamorphoses while both borrowing and recontextualizing the earlier models from which it borrows. With topics ranging from early classics such as *Donkey Kong* and *Super Mario Bros.* to more recent hits such as *Plants vs. Zombies*, the 11 essays in *Music in Video Games* draw on the scholarly fields of musicology and music theory, film theory, and game studies to investigate the history, function, style, and conventions of video game music.

K.J. Donnelly is Reader in Film at the University of Southampton, where he convenes the Film Studies masters program.

William Gibbons is Assistant Professor of Musicology at Texas Christian University. His primary areas of research interest are opera studies and music in video games.

Neil Lerner is Professor of Music at Davidson College, where he is co-coordinator of the concentration in film and media studies. He serves as Editor of the journal *American Music*.

Routledge Music and Screen Media Series

Series Editor: Neil Lerner

The **Routledge Music and Screen Media Series** offers edited collections of original essays on music in particular genres of cinema, television, video games, and new media. These edited essay collections are written for an inter-disciplinary audience of students and scholars of music, film and media studies.

Music in Video Games: Studying Play
Edited by K.J. Donnelly, William Gibbons, and Neil Lerner

The Music Documentary: Acid Rock to Electropop
Edited by Robert Edgar, Kirsty Fairclough-Isaacs, and Benjamin Halligan

Music in Science Fiction Television: Tuned to the Future
Edited by K.J. Donnelly and Philip Hayward

Music, Sound and Filmmakers: Sonic Style in Cinema
Edited by James Wierzbicki

Music in the Western: Notes from the Frontier
Edited by Kathryn Kalinak

Music in Television: Channels of Listening
Edited by James Deaville

Music in the Horror Film: Listening to Fear
Edited by Neil Lerner

Music in Video Games

Studying Play

Edited by

K.J. Donnelly
University of Southampton

William Gibbons
Texas Christian University

Neil Lerner
Davidson College

Routledge
Taylor & Francis Group

NEW YORK AND LONDON

First published 2014
by Routledge
711 Third Avenue, New York, NY 10017

and by Routledge
2 Park Square, Milton Park, Abingdon, Oxon OX14 4RN

Routledge is an imprint of the Taylor & Francis Group, an informa business

© 2014 Taylor & Francis

The right of K.J. Donnelly, William Gibbons, and Neil Lerner to be
identified as the editors of the editorial material, and of the authors for
their individual chapters, has been asserted in accordance with sections
77 and 78 of the Copyright, Designs and Patents Act 1988.

Library of Congress Cataloging in Publication Data
Music in video games: studying play / K.J. Donnelly, William Gibbons,
   and Neil Lerner.
   pages cm.—(Routledge music and screen media series)
   Includes bibliographical references and index.
   1. Video game music—History and criticism. 2. Video game music—
   Analysis, appreciation. I. Donnelly, K.J. (Kevin J.), editor. II. Gibbons,
   William (William James), editor. III. Lerner, Neil William, editor.
   IV. Series: Routledge music and screen media series.
   ML3540.7.M88 2014
   781.5′4—dc23
   2013030028

ISBN: 978-0-415-63443-4 (hbk)
ISBN: 978-0-415-63444-1 (pbk)
ISBN: 978-1-315-88269-7 (ebk)

Typeset in Goudy and Gill Sans
by Florence Production Ltd, Stoodleigh, Devon, UK

Senior Editor: Constance Ditzel
Editorial Assistant: Elysse Preposi
Production Manager: Mhairi Bennett
Marketing Manager: Cedric Sinclair
Project Manager: Charlotte Hiorns
Copy Editor: Andrew Craddock
Proofreader: Jennifer Ide
Cover Design: Jayne Varney

MIX
Paper from
responsible sources
FSC FSC® C014174
www.fsc.org

Printed and bound in the United States of America by Sheridan Books, Inc. (a Sheridan Group Company).

Contents

Series Foreword

While the scholarly conversations about music in film and visual media have been expanding prodigiously since the last quarter of the twentieth century, a need remains for focused, specialized studies of particular films as they relate more broadly to genres. This series includes scholars from across the disciplines of music and film and media studies, of specialists in both the audible as well as the visual, who share the goal of broadening and deepening these scholarly dialogues about music in particular genres of cinema, television, video games, and new media. Claiming a chronological arc from the birth of cinema in the 1890s to the most recent releases, the *Routledge Music and Screen Media* series offers collections of original essays written for an interdisciplinary audience of students and scholars of music, film, and media studies in general, and interdisciplinary humanists who give strong attention to music. Driving the study of music here are the underlying assumptions that music, together with screen media (understood broadly to accommodate rapidly developing new technologies), participates in important ways in the creation of meaning and that including music in an analysis opens up the possibility for interpretations that remain invisible when only using the eye.

The series was designed with the goal of providing a thematically unified group of supplemental essays in a single volume that can be assigned in a variety of undergraduate and graduate courses (including courses in film studies, in film music, and in other interdisciplinary topics). We look forward to adding future volumes addressing emerging technologies and reflecting the growth of the academic study of screen media. Rather than attempting an exhaustive history or unified theory, these studies—persuasive explications supported by textual and contextual evidence—will pose questions of musical style, strategies of rhetoric, and critical cultural analysis as they help us to see, to hear, and ultimately to understand these texts in new ways.

Neil Lerner
Series Editor

Preface

> Music and games share a fundamental property: both are *playable*, offering
> their listeners and operators an expressive experience within the
> framework of melody and rhythm.[1]

As game scholar Ian Bogost has suggested, the act of play is common to both music and video games. In both, the text is enacted by a player who works within a preestablished framework; in both, there are frameworks governed by rules (sometimes to be broken), together with potential frustrations and pleasures. Surviving a difficult level of *Super Mario Bros.* (1985) without losing a life, for example, is a virtuoso task requiring skill, practice, and concentration, not unlike playing a complex Mozart sonata or metal guitar solo with great precision and speed. But this framework is only a part of what it means to play; a game with no player is no game at all. The rest of the "expressive experience" comes from players interpreting the framework. The same freedom of choice—"playability"—that differentiates every musician's version of "I Got Rhythm" (1930) renders each playthrough of *Frogger* (1981), *Angry Birds* (2009), or *Skyrim* (2011) unique.

Perhaps because of this core connection, music has been an important part of video games almost from the medium's beginning (as with early cinema, sound and music seem not to have been crucial parts of video games in their infancy, as the earliest games, such as Steve Russell's *Space War* (completed 1962 on a PDP-1 computer) or *Computer Space* (the first commercial coin-operated game, released in 1971), were apparently experienced without sound or music emanating from their devices). Music has advanced alongside games' narrative and graphics capabilities to become one of the most distinctive forms of the twentieth and twenty-first centuries. In a matter of only a few decades, it has developed from extremely modest beginnings (the primitive bleeps and throbbings of early video games) into a medium of great complexity, affective expressivity, and increasing interactivity. The earliest manifestations of game music were heavily circumscribed by the limitations of the technology (i.e. hardware, amount of memory, the number of voices, and level of sound quality). In more recent years, video game music has taken on a largely technologically defined format. Dynamic or interactive video game music is composed as separate fragments that have the capability to interlock and overlay, all to be masterfully coordinated in the gameplay-responsive game music engine software. In many ways, such video game music is the most technological of contemporary music. In essence, music for video games has not been a live, organic music, but a digital, electronic music, reliant wholly on speakers or headphones. Yet, in recent years, the cultural status of video game music has risen, evident in some music being accorded a status as a concert object and commodified as recordings, underlining that the music is more than a banal sound space filler consumed only as an accompaniment to gameplay. Indeed, video games, much like film and television, are now used to showcase and sell other genres of music, and while many games have distinctive music offering something original to the experience of the game, there are many that use a selection of pop songs in an unremarkable manner.

In the 1990s, when game studies was an emerging discipline, several scholars went to war with the concept of games as "interactive narratives" or "interactive cinema." Drawing deep lines in the sand, these ludologists—most prominently Espen Aarseth and Gonzalo Frasca—campaigned tirelessly against what one scholar called "the threat of theoretical imperialism and the colonization of game studies by theories of other fields."[2] In Aarseth's words, "the (academic) discovery of computer games over the last two decades is accompanied by the most smothering form of generic criticism: the attempt to reform games into a more acceptable form of art, literature or film; i.e., as narratives."[3] In other words, ludology rejects the applicability of narrative-based analyses to games—including (and especially) those types of analysis typically seen in film studies. This attitude continued to impede the application of external theories in the 2000s, when narratological attempts at game analysis—those focusing on games as a medium with significant aspects in common with traditional forms of storytelling, such as film—were often rejected outright as academic nonsense. Consider Markku Eskelinen's pithy turn of phrase from the first issue of *Game Studies*, a leading journal in the field: "Outside academic theory people are usually excellent at making distinctions between narrative, drama and games. If I throw a ball at you I don't expect you to drop it and wait until it starts telling stories."[4]

This ludological preference has seemingly carried over into more specific areas of game studies, resulting in a reluctance to apply or embrace existing methodological frameworks—particularly from film—to examine music in video games. And while game music scholars have not rejected film music theory with the same vehemence ludologists have in game studies writ large, we have nonetheless tended to focus on the aspect of games that most separates them from film: interactivity, the involvement of a player as more than spectator.[5] Exploring the medium's differences from film is crucial, and it is undeniable that the compositional methods and music placement seen in games is quite different from other media. Yet, clearly these media are in close dialogue. Design director Cliff Bleszinski, for example, wrote in the instruction manual to *Gears of War 2* (Epic, 2008) that "this Video Game . . . was designed around the idea of cinematic action. We wanted the gameplay experience to feel like a summer blockbuster where you, the gamer, are the star."[6] The lines between games and other media are wafer-thin, and growing thinner by the moment. Ignoring the medium's obvious similarities to film and existing media is both counterproductive to the field and potentially alienating to scholars and readers who might otherwise be interested in it. Perhaps because of this methodological separation and the resulting jargon barriers, many film and television scholars have ignored games, or at least minimized their interaction with film.

Still, game scholars (and sometimes the players themselves) have tended to ignore music's crucial role in the gameplay experience, focusing (as have film and media scholars) often exclusively on the aural elements. Wikipedia, for example, currently defines a video game as "an electronic game that involves human interaction with a user interface to generate *visual* feedback on a *video* device.[7] Having some sort of visual display becomes a defining feature of a video game, though early handheld games such as Milton Bradley's *Simon* (1978) and Atari's *Touch Me* (1978), which required players to imitate sequences of tones emitted by the device, may offer a reason to broaden a definition built too much around the visual component. Gonzalo Frasca's definition of video games ("any forms of computer-based entertainment software, either textual or image-based, using any electronic platform such as personal computers or consoles and involving one or multiple players in a physical or networked environment") is broader, though the phrase "entertainment software" may leave open some questions of personal judgment similar to, say, Nicholas Cook's definition of music ("humanly generated sounds that are good to listen to, and that are so for themselves and not merely for the message they convey").[8] Such questions of definition can provoke spirited conversation and debate—what one person finds good to listen to might be quite otherwise for another person, and the concurrent matters of taste can be powerfully personal and fraught with meaning—and the essays in this volume are aimed at continuing and expanding such discussion.

A number of key concepts have animated debates about video game music. Earlier writings pursued general concerns about music's place in video games, as evident in David Bessell's "What's that Funny Noise?" from 2002, Axel Stockburger's "The Game Environment from an Auditive Perspective" from 2003, and Zach Whalen's "Play Along—an Approach to Video Game Music" from 2004.[9] Both Whalen and Rod Munday had chapters in Jamie Sexton's *Music, Sound and Multimedia: From the Live to the Virtual* in 2007, and the following year Karen Collins' edited collection *From Pac-Man to Pop Music: Interactive Audio in Games and New Media* was published.[10] All of these writings displayed concerns now traditional to game studies, such as addressing player immersion. This has also inspired psychological research, such as Scott

Lipscomb and Sean Zehnder's "Immersion in the Virtual Environment: The Effect of a Musical Score on the Video Gaming Experience," which confirmed the potential importance for music as part of an immersive gaming whole.[11] More recently, there have been sustained studies of another concern traditional to the discipline, that of interactivity, including Kristine Jørgensen's *A Comprehensive Study of Sound in Video Games: How it Affects Player Action* and Kiri Miller's *Playing Along: Music, Video Games and Networked Amateurs*.[12] One of the most often articulated aspects of video game music is its interactive quality, where it often is constructed to develop alongside gameplay through a process or triggering and overlaying to render a coherent sonic fabric as part of the game's unfolding. As Karen Collins put it in her landmark study *Game Sound*:

> Unlike the consumption of many other forms of media in which the audience is a more passive "receiver" of a sound signal, game players play an active role in the triggering of sound events in the game (including dialogue, ambient sounds, sound effects and musical events).[13]

Indeed, the dynamic interaction of music and gameplay makes not only for an engaging game experience, but also for music with a distinctive character (often defined by looping and layering). Ian Bogost argues that musical games (i.e. rhythm games such as *PaRappa the Rapper* or *Guitar Hero*) can deepen a player's understanding of music listening.[14] Yet, that may happen in all video games with music, as it is likely that all video game playing may, if not deepen our understanding of music, at least make us think of music in a different way. Furthermore, repeated gameplay and the intensive repetition of music accompanying a video game has surely made for some of the most repeated, heard, and remembered music in history. That is remarkable, particularly in the light of the much-touted disposability and ephemerality of contemporary culture, and it indicates that rather than a quickly produced, low-quality product, music for many video games can have a durability well beyond that evident in other forms of music. Some scholars writing about video games have drawn comparisons to the state of video game development and the history of cinema—have video games produced yet a *Great Train Robbery* or *Citizen Kane* (there is much less consensus on the latter than the former)?— and that conversation could be shifted into one relevant to music history and raise the question of whether or not video games have yet had their Ludwig van Beethoven or Bernard Herrmann.[15]

Music in Video Games: Studying Play aims for a wide coverage of video game music, and to that end the essays that follow address a variety of analytical methodologies to games of diverse time periods, genres, and platforms. Chapters 1–3 each focus on the connections between early games and broader cultural questions, shedding new light on the origins of groundbreaking games such as the arcade classic *Donkey Kong* and the hugely popular NES pioneer

Super Mario Bros., while also considering these games' impact—both cultural and musical—in more recent years. Chapters 4–5 apply music-theoretical approaches to games as diverse as *The Legend of Zelda* series, Rockstar Games' cinematic *L.A. Noire*, and the downloadable platformer *BIT.TRIP RUNNER* to explore the relationships between game environments and music. Chapters 6–8 offer more hermeneutic readings of music in more recent games, ranging from the artistically crafted *Shadow of the Colossus*, to survival horror games such as *Dead Space*, to *Plants vs. Zombies*, the popular tower defense game that helped usher in a new kind of player, the casual non-gamer with a mobile computing device. Finally, Chapters 9–11 consider the impact of Western classical music on games (and vice versa), including discussions of *Final Fantasy IX*, *Civilization IV*, and the adventure games of LucasArts. Ultimately, we cannot answer the question of who might be video games' Beethoven or Herrmann, but we can at least begin to outline the rough shape of a highly diverse canon of game music.

K.J. Donnelly, William Gibbons, and Neil Lerner

Notes

All websites were accessed November 4, 2013.

1 Ian Bogost, *How to Do Things with Videogames* (Minneapolis, MN: University of Minnesota Press, 2011), 36.
2 Aphra Kerr, *The Business and Culture of Digital Games: Gamework/Gameplay* (London: Sage, 2006), 33.
3 Espen Aarseth, "Genre Trouble: Narrativism and the Art of Simulation," in *First Person: New Media as Story, Performance, and Game*, ed. Noah Wardrip-Fruin and Pat Harrigan (London and Cambridge, MA: MIT Press, 2004), 48–49.
4 Markku Eskelinen, "The Gaming Situation," *Game Studies* 1/1 (July 2001). More recently, these two fields have begun to find some common ground, with some conciliatory scholars realizing there is common ground between the ludological and narratological approaches. Kevin Veale, for instance, considers, however hesitantly, the possibility that we may have finally reached a point of convergence between game and film in isolated cases. Kevin Veale, "'Interactive Cinema' is an Oxymoron, but May Not Always Be," *Game Studies* 12/1 (September 2012), available online at http://gamestudies.org/1201/articles/veale. This reconciliatory tone has also been struck (on a much broader scale) by such scholars as Henry Jenkins, who has persuasively argued that the idea of narrative could be effectively applied to games on a case-by-case basis. Henry Jenkins, "Game Design as Narrative Architecture," in *First Person: New Media as Story, Performance, and Game*, ed. Wardrip-Fruin and Harrigan, 118–130.
5 The lack of applications of film music theory to games has not stopped some game scholars (and practitioners) from preemptively rejecting their models. The composer Jesper Kaae, for example, lamented (without footnote) in a recent article about "the tendency to transfer the theories and practice of linear film and popular music into computer games without paying attention to the non-linear nature of the media." Jesper Kaae, "Theoretical Approaches to Composing Dynamic Music for

Video Games," in *From Pac-Man to Pop Music: Interactive Audio in Games and New Media*, ed. Karen Collins (Aldershot, UK and Burlington, VT: Ashgate, 2008), 75.

6 Cliff Bleszinski, Instruction Manual to *Gears of War 2* (2008), 2.

7 "Video Games," *Wikipedia*, available online at http://en.wikipedia.org/wiki/Video_game. Emphasis added.

8 Gonzalo Frasca, "Videogames of the Oppressed: Videogames as a Means for Critical Thinking and Debate," Ph.D. dissertation (Georgia Institute of Technology, 2001), 4; Nicholas Cook, *Music: A Very Short Introduction* (Oxford and New York: Oxford University Press, 1998), 4.

9 David Bessell, "What's that Funny Noise? An Examination of the Role of Music in *Cool Boarders 2, Alien Trilogy*, and *Medievil 2*," in *Screenplay: Cinema/Videogame/Interface*, ed. Geoff King and Tanya Krzywinska (London: Wallflower, 2002), 136–44; Axel Stockburger, "The Game Environment from an Auditive Perspective," in *Proceedings: Level Up: Digital Games Research Conference*, ed. Marinka Copier and Joost Raessens (Utrecht: Utrecht University, 2003), available online at www.audiogames.net/pics/upload/gameenvironment.htm; Zach Whalen, "Play Along: An Approach to Video Game Music," *Game Studies: The International Journal of Computer Game Research* 4/1 (2004), available online at www.gamestudies.org/0401/whalen/.

10 Zach Whalen, "Video Game Music: The Case of Silent Hill," in *Music, Sound and Multimedia: From the Live to the Virtual*, ed. Jamie Sexton (Edinburgh: Edinburgh University Press, 2007), 68–81; Rod Munday, "Music in Video Games," in *Music, Sound and Multimedia: From the Live to the Virtual*, ed. Sexton, 51–67; Collins, ed., *From Pac-Man to Pop Music: Interactive Audio in Games and New Media*.

11 Scott D. Lipscomb and Sean M. Zehnder, "Immersion in the Virtual Environment: The Effect of a Musical Score on the Video Gaming Experience," *Journal of Physiological Anthropology and Human Applied Science* 23 (2004), 337–343.

12 Kristine Jørgensen, *A Comprehensive Study of Sound in Video Games: How it Affects Player Action* (New York: Edwin Mellen, 2009); Kiri Miller, *Playing Along: Music, Video Games and Networked Amateurs* (New York: Oxford University Press, 2012).

13 Karen Collins, *Game Sound: An Introduction to the History, Theory and Practice of Video Game Music and Sound Design* (Cambridge, MA: MIT Press, 2008), 3.

14 Bogost, *How to Do Things with Videogames*, 34; see also Miller, *Playing Along: Music, Video Games and Networked Amateurs*, as well as Kiri Miller, "Schizophrenic Performance: *Guitar Hero, Rock Band*, and Virtual Virtuosity," *Journal of the Society for American Music* 3/4 (2009), 395–429.

15 See, for instance, Henry Jenkins, "More on Games Criticism," *Confessions of an Aca-Fan: The Official Weblog of Henry Jenkins* (July 13, 2006), available online at http://henryjenkins.org/2006/07/more_on_games_criticism.html.

Chapter 1

Mario's Dynamic Leaps

Musical Innovations (and the Specter of Early Cinema) in *Donkey Kong* and *Super Mario Bros.*

Neil Lerner

Heading into the second decade of the twenty-first century, it has become possible, expected, and indeed rather commonplace for music to accompany video games in an elaborate and dynamic fashion, with complicated sound design and protean musical cues that shift their character depending on what the player decides to do.[1] That ability of the game's music to respond to things happening in the game makes video game music unlike other genres of music; if the musical gestures are contingent upon player decisions—for instance, a certain melody might sound in conjunction with a player picking up an object or completing a task—then what we might try to describe as the game's score will be a constantly shifting object, a difficult-to-repeat mix of variable intervals and orderings, depending on what occurs in any particular playing of a game. Even *Pong* (Atari, 1972), the earliest video game with musical tones, would create in its soundtrack a minimalistic accompaniment that utilized only three notes (a B-flat each time the paddle hits the ball, a B-flat an octave lower each time the ball hits a wall, and a B natural in the higher octave each time the ball makes it past a paddle and scores a point); its rhythmic unpredictability, together with the aleatoricism of its severely limited pitch collection, should remind us of the contemporaneous minimalistic works of composers such as La Monte Young and Terry Riley.

Yet, despite this exceptional property (of a never-to-be-repeated score), the musical styles arising in video games since the 1970s have nonetheless been rooted in earlier musical traditions. *Circus* (Exidy, 1977), one of the very first (if not the first) games to incorporate recognizable melodies, would sound out either "Ta-ra-ra Boom-de-ay" or the opening melody of the third movement of Chopin's Second Piano Sonata—the familiar funeral music going back to the cinema traditions of the early twentieth century—whenever the player succeeded in clearing out a row of balloons or whenever a clown died, respectively.[2] Karen Collins delineates between *interactive audio* ("sound events that react to the player's direct input"), *adaptive audio* ("sound that reacts to the game states"), and *dynamic audio*, which encompasses both.[3] The idea of dynamic audio can be traced back rather directly to the traditions of live musical accompaniment for early cinema (roughly the late 1890s through

to the 1920s), as pianists, organists, and conductors found themselves impro-
vising their ways through films, generating musical scores that were, in their
own ways, unlimited in their variety, contingencies, and ephemerality.[4] At
some point, video game scores began to move from their primitive monophony
and (for some at least) tedious looping into the marvel of early twenty-first-
century dynamic audio found in so many video games. Nintendo's two groundbreaking games, *Donkey Kong* (an arcade coin-op released in the summer of
1981) and 1985's *Super Mario Bros.* (also an arcade coin-op, but best known
from its inclusion in the Nintendo Entertainment Systems that flooded into
so many homes), are both justifiably lauded for their pioneering innovations
of the genre of the platform game, but their music also deserves attention.
Donkey Kong and *Super Mario Bros.* present key case studies in the way video
game music was beginning to change in the first half of the 1980s. In their
evocation of musical gestures, styles, and techniques associated with the
days of early twentieth-century cinema, they look toward the past, yet their
groundbreaking uses of a series of tonally and motivically related cues point
the way toward the future of game audio.

Donkey Kong's Nostalgia for Early Cinema

Founded as a playing card company in 1889, the Japanese company Nintendo
entered the budding video game market nearly a century later, in the mid
1970s; its release of *Donkey Kong* in 1981 made a deep impression in the U.S.
market, as *Donkey Kong* quickly became one of the most successful games in
the midst of the golden age of the coin-operated video arcade game.[5] The
game established not only Nintendo, but also *Donkey Kong*'s creator, Shigeru
Miyamoto, as major forces within the video game industry. Besides containing
several important innovations in game design, *Donkey Kong* was the first highly
successful example of the platform genre, one where characters moved an
avatar through a space while avoiding obstacles instead of firing at descending
invaders (as in *Space Invaders*) or navigating through a maze (as in *Pac-Man*).
In addition to containing several important innovations in game design,
highlighting a character with no extraordinary abilities (just the capacity to
run, to jump, and to grab a hammer), and introducing what would become
a franchise character for their company (Jumpman, a carpenter who would
later see his name changed to Mario and his career to plumber), Nintendo's
Donkey Kong also stands apart from its contemporary arcade video games for
the relative complexity of its musical accompaniment.[6]

Nintendo's promotional fliers for the game make but brief mention of *Donkey
Kong*'s music, speaking of the "foreboding music" that "warns of the eventual
doom that awaits the poor girl." *Donkey Kong*'s commercial success was such
that it prompted the publication of "how-to" manuals such as *How to Win at
Donkey Kong*, published in 1982.[7] The introduction to this 32-page treatise

mused on the reasons for *Donkey Kong*'s popularity, pointing to the music as one of its many charms:

> Most people will talk about the fantastic animation, with Donkey Kong beating his hairy chest, grabbing the damsel in distress, and dragging her to the top of a building. Others might talk about the sound effects, the growling ape, the honky-tonk music.[8]

The music described as "honky-tonk" in *Donkey Kong* hearkens back to early film music accompanying strategies, alluding stylistically to early twentieth-century piano ragtime and Tin Pan Alley gestures, as well as linking particular musical gestures to elements in the narrative. Furthermore, the various musical cues are constructed such that they establish a tonal center (B-flat major) that provides an important unifying function to the game and its narrative.

The game's efforts at storytelling were groundbreaking for an arcade game of its time. *Donkey Kong* uses introductory and inter-level animated sequences (early examples of what would later be called *cinematics* or *cutscenes*) to reveal a story where a giant ape has taken a woman (Mario's girlfriend) up a ladder and then jumps with such force that it causes the girders to bend.[9] That the woman in the game, first just called "Lady," would eventually be known as "Pauline" is explained by Jeff Ryan as an homage to the wife of the warehouse manager, Polly, who was assisting in the conversion of unsold *Radar Scope* machines into *Donkey Kong* cabinets, but the name Pauline, whether intentional or not, nonetheless draws a connection to the early twentieth-century film series *The Perils of Pauline*.[10] Ben Singer has identified *The Perils of Pauline* as the lone surviving vestige in "popular or scholarly memory" of a genre he labels the *serial-queen melodrama*; these films (approximately 60 films featuring around 800 individual episodes between 1912 and around 1920) stressed "female independence and mastery" and pointed to the youthful film industry's interest in cultivating a female audience—a situation not unlike what the video game industry did in 1981 when it created a game with a female protagonist (*Ms. Pac-Man*) that, like *Donkey Kong*, also deployed the iconography of early cinema (see Figure 1.1).[11] Singer traces this cinematic genre to historical contexts that include the suffrage movement, the rise of the New Woman stereotype, and newspaper stories from the 1890s that featured "plucky girl reporters." One of the images Singer provides (Figure 1.2) creates a powerful contrast between these bold female adventurers and the hapless Pauline of *Donkey Kong*, a traditionally passive feminine character whose purpose in the game's story is to cry out "Help!" and wait to be rescued by the male protagonist (see Figure 1.3). While almost certainly a coincidence, it may still be instructive to consider how both the 1896 image of Kate Swan and the 1981 rendition of Pauline have such similar hairstyles, in particular the way the long hair in the back flows behind them both. *Donkey Kong* takes

Figure 1.1 Beginning of the Act 1 cinematic from *Ms. Pac-Man* (1981)

on some of the visual and narrative trappings of the serial-queen melodrama while actually subverting them in retrograde ways: we can see in the eyes of plucky Kate Swan that she would not stand up on a high girder crying out "Help!" If we can conceive of *Donkey Kong*, though, as a nostalgic and even perhaps postmodern reworking of early cinema conventions, it is also relevant to note that the narrative device of the cliffhanger, such a central feature of early serial cinema, finds a modern parallel in the way that games such as *Donkey Kong* lead the player through a level, only to discover that the damsel is still in distress and will need saving in the next level.[12]

Beyond its fairly oblique reference to *The Perils of Pauline* and its use of early cinema conventions such as the chase, the damsel in distress, and the cliffhanger, *Donkey Kong*'s music also points back in several ways to the traditions of early cinema. For instance, the introductory animation that begins every game of *Donkey Kong* is accompanied by a melodramatic cue, in parallel fifths, whose penultimate note trills in a manner approximating the way a pianist might apply tremolo to a suspenseful scene (see Example 1.1)[13] That melodic phrase is, in fact, part of the famous opening from the *Dragnet*

Figure 1.2 "Kate Swan, at a Dizzy Height," from the *New York World* (April 12, 1896)

Figure 1.3 The Lady (later known as Pauline) screaming "Help!" in *Donkey Kong*

television series that Jon Burlingame describes as "the decisive and melodramatic four-note phrase [that] became a kind of American musical code for 'you're in trouble now'."[14] Although the *Dragnet* phrase does not appear to be a direct quotation from the early twentieth-century photoplay books, its diminished harmonic structure and exaggerated character nonetheless

Example 1.1 Introductory music from *Donkey Kong*

tie it to that musical world. Other games from the early 1980s utilized this same melody: *Wizard of Wor* (Midway, 1980) opens each level with the first four notes of the phrase, withholding the final chord until a successful completion of a level, while *Pitfall!* (Activision's 1982 game for the Atari 2600) accompanies each (temporary) death of its main character with the same tune.

After the opening *Dragnet* phrase in C minor, each level of *Donkey Kong* then begins with an opening cue that playfully establishes B-flat major as its key (V to I) and the key for the rest of the game (see Example 1.2). The first level has a constant syncopated bassline that spells out a B-flat triad, while each time Mario successfully jumps over one of the barrels thrown at him by the ape, it is accompanied by a rapid five-note melody that momentarily introduces an E-flat chord, the subdominant harmony, into the mix (see Examples 1.3 and 1.4). That melody's rapidly rising and falling contour matches Mario's physical movements as he rapidly jumps up and down over a barrel, thus offering an early example of Mickey Mousing from a video game (Figure 1.4 comes from the first level, as Mario successfully leaps over a barrel thrown by Donkey Kong). Should Mario grab a hammer, the time during which he wields it will be accompanied by a B-flat major fanfare (see Example 1.5). Each of Mario's deaths unleashes a torrent of chromatically related sixths and fifths before delivering a return to the relative stability of diatonicism and the familiarity of B-flat major (see Example 1.6). If the player has remaining lives after a death, the death music is then followed by the level introductory music, returning to the key of B-flat major.

Example 1.2 Opening level music from *Donkey Kong*

Example 1.3 Level one bassline from *Donkey Kong*

Example 1.4 Jumping music from *Donkey Kong*

Example 1.5 Hammer music from *Donkey Kong*

Example 1.6 Death music from *Donkey Kong*

Completing each level brings a musical reward, although each respite from the ape's assaults lingers but for a moment. Successfully completing the first level elicits a short, happy moment in the music before three ominous low F-sharps sound, which accompany Donkey Kong again stealing Mario's girlfriend and causing the heart above them to break, only to be followed again by the introductory level music (see Example 1.7 and Figure 1.5). Three of *Donkey Kong*'s four levels have continuous musical accompaniments; the basslines of the rivet level and the conveyor belt level, seen in Examples 1.8 and 1.9, also support the B-flat tonality. (The fourth level, the elevator level, has no musical accompaniment, only the constant sound effect of the bouncing Springese.) Defeating the rivet level on the first stage causes the ape to fall, allowing Mario and Pauline a brief moment together and triggering a ragtime-inflected cue that ends with a B-flat seventh chord; defeating the rivet level on the second stage also carries with it a brief whiff of ragtime syncopations and blue notes (see Examples 1.10 and 1.11 and Figure 1.6). With the start of the next level, B-flat major returns as the primary tonality. The entire game thus uses a single key area to unify the various levels and actions, using the brief disruption of the chromatic death music as contrast to the rest of the music that occurs as frame and within each level (i.e. the level introductory music, the ostinato bassline, plus any jumping and hammering that the player may elect to do) and to add momentum back into the home key. This level of tonal unity was unusual for a video game soundtrack of its time, though such coherence was also a quality prized in early film accompanying: J.S. Zamecnik composed his photoplay cues in related keys, and manuals advising film accompanists emphasized the need for smooth modulations between cues.[15]

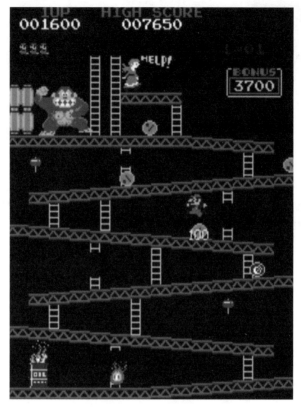

Figure 1.4 Jumpman (later known as Mario) successfully jumps over a barrel in *Donkey Kong*

Example 1.7 Level one ending music from *Donkey Kong*

Example 1.8 Rivet level bassline from *Donkey Kong*

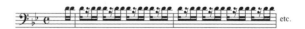

Example 1.9 Conveyor belt level music from *Donkey Kong*

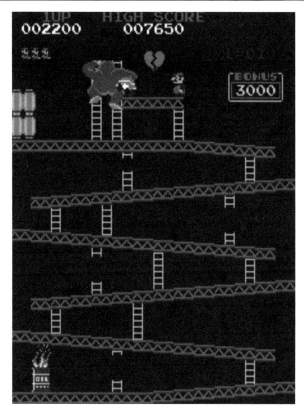

Figure 1.5 Completing the first level in *Donkey Kong* allows Jumpman only a brief moment with the Lady before Donkey Kong again kidnaps her, causing their hearts to break

Example 1.10 First rivet level victory music from *Donkey Kong*

Besides having no earlier precedent in any video game soundtrack, this remarkable tonal coherence operates in interesting ways next to Jesper Juul's categories of incomplete versus incoherent story worlds.[16] Incomplete worlds leave out information about the fiction; Juul gives as an example the way that the *Super Mario Bros.* games tell us the names of the brothers Mario and Luigi but do not name their parents. Incoherent worlds present inexplicable

Example 1.11 Second rivet level victory music from *Donkey Kong*

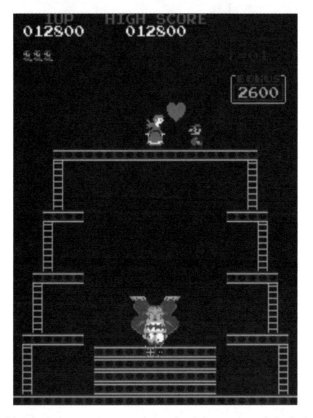

Figure 1.6 After a victory on the second rivet level, Jumpman and the Lady enjoy a romantic moment accompanied by a ragtime-like cue

contradictions, such as in *Donkey Kong*, where Mario's girlfriend finds herself repeatedly kidnapped, no matter what else happens in the game; even if a player, as Mario, successfully saves the girlfriend in levels one and two, by level three, she has been kidnapped again and apparently returned to the original hideout. In bleakly Sisyphean fashion, Mario must again ascend to the top of the ramp only to eternally see the woman snatched away (one must imagine Mario happy, to paraphrase Camus). To further flesh out the idea of incoherent worlds, Juul asks the question, "Why does Mario have three lives?" Mario's ability to die and then be reborn three times (in most settings of the game), or to earn an extra "life" after achieving a certain number of points, are two more examples of how Juul finds incoherence in the world of *Donkey Kong*. Juul proposes "that we call this type of fictional world an *incoherent world*, meaning that there are many events in the fictional world that we cannot explain without discussing the game rules."[17] Apart from the opening C minor cue—perhaps a musical example of incoherence following Juul's categories for story worlds—the *Donkey Kong* underscore actually creates a powerful thread unifying the game from start to finish, thereby defying its narrative incoherence. Such variety and cohesion in a video game was unprecedented in games such as *Space Invaders* (1978), *Asteroids* (1979), and *Pac-Man* (1980): video game players had seen, and heard, nothing like it up to its time.

Super Mario Bros.: Musical (and Other) Links to Early Cinema

Nintendo's popular Jumpman character from *Donkey Kong* reappeared in 1982 with the new name "Mario" in the follow-up arcade games *Donkey Kong Jr.*, and then a year after that with a new character, his brother Luigi, in *Mario Bros.* (1983).[18] The introductory music in both *Donkey Kong Junior* (the famous opening of Bach's *Toccata*, usually heard on organ) and *Mario Bros.* (the opening of Mozart's *Eine Kleine Nachtmusik*) continued the use of stylistic features borrowed from early cinema, as both games turned to preexisting music from the European concert hall tradition in their opening sequences (just as it was not uncommon in early cinema accompaniment to find works by Beethoven and Mendelssohn next to nineteenth-century marches and Tin Pan Alley songs). When Nintendo's video game unit for the home (the Family Computer, or Famicom, as released in Japan, and then called the Nintendo Entertainment System, or NES, when released in the United States) was introduced in the US in 1985, the next appearance of Mario—in the game *Super Mario Bros.*, which was bundled in the US together with *Duck Hunt*—helped to solidify his centrality as a franchise character.[19]

Just as in *Donkey Kong*, the story in *Super Mario Bros.* revolves around a helpless woman in distress, waiting to be rescued by Mario. Here, the female is a princess (instead of Jumpman's girlfriend, Pauline), and the setting moves from the construction site of *Donkey Kong* to the colorful Mushroom Kingdom, a whimsically hallucinogenic land full of platforms, bridges, pipes, and castles. Giant mushrooms that turn Mario twice his size can be found hidden throughout, and the whole place is populated by odd little creatures called "Goombas" and turtle-like creatures called "Koopas" who sometimes throw hammers. Antagonists can be crushed, immobilized, or kicked by Mario leaping on them, or Mario may pick up objects such as Fire Flowers or Starmen that allow him to shoot fire at them or run through them with invincibility; alternately, Mario can just opt to avoid and run or jump around these antagonizing characters. Chris Kohler has estimated that nearly 5 million copies of the game were sold in Japan, and probably over 20 million copies sold worldwide, and the game was distinctive because of the centrality of its narrative.[20] Points could be scored for various actions throughout the game, although these may be secondary to the effort to reach the conclusion of the game's story and to discover if Mario would indeed save the Princess; after successfully completing each of the first seven (of eight) levels in the game, the player is told that "our princess is in another castle," thus providing motivation (beyond getting more points) to continue on in the game.[21] A rich fan culture has filled in the story, such as can be seen in things such as the machinima that has grown up around the Mario franchise.[22]

Paradoxically, the narrative eschews character development: Mario is famously underdeveloped as a character, perhaps to maintain versatility for his appearance in a wide range of games. First introduced to the public as a carpenter, Mario became a plumber in later games. He may have been based on an Italian-American landlord, Mario Segale, who had threatened to evict Nintendo (but granted some extra time) from the warehouse it was renting in Tukwila, Washington as they were in the early days of converting *Radar Scope* machines into *Donkey Kong* units in the summer of 1981.[23] But the pixelated Mario has no voice, audible or otherwise, until later in the franchise, and certainly not anywhere in *Donkey Kong* or *Super Mario Bros.* (the small bits of dialogue from Mario reveal him to have a heavy Italian accent). He's a mute character, as was the norm in the era before synchronized sound, and Mario functions essentially as a character from a silent (or mute) film. The representational system that gives us Mario relies on several features of early cinema, including occasional title cards, the use of a largely nonverbal communication system, and also a continuous musical accompaniment composed by Koji Kondo.[24] A new vocabulary had to develop that would signal different events in the game itself. For instance, how could one signal the beginning of a film or a video game? An easy answer would be an overture or a fanfare (which assumes that the film screening has a clear beginning, which was not quite the case in the age of the nickelodeon). What about signaling a pause in a game? Pausing was not possible in arcade units, but for home games it became an important feature (in *Super Mario Bros.*, pausing triggers a quick four-note melodic figure of E-C-E-C). As Zach Whalen has observed, Mario's jumping action is matched with a rising octave (a rising C leaping up that begins on a higher or lower octave depending on whether or not Mario is powered-up).[25] The music in *Super Mario Bros.* continues the development of an early film aesthetic begun in 1970s games.

Kondo's music for *Super Mario Bros.* sounds almost continuously throughout the game, yielding to silence only at the start of each level.[26] Actions such as powering-up, grabbing a coin, or getting a Starman each come with their own melodic markers. Furthermore, different territories in the game are accompanied by different music. The most famous of all of the music in *Super Mario Bros.*, and indeed among all video game music to date, must be the opening bars from the "Above Ground" music (see Example 1.12).[27] This cue consists of an introduction (a D^9 chord that acts as a secondary dominant of C major; it is labeled **I** in the example) and four different melodic ideas (indicated as **A, B, C,** and **D**) that all work to support and ultimately lead

Example 1.12 "Above Ground" music from *Super Mario Bros.*

Example 1.12 continued

back into the key of C major. The syncopated rhythms, which are often described as sounding Latin, bring a playful mood to the music. The interval of the third serves as an important melodic and harmonic feature to this cue, along with the surprise of a sudden chromatic slippage such as the G-flat major chord in the fourth measure. The unexpected deviation from C major

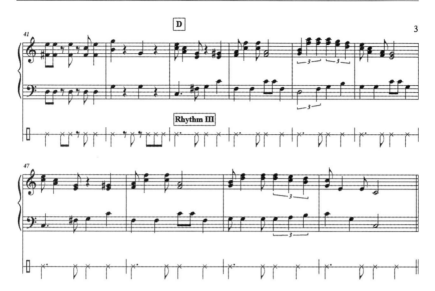

Example 1.12 continued

there hints at the further chromatic moments that will develop throughout the score in a manner perhaps not unlike the famous D-flat in the opening of Beethoven's *Third Symphony*. The four principal melodic modules are constructed harmonically such that they can all be repeated and also lead back into each other. Accompanying each of these four phrases is one of three different rhythmic patterns sounding generated by the noise generator and acting as a largely swinging percussion part; that both melodic modules **A** and **C** occur with rhythmic pattern I, thus cycling through more melodic phrases (color) than rhythmic patterns (talea), might be viewed as a vestige of isorhythmic technique making an unexpected appearance in the 1980s (see Table 1.1).

Occasionally, Mario finds himself underwater, a condition that brings with it the waltz titled "Underwater" (an oddly charming piece, given the dangers of being submerged for such an extended period), which could easily fit within the early twentieth-century harmonic and melodic language of Tin Pan Alley songs, or waltzes composed to accompany film scenes such as J.S. Zamecnik's "Garden Love Scene" (from *Sam Fox Moving Picture Music*, volume 3, 1914) that, like "Underwater," also contain occasionally unfolding chromatic movement (see examples 1.13 and 1.14).[28] The "Underground" theme, occurring whenever Mario descends down a pipe into the territory beneath the ground, has an ominous melody in the low range, doubled in octaves that circle chromatically around the central pitches of B-flat and E-flat before descending into eighth note and triplet patterns that contain several leaps

Example 1.13 "Underwater" music from *Super Mario Bros.*

Example 1.13 continued

Example 1.14 J. S. Zamecnik, "Garden Love Scene" (excerpt) (from *Sam Fox Moving Picture Music*, volume 3, 1914)

of a tritone; and very much in the tradition of a *misterioso* from early cinema, such as Zamecnik's "Misterioso" (from *Sam Fox Photoplay Edition*, volume 1, 1919) or the "Pizzicato" (from Gregg A. Frelinger's *Motion Picture Piano Music*, 1909) (see Examples 1.15, 1.16, and 1.17). As in *Donkey Kong*, losing a life triggers "Mario Loses a Life," a cadential figure that borrows from one of the gestures (D) from the "Above Ground" music (see Example 1.18 and Figure 1.10). Successfully completing a stage or level brings with it the "Course Clear Fanfare" (see Example 1.19 and Figure 1.11). When time begins to run out, the music signals that by sounding a series of chromatically rising diminished triads called "Hurry Up!" and then going to a quicker tempo, in the tradition of a cinematic and melodramatic "hurry"; also, that "Hurry Up!" ends on a B diminished triad gives the cue a strong sense of harmonic momentum heading into the numerous cues that begin with C, such as "Above Ground" and "Underground" (see Example 1.20). The music found in the castles ("Koopa Stage") hearkens back to the character of *agitatos* or *furiosos* such as Langey's "Furioso No. 3" (1918) or Zamecnik's "Furioso" (from *Sam Fox Photoplay Edition*, volume 1, 1919) (see Examples 1.21, 1.22, and 1.23).

Successfully defeating the King Koopa will bring another musical fanfare figure ("Koopa Defeated Fanfare"), this time a phrygian ascent of parallel diatonic triads ending on G (see Example 1.24). After losing one's final life in a game, a special cadential figure occurs that has the same opening figure of the main theme (A) from "Above Ground" but then moves to F major, F minor, and finally C major, but with a nostalgic lower mordent (see Example 1.25). Kondo's various cues interlock together to support a C major tonal framework, following the model of *Donkey Kong* in using tonal coherence as a way of unifying a video game; *Super Mario Bros.* goes much further, however, in beginning to contain a stronger sense of motivic connection (such as the melody in part D of the "Above Ground" music that occurs each time Mario dies).

Figure 1.7 Mario chases a 1-Up mushroom in *Super Mario Bros.*

Example 1.15 "Underworld" music from *Super Mario Bros.*

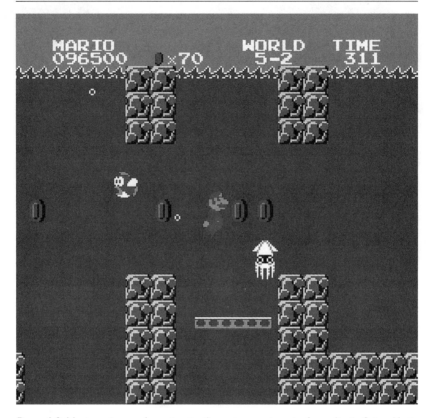

Figure 1.8 Mario swims underwater to the accompaniment of a waltz in *Super Mario Bros.*

Table 1.1 Melodic modules and rhythmic patterns as they cycle through the "Above Ground" music of *Super Mario Bros.*

Melodic modules (color)	Rhythmic pattern (talea)
I	I
A	I
A	I
B	II
B	II
C	I
I	I
A	II
A	II
D	III
D	III
C	I
D	III

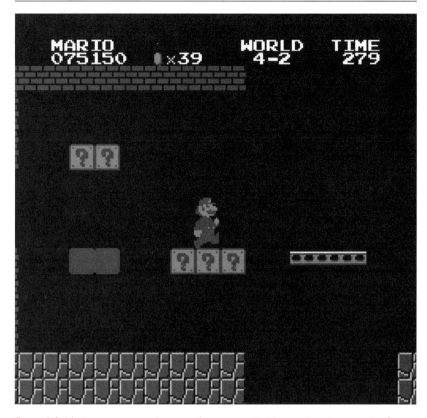

Figure 1.9 Mario ventures underground, accompanied by a misterioso cue, in *Super Mario Bros.*

Example 1.16 J. S. Zamecnik, "Misterioso" (excerpt) (from *Sam Fox Photoplay Edition*, volume 1, 1919)

Figure 1.10 Mario's death triggers "Mario loses a life" (Example 1.18)

Example 1.17 Gregg A. Frelinger, "Pizzicato" (excerpt) (from *Motion Picture Piano Music*, 1909)

Example 1.18 "Mario Loses a Life" music from *Super Mario Bros.*

Example 1.19 "Course Clear Fanfare" music from *Super Mario Bros.*

Example 1.20 "Hurry Up!" music from *Super Mario Bros.*

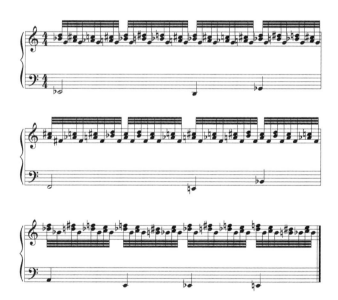

Example 1.21 "Koopa Stage" music from *Super Mario Bros.*

Example 1.22 Otto Langey, "Furioso No. 3" (excerpt) (1918)

Example 1.23 J.S. Zamecnik, "Furioso" (excerpt) (from *Sam Fox Photoplay Edition*, volume 1, 1919)

Figure 1.11 Successfully leaping onto a pole at the end of a level triggers a brief fanfare in *Super Mario Bros.*

Example 1.24 "Koopa Defeated Fanfare" music from *Super Mario Bros.*

Example 1.25 "Game Over" music from *Super Mario Bros.*

Conclusion

It does not seem hyperbolic to claim that the music from *Super Mario Bros.* has become so widely known that it has the familiarity of folk music for the generation that came of age playing it as young people—is it too much to call it the childhood soundtrack for the post-baby boomer generation? The music has been included in later games within the Nintendo world, as well as having been re-performed in a wide variety of styles, from *a cappella* arrangements to Lisztian piano solos such as those done by a young pianist who calls himself the Blindfolded Pianist: he achieved Internet fame by posting YouTube clips of himself playing medleys from *Super Mario Bros.* and other games. Part of the music's powerful appeal derives from Kondo's inspired compositional decisions, but part of the appeal also comes from Kondo's use of an existing set of signifying codes that ranged back through cartoon music to early twentieth-century cinema practices. No other game scores from the first half of the 1980s contained as much tonal coherence as *Donkey Kong* and *Super Mario Bros.*; they are pivotal examples in the rapid stylistic and functional development of video game music.

Notes

All websites were accessed November 4, 2013.

1 Parts of this essay were read, under different titles, at the Music and the Moving Image Conference in New York City (May 22, 2011) and for the Audiovisualities Working Group of the Franklin Humanities Institute at Duke University (April 10, 2012). For assistance with Japanese translations and other feedback on the arguments in this essay, I gratefully acknowledge Micah Auerback and Shoko Whittemore; Jessica Cooley, Kevin Donnelly, Will Gibbons, Van Hillard, and Aaron Major offered valuable feedback on earlier drafts.

2 The Chopin funeral march would only burst forth from the cabinet of a *Circus* machine when a clown in the game died, not whenever a clown anywhere in the world died.

3 Karen Collins, *Game Sound: An Introduction to the History, Theory, and Practice of Video Game Music and Sound Design* (Cambridge, MA: MIT Press, 2008), 4.

4 In Neil Lerner, "The Origins of Musical Style in Video Games, 1977–1983," in *The Oxford Handbook of Film Music Studies*, ed. David Neumeyer (Oxford: Oxford University Press, 2014), 319–47, as well as in Neil Lerner, "Investigating the

Origins of Video Game Music Style, 1977–1983: The Early Cinema Hypothesis," presented at the national meeting of the American Musicological Society (November 3, 2013), I have argued for several ways that video games of the 1970s and early 1980s adopted many of the strategies for fitting music to early film accompanying practices, noting the intermediary step of cartoon scores from the mid twentieth century as a key link, as cartoon composers such as Carl Stalling brought early film music traditions with them to animation. Video games, after all, may be seen as interactive animated films.

5 Extended histories of Nintendo and its rise in the video game industry include: David Sheff, *Game Over: How Nintendo Conquered the World* (Wilton, CT: Gamepress, 1999); Steven L. Kent, *The Ultimate History of Video Games* (New York: Three Rivers Press, 2001); Tristan Donovan, *Replay: The History of Video Games* (East Sussex, UK: Yellow Ant, 2010); and Jeff Ryan, *Super Mario: How Nintendo Conquered America* (New York: Portfolio/Penguin, 2011).

6 As was common with arcade games, *Donkey Kong* offers no credits for designer or programmer, much less composer, within the game itself or on the cabinet. Shigeru Miyamoto's role as the chief designer of *Donkey Kong* appears in Sheff, Kent, Donovan, and Ryan, though only Sheff offers an answer to the question of who composed the music for the game: "Miyamoto was nearly finished, but the game needed background music. He wrote it himself, on an electronic keyboard attached to a computer and stereo cassette deck." Sheff, *Game Over: How Nintendo Conquered the World*, 48. Contradicting Sheff's account, however, are the credits in the CD *Famicom 20th Anniversary Original Soundtracks*, volume 1 (Sony/Columbia, B0000VSBKK, 2004); the liner notes offer Yukio Kaneoka, and not Miyamoto, as the composer for *Donkey Kong*. Collins writes that Kaneoka invented the sound chip used in the Nintendo Entertainment System. Collins, *Game Sound: An Introduction to the History, Theory, and Practice of Video Game Music and Sound Design*, 25. The *Famicom 20th Anniversary Original Soundtracks* liner notes gives as its first track for *Donkey Kong* something called "Title," a tune that does not appear in the 1981 arcade version of the game but does serve as accompaniment for the title screen of the 1983 port of the game for the Famicom system. Complicating this matter of compositional attribution even further is the website of composer Hirokazu Tanaka, which claims *Donky* [sic] *Kong* as one of his credits: www. hirokazutanaka.com/works/. Tanaka's first work with Nintendo was to design the sounds for *Space Firebird* (1980); see Alexander Brandon, "Shooting from the Hip: An Interview with Hip Tanaka," *Gamasutra* (September 25, 2002), available online at www.gamasutra.com/view/feature/2947/shooting_from_the_hip_an_.php.

7 Published by Pocket Books in 1982, the book names no author, although the 2007 documentary *The King of Kong: A Fistful of Quarters* attributes the book to Steve Sanders.

8 *How to Win at Donkey Kong* (Pocket Books, 1982), 3.

9 1980's *Pac-Man* has earlier examples of cutscenes that occur between certain levels.

10 Ryan, *Super Mario: How Nintendo Conquered America*, 29–30.

11 See Chapter 8, "Power and Peril in the Serial-Queen Melodrama," in Ben Singer, *Melodrama and Modernity: Early Sensational Cinema and Its Contexts* (New York: Columbia University Press, 2001); the quotation is from page 224. The "popular and scholarly memory" quotation comes from the earlier version of the essay: "Female Power in the Serial-Queen Melodrama: The Etiology of an Anomaly," *Camera Obscura* 8 (January 1990), 91.

12 As but one other way that *Donkey Kong* indulges in postmodern pastiche, consider the use of the King Kong tropes of the giant ape kidnapping a blonde woman and taking her to a high place. All of the histories of Nintendo go into some detail

about the story of Universal's colossally unsuccessfully infringement suit against Nintendo (*University City Studios, Inc. v. Nintendo Co. Ltd.*) in which Universal claimed ownership of the King Kong property (in a lovely irony, Nintendo's lawyer pointed to a 1975 suit of Universal's against RKO where Universal had successfully argued that King Kong was in the public domain). Nintendo's fascination with the figure of King Kong, a movie character made famous in RKO's original 1933 film (remade in 1976), may be seen as evidence supporting Stuart Hall's statement that postmodernism "is about how the world dreams itself to be 'American'." Lawrence Grossberg, "On Postmodernism and Articulation: An Interview with Stuart Hall," *Journal of Communication Inquiry* 10 (1986), 46.

13 All musical examples have been transcribed by the author.

14 Jon Burlingame, *TV's Biggest Hits: The Story of Television Themes from "Dragnet" to "Friends"* (New York: Schirmer Books, 1996), 15.

15 Rick Altman, *Silent Film Sound* (New York: Columbia University Press, 2004), 261–263. In Edith Lang and George West, *Musical Accompaniment of Moving Pictures* (Boston: Boston Music Company, 1920), 14, they include a section titled "Transition and Modulation" where they assert that "as a general rule the player should bear in mind that his transitions should never be abrupt, unless a special graphic end may be gained thereby. He should take time and care with his modulation." George W. Beynon, *Musical Presentation of Moving Pictures* (New York: G. Schirmer, 1921), 53, declares that "a score must have key-sequence; in other words, each successive number must be in a key related to the one immediately preceding it." David Neumeyer and James Buhler discuss the question of large-scale tonal design in film music from the era of recorded sound in David Neumeyer and James Buhler, "Analytical and Interpretive Approaches (I): Analysing the Music," in *Film Music: Critical Approaches*, ed. K.J. Donnelly (Edinburgh: Edinburgh University Press, 2001), 26–28.

16 See Chapter 4 of Jesper Juul, *Half-Real: Video Games Between Real Rules and Fictional Worlds* (Cambridge, MA: MIT Press, 2005).

17 Juul, *Half-Real: Video Games Between Real Rules and Fictional Worlds*, 130.

18 The trade publication *Play Meter* offered a middling review of *Mario Bros.*, calling it "a big disappointment" and claiming that it "is just an average game." See Gene Lewin, "Gene's Gudgements," *Play Meter* (September 15, 1983). Lewin was more optimistic about *Donkey Kong 3*, writing that "the cute musical Nintendo tunes are there. Every game it comes up with new sounds and songs" and predicting that "the game may have a short life as the levels are very similar to each other, but it should earn well for a while." See "Gene's Gudgements," *Play Meter* (March 15, 1984).

19 Marsha Kinder discusses the rise of Mario and the Nintendo Entertainment System along with the TV show "The Super Mario Brothers Super Show" in Chapter 3 of *Playing with Power in Movies, Television, and Video Games: From Muppet Babies to Teenage Mutant Ninja Turtles* (Berkeley: University of California Press, 1991). In 1993, a live-action film version of *Super Mario Bros.* was released in the US.

20 Steven E. Jones cites Chris Kohler's figures in *The Meaning of Video Games: Gaming and Textual Strategies* (New York and London: Routledge, 2008), 138.

21 In connection to *Super Mario Bros.*, Kinder writes of the "oedipalization of video games" (101) and points to the "strong male orientation in video games" (102) that account for the "heavy reliance on action genres ... in which males have traditionally grown into manhood and replaced father figures, and on myths ... in which little guys beat giants" (104–105).

22 Machinima uses existing video game imagery, sometimes via a sort of digital puppetry, to generate sequences that can be made into their own films. An excep-

tional example that purports to explain the backstory to the game's narrative may be viewed here: www.newgrounds.com/portal/view.php?id=107784.

23 Several variants of this story abound. See, for instance, Ryan, *Super Mario: How Nintendo Conquered America*, 29–30; Sheff, *Game Over: How Nintendo Conquered the World*, 109 (where he spells the last name "Segali"); Kent, *The Ultimate History of Video Games*, 159; and Donovan, *Replay: The History of Video Games*, 100, although neither Nintendo nor Segale confirm it.

24 Unlike *Donkey Kong*, the identity of the composer for *Super Mario Bros.* (Koji Kondo) is widely reported. See, for instance, the brief discussion of Kondo's music for the game by Eric Pidkameny, "Sound in Video Games," in *The Video Game Explosion: A History from PONG to PlayStation and Beyond*, ed. Mark J.P. Wolf (Westport, CT: Greenwood Press, 2008), 253.

25 Zach Whalen, "Play Along: An Approach to Videogame Music," *Game Studies* 4/1 (November 2004), available online at www.gamestudies.org/0401/whalen/.

26 The NES could produce three independent lines of synthesizer melody along with a noise channel that could create percussion effects; see Collins, *Game Sound: An Introduction to the History, Theory, and Practice of Video Game Music and Sound Design*, 25. Where appropriate, I have transcribed the percussion parts as well as the melodic lines.

27 For titles here of the cues from *Super Mario Bros.*, I am following the names as given in the CD *Famicom 20th Anniversary Original Soundtracks*, volume 1.

28 Kondo's "Underwater" music has similarities (particularly the opening part of the main melody) to a waltz that Danny Elfman composed to accompany the character of The Joker in *Batman* (1989). Janet K. Halfyard describes Elfman's waltz as "Straussian" in *Danny Elfman's Batman: A Film Score Guide* (Lanham, MD: Scarecrow Press, 2004), 59.

Chapter 2

The Temporary Avatar Zone
Pico-Pico Parties in Tokyo

Chris Tonelli

My friend Maki was a metalhead fish out of water at the hyper-cute Usagi-Chang Records showcase. She looked around and commented, "The girls are cute, but the guys are all otaku." "Otaku?" I asked. "Yeah, you know . . . nerds."

Field Note, Tokyo, August 21, 2004

Usagi-Chang Records was one of the most important labels in the "pico-pico" scene and this event was their second annual *Usagi-Chang Night Fever*—an epic six-hour showcase of live bands and DJs on or associated with the label.[1] In the Japanese language, "pico-pico" is an onomatopoeic term signifying video game sound. In Tokyo, in 2004, it was also serving as the genre term for a new form of popular music, a bright, jarring, hyperactive form that often tended toward dense, highly ornamented textures, and sudden, radical timbral and stylistic shifts.

Pico-pico, or picopop as it is sometimes called, began to emerge around 1999 and was often described by writers, fans, and musicians as an offshoot of the popular Shibuya-kei genre.[2] Pico-pico was more frenetic than Shibuya-kei ever was, but the comparison is understandable; both genres frequently borrowed freely from a wide range of contrasting musical styles while retaining a bright, energetic approach to pop music as their core.[3] However, true to its name, pico-pico can be differentiated from its predecessor through the presence of aspects of video game aesthetics that were not characteristic of Shibuya-kei. Pico-pico musicians often incorporated or emulated the limited sonic capacity of the sound chips of early video gaming systems, which employed simple periodic waveforms (such as pulse waves, triangle waves, and sawtooth waves) to produce melodies, countermelodies, and basslines whose uniform envelopes and limited spectral content caused listeners to refer to them as "bleepy." In most cases in pico-pico, these "bleepy" sounds were used sparingly alongside more common pop timbres, though at least one prominent group, YMCK, made music almost entirely composed of this "chip sound."[4] Beyond the use of these timbres, pico-pico artists followed video game sound design by creating textures where stable musical voices exist alongside a varied barrage of sonic ornaments. In most video games, a stable musical element is accompanied by a variety of isolated sounds that represent actions occurring in the game world. Similarly, in pico-pico, much more so than in Shibuya-kei, the soundscape was littered with isolated ornamental sound events that made the music sound busier by drawing the listener's attention to a wide range of distinct elements in and around the musical texture.

However, it was not only video game sound aesthetics that informed the culture in and around pico-pico music; aspects of the wider experiential domain of video gaming were equally present in the ways listeners were receiving and participating in the genre around the time of *Usagi-Chang Night Fever Vol. 0002*. The visual culture around pico-pico, its themes of travel, and the musical characteristics of the genre encouraged listeners to draw on their memories of video games and allowed the pico-pico listening space to become what I call a "Temporary Avatar Zone"—a space in which listeners could engage in mimetic intersubjective experience with the avatar "bodies" at the center of video games.

Imagined Travel and Avatar Intersubjectivity

The term "avatar" comes from Hinduism, Ayyavazhi, and Sikhism, where it refers to an incarnate form that a deity has crossed over into. In mid-1980s gaming discourse, this order of materiality and immateriality reversed—the term "avatar" came to mean the virtual body incarnate gamers controlled and occupied while in the act of gaming. In her book *Hello Avatar: Rise of the Networked Generation*, Beth Coleman explains that the commonplace use of "avatar" in gaming discourse refers to "a computer generated figure controlled by a person via a computer . . . often a graphical representation of a person."[5] At the same time, however, she "make[s] the case for an expanded definition of avatar that includes a wider array of media forms and platforms such as Voice over Internet Protocol (VoIP), instant messaging (IM) and short message service or text messaging (SMS), and uses of social and locative media."[6] Though her expanded definition is evidence that the notion of what constitutes an avatar is changing in the world of digital culture, it is the "unexpanded" avatar that is most relevant to the genre of pico-pico music. Yet, these simpler avatars are not as simple as they may seem. James Newman helps us understand that game avatars are not merely characters that a player identifies with, but are also "sets of available capabilities and capacities."[7] Invoking the avatar also invokes players' memories of the imagined mobility they experienced during gameplay. Further, it also invokes aspects of the world in which that avatar exists. Referencing the *Super Mario* series of video games, Newman writes:

> The very notion of the primary-player relating to a single character in the gameworld may be flawed. Rather than "becoming" a particular

character in the gameworld, seeing the world through their eyes, the player encounters the game by relating to everything within the gameworld simultaneously. Perhaps the manner in which the *Super Mario* player learns to think is better conceived as an irreducible complex of locations, scenarios and types of action. Certainly, it is difficult to dislocate Mario the "character" from Mario World, with its interconnecting pipes, or from running, jumping, and puzzling, or even from the enemies, adversaries and opponents encountered in Dinosaur Island. In this way, perhaps the very notion of player–character relationships, and characters in locations performing actions and encountering other non-player-characters, still betrays an insensitivity to the experience of videogame play.[8]

Accordingly, we should be open to the notion that images of avatars that appear in the visual culture outside of gamespace may, for gamers, invoke memories of the experiential aspects of gamespace. As such, "Avatar" in "Temporary Avatar Zone" stands not just for an identificatory relation to a character at the center of a game, but also for all the affordances of gameplay and of avatar worlds.

One immediately registers the significance of the graphical avatar upon encountering the artwork on recordings and in music videos in the pico-pico genre. We can begin with the example of the group YMCK, who have featured images of the group members in avatar form on all six of the albums they have released to date (see Figure 2.1). The group has also created several music videos featuring these avatars traveling in automobiles, space shuttles, and roller coasters through forests, distant planets, and skyscraper-filled urban spaces. Often, these videos were present in the performance space, as YMCK frequently screened them during their live performances.[9]

MIDORI
Vocal

YOKEMURA
Music·Lyrics·Chorus

NAKAMURA
Music

Figure 2.1 Avatar representations of the three members of YMCK

What is less obvious from encounters with avatar-related artwork or the sounds of recordings of pico-pico music is the extent to which an avatar's original sense of the immaterial occupying the incarnate was an important part of pico-pico culture. Live performances by pico-pico groups afforded a kind of feedback loop between the material and immaterial bodies crossed between in avatar exchanges. The mobility and dynamics of the gaming avatar can be invoked through pico-pico's reference to the sound worlds of gaming, and both listeners and audience members showed evidence that avatars often became present in their absence once pico-pico music appeared. We can begin to see the ways pico-pico music invoked the dynamics of avatar mobility by examining YMCK frontwoman Midori Kurihara's performance at *Usagi-Chang Night Fever Vol. 0002*. My first impression of her performance style was that it was highly referential, intended to invoke a range of contemporary and bygone femininities associated with both the domestic and private spheres. She performed that night in an outfit she often uses, notable for more closely resembling a public service-level corporate uniform than the street clothes worn by most other performers at pico-pico shows. Corporate uniforms worn by professionals such as flight attendants or in retail environments in Japan often underscore the gender of the employee and signify the corporate brand through the strategic use of mono or duochrome color schemes associated with the brand. Midori's dress was duochrome, red and white, and its flared skirt exaggerated the femininity of the garment while giving it a retro feel augmented by her short-bob-style-with-bangs haircut. This haircut is capable of invoking both the then-threatening femininities of 1920s flapper culture and the staid stay-at-home moms of the 1950s and 1960s depicted on television by characters such as Mary Tyler Moore's Laura Petrie on *The Dick Van Dyke Show*. The public and domestic femininities invoked by her clothes and hair were amplified by the controlled gestural vocabulary she employed. In Christine Yano's book *Tears of Longing: Nostalgia and the Nation in Japanese Popular Song*, she describes the ways singers in the musical genre of enka engage in carefully crafted gendered display through the ways they hold and move their mouths, shoulders, arms, hands, fingers, chest, hips, legs, knees, and feet. Midori's performance was comparably refined and she invoked some of the same means of marking her femininity used by female enka performers: bent elbows held close to her body, unevenly distributed weight on her hips, legs held closely together, frequent bending at the knees.[10] As she sang, she sported an exaggerated smile, danced using simple repetitive movements, and bent her knees frequently in a kind of curtsy gesture. Her movements recalled scenarios in which women are called into public service and their bodies policed in the production of a standardized feminine ideal, invoking the obligatory cheery demeanor and gendered gestural vocabulary we might see employed by flight attendants, in retail environments, or by television moms such as Laurie Petrie. Midori's performance pointed to the gendered politics of the body in public and private spheres.[11] But, at the same time as her calculated gestures invoked real-world performances of femininity, the simplistic, repetitive style of movement she employed was also analogous to the limited graphic vocabulary used to convey movement in the kinds of early video games YMCK's avatars make reference to. Similarly, her duochrome dress, while reminiscent of corporate uniform color branding, also invoked the simplistic, usually also duo or trichrome color schemes used to render the outfits of early video game avatars.[12]

Consider, for a moment, the aforementioned avatar Mario in the form in which he appeared in Nintendo's original *Super Mario Bros.* video game. Mario's clothing was rendered using a trichrome scheme that represented a brown shirt under a pair of red overalls. Two yellow pixels were added to this red and brown scheme that represented the clasps of Mario's overalls. Midori's outfit contained large white buttons on a red background whose exaggerated size was capable of referencing the pixel size used to render early game avatars. It was as if the aesthetics of both avatar movement and avatar composition had become incarnate in her performance style.

Behind Midori, Takeshi Yokemura and Tomoyuki Nakamura complemented the color scheme of her dress with white shirts and thin red ties. These outfits, though not as strongly referential of bygone fashions as Midori's, were still capable of referencing the period before rock music, when popular musicians almost always performed in matching uniforms and formal attire. The outfits worn by their avatars are more strongly referential. The monochrome green and blue suits and white cravats that adorn their avatars strongly reference the sartorial conventions of music of the 1950s and 1960s.[13]

YMCK's referencing of the 1950s and 1960s invokes not only the period in which television became a ubiquitous force affording quotidian imagined travel, but also the beginning of the jet age, a period where both imagined and actual travel occurred in new accelerated forms. YMCK, however, were not the first Japanese popular musicians to underscore connections between the rise of video games and beginnings of the jet age. We can understand pico-pico better by considering themes explored in the Shibuya-kei genre. A central image in the CD insert for Shibuya-kei artist Yoshinori Sunahara's 1998 *Take Off and Landing* contains a former slogan of Pan-American World Airways: "For once in a lifetime get into this world" (see Figure 2.3).

Underneath the text are 18 images with borders shaped like television screens and displaying dated images of smiling pilots, in-flight meal service, palm trees at dusk, the sphinx, a sexual encounter, and an airline concourse. The design of this album art is a pastiche of the image contained on the packaging of the Atari 2600 Video Computer System. On that packaging, the "screens" displayed screenshots from a variety of Atari games alongside images of children and adults looking joyful, presumably from the pleasure and bonding experiences provided to them by the Atari VCS (see Figure 2.4).

Figure 2.2 YMCK live at *Usagi-Chang Night Fever Vol. 0002*

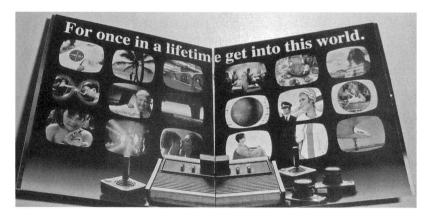

Figure 2.3 Album art from Yoshinori Sunahara's *Take Off And Landing*

Figure 2.4 Packaging image from the Atari 2600 Video Computer System

In both Sunahara's image and the packaging image it pastiches, in the foreground, in front of the screens, sits the Atari VCS itself. While Sunahara's "screens" present images associated with travel, they also seem to suggest inaccessibility. Even if viewers can afford to get themselves physically in the presence of the sphinx, they cannot transport themselves into the bygone era the images invoke. There is also a racial component to this inaccessibility; despite the fact that Sunahara's album was produced in Japan by a Japanese artist, all of the bodies in the images, with the exception of one image of Sunahara himself, are "white" bodies.[14] Inaccessibility also appears through the fact that Japanese viewers cannot occupy the forms of whiteness these dated images seem to celebrate. Further, the presence of a bank of 18 "screens" makes it difficult for the viewer to escape into any single image for long without being drawn toward the others, and the frames themselves have a distancing effect; while one can suspend attending to the frame while watching a single screen, it is much harder to do so when multiple screens are presented alongside one another. As such, the viewers are reminded of the distance between themselves and the space depicted in the image, of the impenetrability of the image, through the way the layout of the screens draws them back to the frames. Conversely, the gaming system sits in the frame that is the border of the album sleeve. Its placement in the foreground makes it seem real, tactile, and accessible relative to the content of the "screens." The viewer is not drawn to the frame that contains it, but is instead drawn by the frame to the gaming system as the focal point of the image. Against the "screens," the gaming system seems the only accessible way to respond to the imperative of the Pan-Am slogan.[15] The viewer may not have access to the sphinx or to whiteness, but the gaming system and the imagined travel it affords are within reach.

Regardless of how this insert image is interpreted, imagined travel is the central theme in *Take off and Landing*. The album begins with the announcement:

> Ladies and Gentlemen, welcome to the Tokyo Underground Airport on its opening day. The first plane is about to take off. Let's take a state of the art elevator to the satellite of the 340th floor underground.[16]

An image beneath the clear CD tray offers a guide to this Tokyo Underground Airport, which takes travelers from Tokyo to the furthest metropolises of the globe in less than 120 minutes. The reference to "underground," and the fact that the album's musical content begins after the announcement, suggests that the airport is a metaphor for musical affordance—music, like gaming, is a tool that affords types of imagined travel.

Travel is also a central theme in the pico-pico genre. Clearly related to, but faster than, the Tokyo Underground Airport is the group Capsule's Tokyo Portable Airport. Unlike Sunahara, Capsule can be considered part of the pico-pico scene; they have often performed and collaborated with other pico-pico groups, and much of their music conforms to key stylistic elements common in the genre.[17] The Tokyo Portable Airport, described on the 2004 album *S.F. Sound Furniture*, imagines instantaneous travel via portals above the city. Instantaneous is, obviously, the only acceptable speed for those used to the imagined travel afforded by video games and the Internet.

The transformative nature of instantaneous imagined travel is explored by another group featured at *Usagi-Chang Night Fever Vol. 0002*, The Aprils.[18] In their song "Net-surf Music," they sing of racing in a "web-jet" through a "digital-slide"; after reaching top speed they ask: "頭の中 繋がっていく新しい声が響くだろう？" (Can you hear the new voice echoing inside of your head?).[19] Here, the divide between "real" and "imagined" travel is blurred; their song "STRO-B" begins, "世界が部屋へと注ぐ 嘘だらけの現実を抜け出してさ" (The world flows into my room. It slipped out from the false reality). Similarly, travel to both "real" and "imaginary" locations occur in the genre. Pico-pico songs present hyperreal Nevada (Plus-Tech Squeezebox's "Hoky-Poky a la mode"), Wyoming (Plus-Tech Squeezebox's "Uncle Chicken's Drag Rag"), and the African savannah (Hazel Nuts Chocolate's "ポコポン探検隊" transla-tion: Pocopon Adventure) as destinations for imagined travel alongside "Dough-Nuts Town" (Plus-Tech Squeezebox's "Dough-Nuts Town's map") and "Pants Country" (Hazel Nuts Chocolate's "パ・パ・パ・パ・パンツで GO!" translation: In Pa-Pa-Pa-Pa-Pants, GO!).[20]

This blurring of real and imagined travel is in accordance with the blurring between performer and avatar suggested in the work of YMCK. YMCK, however, is not the only pico-pico group who invoke the avatar in its work. In the album art that accompanies Plus-Tech Squeezebox's 2004 album *Cartrooom!*, an interesting tension is created between a photograph of the group members and several images of their animated counterparts. The photograph depicts the two male members of the group, Tomonori Hayashibe and Takeshi Wakiya, in lab coats and safety goggles. In front of the pair is the vocalist Junko Kamada, wearing a short orange dress, looking like a prisoner in bare feet and with one ankle and one wrist restrained with cables that trail off beyond the borders of the image.[21] She stares unsmiling at the camera, looking somewhat lifeless with her arms straight at her sides. Captive in non-avatar form, the illustrated images depict avatar-Junko breaking free of her restraints and retaliating against her captors. Here, Plus-Tech Squeezebox depict the avatar space as one in which power imbalances are turned on their heads. Reversals of this sort have, of course, long been an explanation for the appeal of gaming; many theorists have positioned avatars as a means through which empowerment can be achieved.[22]

The presence of avatar-centered album art on the merchandise tables at pico-pico events brings the avatar into the pico-pico performance space, as do listeners' memories of pico-pico album art and music videos they have taken in on past occasions. At the same time, the presence of the avatar is invoked in the performance space in other ways. At *Usagi-Chang Night Fever Vol. 0002*, the duo Hazel Nuts Chocolate performed a live set where one of the members deejayed their recorded material while the other created an elaborate chalkboard drawing of avatar versions of herself and her partner that took form over the duration of the set.[23] Game avatars such as those that appear in most of the games of the Nintendo Entertainment System are relatively expressionless and portray movement through switching repetitively between simple binary pairs of graphics that suggest various types of motion such as running, raising an arm, or jumping. At *Usagi-Chang Night Fever Vol. 0002*, I had the momentary impression that I was present at a low-intensity exercise class. The audience around me performed simple repetitive movements that seemed to me more like calisthenics than a form of dance. After some time, I was struck by the impression that their dancing recalled the on/off switch binary graphics of early game avatars. The binary graphic set that depicts classic avatar running is composed of an image of the right arm of the avatar raised while the left is lowered and an image where the left is raised but not the right. This, too, describes the dance I was surrounded by during much of the night. This steady on/off switch arm movement was accompanied by static hips and torso and often by a static facial expression. The spectral body of the game avatar had indeed become incarnate, both onstage and off.

The Sounds and Space of Pico-Pico Music

This blurring of self and avatar and these themes of imagined travel were both core components of the genre that prompted listeners to draw on memories of video gaming in the pico-pico performance space. The sounds of the genre also point us toward pico-pico's invocation of memories of the imagined travel of video gaming and its affordance of an incarnate expression of avatar mobility. By imitating aspects of the sound design of video gaming, the sounds of pico-pico music work to position the listener as an avatar hero on a journey through gamespace.

Pico-pico was a genre that accommodated a relatively wide range of musical styles. The jazz harmonies and ubiquitous chip timbres of YMCK's sound were distinct from the guitar pop style of The Aprils, and both of these diverged substantially from the collage of styles that comprised the music of groups such as Plus-Tech Squeezebox or Hazel Nuts Chocolate. Yet, these groups all tended toward the frequent use of dense, highly ornamented textures. This stylistic component was essential because it was the element that afforded an experiential blurring between real world space and gamespace; it was what made the listening space reminiscent of the game world. The blurring of avatar and performer was more than imagery and was fueled by more than memories; it was also an experiential component afforded by the music itself.

Given the stylistic diversity of the pico-pico genre, illustrating the sonic characteristics that allowed the listening space to become reminiscent of gamespace will require close readings of examples from different corners of pico-pico's stylistic domain. One of the characteristics of a number of pico-pico groups was their incorporation of a wide range of stylistic appropriations in a single piece. Hazel Nuts Chocolate's "Humpty Dumpty Rag" is a song appropriately representative of this approach. YMCK, on the other hand, represents a pico-pico group whose songs adopted a relatively consistent style throughout. "Starlight" is a track from its third full length album, *Family Genesis* (2008).[24] Placing these two songs alongside one another highlights the considerable musical diversity contained within the genre of pico-pico; at the same time, it can show how songs of notably different styles shared musical characteristics essential to the genre, characteristics that afforded the blurring of real and gamespace.

"Humpty Dumpty Rag" was one of the songs included in Hazel Nuts Chocolate's D.J. set at *Usagi-Chang Night Fever Vol. 0002* and is the first full track (after a short introduction track) on its 2004 debut album *Bewitched*.[25] The song begins with a sonic code that signifies imagined travel, a descending harp flourish that has been used in countless film and television sequences to signal that a character is travelling back in their memory or entering a dream state. When this flourish appears in the absence of a televisual image, it seems to interpellate the listeners themselves as travelers. Like the intercom announcement that begins *Take Off and Landing*, this harp flourish suggests to listeners that the music that follows is not just music, but a new environment through which they will travel. Another common television soundtrack technique appears alongside the harp flourish: it is common, over such

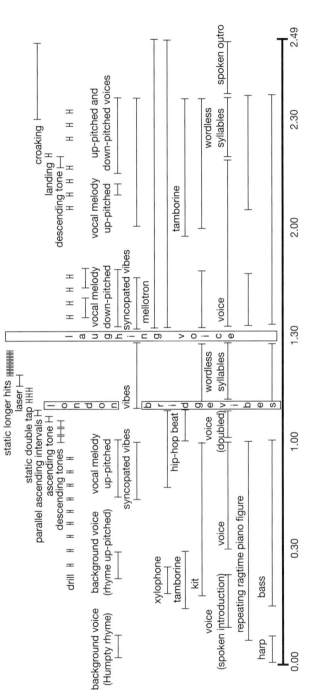

Figure 2.5 Graphic Map of "Humpty Dumpty Rag" by Hazel Nuts Chocolate. This style of graphic mapping was previously used by Eric Clarke and Nicola Dibben in their 2000 article, "Sex, Pulp, and Critique." Unless relabeled, each horizontal plain represents the same instrument or instrument group as the label to its left

Example 2.1 Repeating ragtime figure from "Humpty Dumpty Rag"

figures, to use repetition of a word or phrase to mark that word or phrase as the trigger to the reverie. This technique sonically signifies the act of running a memory over again in one's thoughts in contemplation. Here, low in the mix, a voice can be heard repeating "Humpty Dumpty" in such a manner. What enters next is a four-measure ragtime piano figure that repeats throughout much of the song, serving as a motor rhythm and harmonic anchor (see Example 2.1).[26]

This figure may invoke a vehicle in motion, given the motor function it serves as it carries the listener out of the transition between reality and reverie (the rhythms are almost train-like and many listeners associate ragtime music, rail travel, and early American modernity). With this vehicle in motion, the lead singer enters with a spoken welcome to the listener. This greeting is somewhat odd given the fact that the first track of the album already provided a spoken welcome. But if we have entered some new space, perhaps a second welcome is appropriate. Under this welcome, the texture builds with a bass and tamborine entry, followed by drum kit and xylophone. The voice low in the mix reciting the "Humpty Dumpty" poem in English can be heard again before the start of the first verse, but here it is up-pitched, making the voice sound somewhat alien.

The first verse proceeds in a relatively conventional manner. The texture thins as the verse starts, with the tamborine and xylophone dropping out before it begins. It thickens again midway through the verse to build toward the next section. However, one unusual and jarring element of the verse is a percussive ornament that begins two measures before the verse; in the graphic map in Figure 2.5, I have labeled the ornament—which accents beat four of measures two and four of the hypermeter, eventually coming to color the ends of vocal phrases as the verse begins—"drill" because the abrasive timbre of the sample is reminiscent both of a drill and of the kinds of samples that occur frequently in drillcore music. This drill sits surprisingly high in the mix and inevitably jolts the listener wherever it occurs.

When the verse ends, a break occurs that sees the ragtime figure, the bass, and the drum kit drop out. A hip-hop rhythm accompanies a short rapped vocal that restates, in Japanese this time, the core elements of the "Humpty Dumpty" rhyme. This portion also contains a series of ornaments that I find significant. Three descending tones occur in sequence, each lasting two beats and pausing two beats before recurring. Following these three descending tones is one ascending tone of equal length. This pattern is followed immediately by a different style of ornament that features two beats worth of sixteenth notes rising in parallel sequence.

All of the instruments drop out after this brief hip-hop interlude and a vibraphone timbre delivers a brief quotation of "London Bridge is Falling Down," likely in reference to "Humpty Dumpty's" theme of falling, but also significant for its contribution to the song's mélange of shifting references. The section that follows this quotation serves as an instrumental interlude that builds toward a denser and more frenetic second verse. Over the eight measures of the section, the harmonic rhythm moves from one chord change per measure, to changing every two beats, and finally to a chord change every beat as the rhythms of the instruments get progressively more frantic, building toward a climactic break where all that is heard is a sample of uproarious laughter. This section consists largely of ascending and descending runs on the vibraphone that recall practice exercises for Western classical piano students. But, like previous sections, the consistent presence of strange percussive ornaments disturbs the overall stylistic conventionality of the section. Here, three types of ornament exist. The first sounds like radio static; what I have labeled "static double tap" is a pattern of two quick pulses followed by a single pulse that recurs each measure for three measures. This "static" timbre disappears momentarily and a steady eighth note figure in a timbre that could be used to represent laser blasts in a video game or film occurs in its place for a single measure. After this, the "static" timbre recurs, but here it keeps a steady quarter note pulse for two measures. One more ornament can be heard before the climactic laughing break. It is another "drill" sound that helps the passage to reach its maximum density before the break.

After the break, the second verse appears. It is twice the length of the previous verse. From the outset, the texture is denser than the previous verse: an instrument resembling a mellotron or accordion fills out the texture alongside an ascending sample that is voice-like, and may be a voice, a theremin, or some other processed sample. The second quarter of this section sees the texture thinning drastically in preparation to end the section and song with even greater density. The voices that dropped out for this second quarter re-enter for the final half of the section. The drill ornaments continue, but pause midway through the second half to make space for two other ornaments. The first is a long descending tone, reminiscent of those heard in the first verse, but double the duration. This long falling tone is followed by an ornament that I have labeled "landing," due to the fact it follows the long falling tone. It resembles the sound of tearing paper or running through gravel.

Overall, the song is incredibly dense and busy, filled with a variety of timbres and a series of attention-grabbing ornaments. The drill ornament that recurs with the most consistency throughout the song is not a single repeated sample; it comes in a variety of forms. Some instances of it appear as a double tap, some ascend in pitch and others descend. The variety with which they appear ensures that the listener cannot easily acclimatize to them and thus cease to be jolted. A texture in which the melodic and harmonic elements of the song are accompanied by an intense variety of distinct ornaments is one that bears striking resemblance to the sound design of most video games, whose melodic and harmonic components exist alongside a variety of distinct sound events that represent actions occurring in the gamespace. When we play a video game such as *Super Mario Bros.*, we hear melody, countermelody, bassline, and steady percussion, but alongside that we hear isolated sound events that represent our avatar jumping, collecting a coin, stomping a Goomba, or a number of other events. Each of these events has a distinct sound that adds to the sonic texture of the game world. Ascending and descending tones such as those that can be heard in "Humpty Dumpty Rag" are used in video games to signify objects rising or falling in gamespace, the drill sounds resemble sounds used to indicate forms of contact between bodies in the game world, and the "laser"-type sounds resemble, of course, lasers. The variety and frequency with which these ornaments occur in "Humpty Dumpty Rag" position the listener not just within a musical work, but within a game world where his or her body is the center and audible events are occurring all around him or her.

Alongside its percussive ornaments, "Humpty Dumpty Rag's" texture is filled with a variety of processed vocal sounds, many cartoonishly high and low. Rather than simply presenting a single vocalist, a din of vocal sound often appears behind the foregrounded vocal, suggesting a space occupied by multiple bodies. The "static" sounds in the instrumental bridge sound almost like an alien vocal din, as do the sounds toward the end that I labeled "croaking" (which seem to be strangely processed vocal samples). The stylistic leaps in the song from carnivalesque ragtime, to hip-hop, to classical piano exercises, recall the way many video games consist of the exploration of a variety of unique lands; the listener's journey takes him or her through a series of radically distinct stylistic spaces.

Unlike Hazel Nuts Chocolate, YMCK's sound does not employ wide-ranging timbral diversity and frequent genre-hopping. YMCK's nearly exclusive use of "chip sound," the limited timbral sphere of early video game sound, prevents the kinds of diversity prevalent in "Humpty Dumpty Rag." Yet, much of their music features a similar density of ornament and a comparable approach to sectionality. "Starlight" has an unusual structure that can be summarized as:

chorus (8 bars), verse (8 bars), bridge 1 (16 bars), verse (8 bars),

chorus (16 bars), instrumental solo (16 bars), bridge 2 (18 bars),

break (1 bar), chorus (16 bars), verse (8 bars), outro (2 bars).

The chorus consists entirely of the repetition, in English, of "starlight" and "fall down," "light" and "down" being held for nearly the full duration of the hypermeter. Each line of the verses begins with the refrain "parara," an onomatopoeic term meant to invoke the sound of engines.

The chorus sections provide the thinnest textures. They feature Midori's voice accompanied by a male vocal harmony, and three layers of chip sound: countermelody, harmony, and percussion. The rhythmic activity in the section is fairly calm and there is relatively little ornamentation. A sound that in the textural map below is labeled "rocket," which is a cloud of static that ascends in pitch, appears to color the end of the first hyper-metrical unit and a drum rush appears to create energy as the section changes to the verse.

The first verse is also relatively thin. The midrange chip sound voices drop out, but are replaced with a chip sound bassline. The regularity and "brush" timbre of the chorus percussion transforms into an erratic breakbeat style of rhythmic accompaniment that continues throughout most of the song. The vocal phrase rhythm changes to a pattern of short phrases that accent the downbeat of the first and third measures. In the measures of the hypermeter that contain the emphasis of the vocal activity (1 and 3), we can also hear an ornament I have labeled "coin tones." These are a series of two or three upper-range pitches, the first and third of which possess an envelope and brightness that resembles the tones that sound in *Super Mario Bros.* when a coin is collected. These sets of two or three tones ornament all three verses and the first bridge. The second pitch is always a descending fifth below the first and has a differing envelope that gives it a pulsing character. The third pitch (where it occurs) always ascends upward from the second but varies in pitch. In the first verse, in the space between these ornaments, few other ornaments occur; only between the first and third set of "coin tones" does an ornament, a descending gesture, occur.

The first bridge is nearly identical texturally to the first verse. The voice changes from a male and female harmony to Midori alone, singing phrases that repeat a single pitch and are highly processed in a manner that signifies the synthesized voice of a robot. A new ornament appears in this section, a "rising echoing flourish" that opens the section and colors the ends of its first two lines.

In the second verse, the ornamentation between the "coin tone" patterns increases in frequency and diversity. The space between each of the "coin tone" patterns contains a different series of sounds. After the first, at 0:53 in

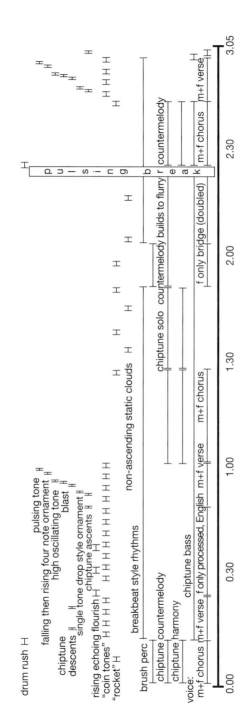

Figure 2.6 Graphic map of "Starlight" by YMCK

the song, a rising line can be heard followed by a single tone that has an envelope and effect similar to a "bass drop." After the second, a descending figure occurs, followed by what I have labeled as a "blast," which itself is followed by a high oscillating tone. After the third "coin tone" pattern, we hear a four-note ornament followed by a pulsing tone. Altogether, this section, and the final appearance of the verse (which repeats the same sequence of events), creates a texture littered with a diversity of ornaments. As in the densest sections of "Humpty Dumpty Rag," a barrage of distinct sounds command the attention of the listener.

I labeled the "blast" ornament as such in following with the video for "Starlight," which depicts a sequence of events, displayed in Figure 2.7. The ornament I refer to with the label "blast" is a moment of noise that can be heard in the music video for "Starlight" at the point where the third image contained in Figure 2.7 occurs. The descending gesture that precedes the noise accompanies the images of the red squares descending toward the gray, T-shaped object. These images being paired with the occurrence of these ornaments in the song suggests that these ornaments are not heard only as sonic events in the space of the song, but also as actions occurring in a game-type environment the listener inhabits. The care taken in pico-pico music to offer a breadth of ornaments and to offer ornaments that change character as they recur is a feature of the genre that invokes memories of game sound environments where music coexists with a series of isolated, momentary sonic events meant not just to add color to the game's soundscape, but also to signify that actions are occurring within gamespace.

Conclusion

In the pico-pico scene, the frequency of depictions of the performers as avatars, the themes of travel prevalent in lyrics and imagery, and the textures and timbres of the music itself all worked to encourage listeners to re-conceptualize themselves as avatars. The busy, highly ornamented textures of pico-pico suggested a game world was present, and in the absence of an avatar to occupy that imagined world, the listener's own body and the bodies of the performers and other listeners around him or her became the occupants of that world. As these sonic elements positioned the listener as a traveller in a game world, the lyrics and imagery of the genre celebrated imagined travel in a multiplicity of forms—from the new cosmopolitan imaginations of the jet age, to the orientation of the domestic space toward the shared televisual travel of nuclear families, to the imagined travel of Web surfing and gaming technologies.

I do not intend to argue that these kinds of imaginations will inevitably be part of the way listeners experience this music. Like all forms of music, what pico-pico affords will differ in different environments. However, I think

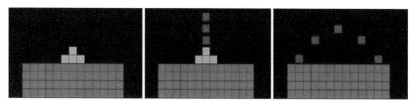

Figure 2.7 Rendering of "Blast" sequence from YMCK's "Starlight" video

these observations can help us understand a part of how the music was functioning and what it was affording in live performance, and, perhaps, private listening environments in the early years of the pico-pico scene.

But if the avatar experience was so powerful, why not just return to gamespace? Why invoke it outside of the space of video gaming? Sean Fenty provides us with one possible answer. In an essay theorizing nostalgia for early video games, he writes:

> The nostalgia felt for video games is not nostalgia for a past state before the trauma of games disrupted us, but a desire to recapture that mind-altering experience of being in a game for the first time. It is a yearning for liminality itself—for the moment of transition. Not the liminality of being caught between the two worlds of pre-video games and video games, but the liminality of being between the two worlds of the real and the game world—of being on the threshold.[27]

The pico-pico genre used sound, imagery, and lyrics to invoke the worlds of gaming in their absence. By absenting the game while using sound to remake the "real" world in its image, pico-pico created a new means of fostering liminality between the real and the game, between our biological bodies and the speeds and slownesses of the avatar. Events such as *Usagi-Chang Night Fever* afforded, for some, the experience of being on this threshold. With the help of this unique genre of music, avatar and actual bodies and real and gamespace were collapsing into one another in new ways in pico-pico's Temporary Avatar Zones.

Notes

All websites were accessed November 4, 2013.

1 The concept of the music "scene" is discussed in Andy Bennett and Richard Peterson, *Music Scenes: Local, Translocal, and Virtual* (Nashville, TN: Vanderbilt University Press, 2004). My use of the term conforms to Bennett and Peterson's understanding that "scene" describes a group of "performers, support facilities, and fans com[ing] together to collectively create music for their own enjoyment" and that this contrasts with the industry model in which "relatively few people

make music for mass markets" (p. 3). The other small independent labels active in the scene at the time of this event included abcdefg records, Softly!, and Vroom Sound (later renamed Stubbie Records).

2   Shibuya-kei is a genre that was popular throughout the 1990s in Japan. The term "neo-Shibuya-kei" has sometimes been used to describe artists in the pico-pico scene.

3   The comparison is also directly historical; pico-pico groups often described Shibuya-kei musicians such as Kahimi Karie, Flipper's Guitar, and Cornelius as notable influences on their work.

4   Given this fact, YMCK moved fluidly between the genres of pico-pico and chiptune. Chiptune is a musical genre characterized by its complete devotion to the limited sound world of early video gaming systems. With the exception of YMCK, no other group active in the pico-pico scene that I am aware of would qualify as chiptune music, in seemingly dominant understandings of the term, as any chip sound they employ makes up only a small portion of the music's instrumentation. However, in other uses of the term, pico-pico is considered a subgenre of chiptune despite its relatively small reliance on chip sound. For more on chiptune, see Chris Tonelli, "The Chiptuning of the World," in *The Oxford Handbook of Mobile Music Studies*, ed. Jason Stanyek and Sumanth Gopinath (Oxford: Oxford University Press, forthcoming).

5   Beth Coleman, *Hello Avatar: Rise of the Networked Generation* (Cambridge, MA: MIT Press, 2001), 12.

6   Coleman, *Hello Avatar: Rise of the Networked Generation*, 12.

7   James Newman, "The Myth of the Ergodic Video Game," *Game Studies* 2/1 (July 2002), available online at www.gamestudies.org/0102/newman.

8   Newman, "The Myth of the Ergodic Video Game."

9   This was not the case, however, at *Usagi-Chang Night Fever Vol. 0002*.

10 See Christine Yano, *Tears of Longing: Nostalgia and the Nation in Japanese Popular Song* (Cambridge, MA: Harvard University Press, 2002), 115–122. My intention in making this comparison to enka is not to underscore Midori's Japaneseness by comparing her performance to those of other Japanese musical genres, particularly to a genre so strongly articulated with ideas of the Japanese nation, but, rather, to make a comparison between two styles of musical vocal performance with highly conscious and constructed gestural vocabularies.

11 The politics of the domestic sphere is further underscored by the recurring theme of "Family Music" that runs through YMCK's work. Four of their six albums contain the word "Family" in their titles: *Family Music* (2004), *Family Racing* (2005), *Family Genesis* (2008), and *Family Cooking* (2009). The family association is likely received by much of their audience as a reference to the fact that the video game system known as the "Nintendo Entertainment System" in North America was branded in Japan as the "Famicom," which was a shortened version of "Family Computer," a name that betrayed the early marketing strategies of home video gaming systems, which positioned them, much in the way board games have often been positioned, as a tool of nuclear family unity. The chiptune timbres of YMCK's music and the aesthetics of their avatars make strong references to the sights and sounds afforded by the Famicom/Nintendo Entertainment System.

12 Midori has used this outfit in many of her performances with YMCK. At times, she has worn this outfit with the addition of a pillbox hat and elbow-length white gloves that further amplify many of the associations discussed above. A second outfit she has also frequently employed is notably similar to the one I describe here, with the same color scheme and general characteristics.

13 In another example of "the real" imitating the avatar, Yokemura and Nakamura later began to perform in suits that imitated the green and blue outfits of their avatars.

14 This image of Sunahara is distinct from the other images in that it looks contemporary, depicts a blank white background rather than a more specific real-world space, and contains a visibly Asian body. This "screen" is, notably, positioned closest to the video game system depicted in the foreground beneath the "screens."

15 An oppositional reading is, of course, possible and likely to have manifested in different viewers' encounters with the image. The Pan-Am slogan may well have been taken literally by viewers, and the image interpreted as advocacy for actual travel over the imagined travel of video gaming. When dealing with the texts of popular culture, we must always leave open the possibility of the co-presence of opposing readings. However, as I explore in the following paragraphs, imagined travel remains both a theme of the album and an effect of it.

16 Yoshinori Sunahara, *Take Off and Landing* (Sony, 2000).

17 Capsule has made music that is stylistically distinct from pico-pico and has contributed to other genres. Its collaboration with groups more firmly located in the pico-pico genre can be found on albums such as *Phony Phonic* (2003), which features collaborations with pico-pico groups Hazel Nuts Chocolate and Sonic Coaster Pop.

18 The Aprils released its music at this time on the Softly! label, rather than on Usagi-Chang. Their appearance at *Usagi-Chang Night Fever* is evidence of the collaborative, interconnected nature of a variety of the small independent labels active in the pico-pico scene.

19 All translations of song lyrics from Japanese were completed by Yumiko Morita and myself.

20 Japanese popular musicians in many genres commonly employ English-language titles for album and track names. In this chapter, song and album titles that appear in English and not in Japanese were listed in English on the original domestic Japanese album release.

21 Hayashibe and Wakiya are the core members of the group. A variety of vocalists have appeared on various tracks they have recorded.

22 These theorists include Charles Bernstein, who wrote in his 1989 essay "Play It Again, Pac-Man," that the "Nerdy kid who can't get out a full sentence and whose social skills resemble Godzilla's is the Star of the arcade," and Mackenzie Wark whose recent notion of the "gamer as theorist" in *Gamer Theory* (Cambridge and London: Harvard University Press, 2007) suggests a variety of game player who has the power to disrupt the logic of capitalist agon.

23 Though a cartoon of oneself in an imagined world is not an "avatar" per se, such an illustration, in the environment of a pico-pico performance space can invoke memories of avatar mobility. As the pico-pico music plays, listeners in this context may draw on memories of game mobility to dynamize the illustration, to imagine the cartoon figure moving through their imaginary world. As the music invokes gaming, the illustration is likely to form a palimpsest with memories of gaming and become avatar-like.

24 YMCK, *Family Genesis* (Avex Entertainment, 2008).

25 Hazel Nuts Chocolate, *Bewitched* (Trolley Bus, 2004).

26 Hazel Nuts Chocolate's "Humpty Dumpty Rag" bears a slight resemblance to "Humpty Dumpty," a "novelty rag" by the American composer Charley Straight, recorded by the New York Military Band in 1914. Both Straight's composition and the ragtime figure in Hazel Nuts Chocolate song begin with a repeated three-

note arpeggio. But these kinds of arpeggiated passages were ubiquitous in ragtime, and beyond this and the similar titles, no other obvious similarities or connections appear.

27 Sean Fenty, "Why Old School is 'Cool': A Brief Analysis of Classic Video Game Nostalgia," in *Playing the Past: History and Nostalgia in Video Games*, ed. Zach Whalen and Laurie N. Taylor (Nashville, TN: Vanderbilt University Press, 2008), 23.

Chapter 3

Nintendo's Art of Musical Play

Roger Moseley and Aya Saiki

My way of thinking is to make old things possible with current technology.[1]
(Gunpei Yokoi)

The audiovisual elements of North American and European digital games
have often been conceptualized in the light and shadow cast by cinematic
and televisual theories, operations, and discourses.[2] In the wake of "blockbuster"
console games such as the post-apocalyptic *Gears of War*, which inspired
(as well as reflected) recent Hollywood themes and techniques, screen-based
analogies now extend to almost any game designed for optimal play in the
hushed darkness of the home theater.[3] Critics craving legitimacy for digital
games routinely invoke *Citizen Kane* as a litmus test for software with the
potential to transform the medium from a conduit for childish entertainment
to an art form capable of sophistication, ambiguity, beauty, and profundity.[4]
Why should this be so?

One reason has to do with media technology. Over the last two decades,
both films and games have been distributed on optical media (especially DVDs
and Blu-ray Discs), enabling the domestication of content whose exorbitant
data and hardware requirements had previously driven customers to attend
cinemas and arcades. Particularly in the United States, these new economic
conditions helped promote the ideal of privatizing public experiences: both
the cinema and the arcade could be brought home with minimal loss of quality.
In the gaming realm, this model had been established by the Atari VCS/2600
(1977), which found success by bringing Japanese arcade hits such as *Space
Invaders* and *Pac-Man* into the living room, despite the shortcomings of the
domestic versions in comparison to their arcade counterparts.[5] Only at the
turn of the millennium, with the introduction of ever-growing plasma and
LCD screens, audio receivers capable of Dolby Digital and DTS surround
sound, and the burgeoning capacity and 3D graphical power of DVD-based
consoles such as Sony's PlayStation 2 and Microsoft's Xbox, did console games
break decisively from the arcade paradigm and simulate cinematic techniques
and effects as a matter of course. Games developed for the subsequent

generation of consoles, such as *Heavy Rain* and *Alan Wake* for Sony's Blu-ray-equipped PlayStation 3 and Microsoft's Xbox 360, respectively, aimed to present narrative-driven gameplay with cinematic production values.[6] In doing so, they conformed to Lev Manovich's definition of visual culture in the computer age: "cinematographic in its appearance, digital on the level of its material, and computational . . . in its logic."[7] Accordingly, the qualities of photorealism and sonic immersion have been embraced by many as a self-evident *telos* for the future development of the digital game.

Manovich makes a compelling case for cinema as the master trope that informs the structure of "new" media. When applied to prominent console games in the Western marketplace, his argument draws further support from Marshall McLuhan's famous declaration that "the 'content' of any medium is always another medium" and Jay David Bolter and Richard Grusin's more recent theory of remediation.[8] As a generalization about the medium of the digital game *in toto*, however, it is problematic for at least two reasons. First, it fails to reflect global diversity, based as it is on European and North American theories and practices.[9] Second, its privileging of the cinematic underplays other configurations of audiovisual elements in the medium's historical and archaeological records. Moreover, while Manovich observes that attributes such as digitality and interactivity that are broadly ascribed to "new" media can also be found in film, he does not take full account of the way that interactivity is integral to the ludic systems of digital games.[10]

In all these regards, it is telling that Japanese media artist Toshio Iwai, who developed the multimedia "art game" *Electroplankton* for Nintendo's handheld DS system in 2005, locates the origins of the medium in the pre-cinematic technologies of the flip book and the music box.[11] In his view, digital game systems are "musical instruments with which one can play with moving images and music simultaneously."[12] For Iwai, the manually activated flip book marks the "starting point of the moving image," while the music box represents a corresponding breakthrough in the transduction of sound into image (and vice versa).[13] Iwai thus considers antique technologies associated with cel animation and musical recreation to be more directly relevant to the digital game's prehistory than film or television.[14]

Insofar as player input is routed through fingers and thumbs (via controllers and discrete systems) and conveyed through gestures (relayed by Nintendo's Wii controller or registered by Microsoft's Kinect multimedia sensor) or even vocalizations (captured by Kinect and the DS), digital gameplay has more to do with musical performance than with spectatorship. Whether instrumental or vocal, the rhythmic corporeality of ludic performance suggests that investigations into its origins should pay as much heed to the history of sound and music as to image and text. We thus propose that the complex ways in which games negotiate between sound and image should be reflected by critical methods flexible enough to register and interpret a broad range of audiovisual formations at the interfaces of bodies and code. In order to map complex cultural configurations, such methods should be genealogical (in that they acknowledge epistemological and discursive prerequisites instead of relying on the notions of origin and causality as self-evident) and media-archaeological (in that they are concerned with the persistence and transformation of material phenomena across time and space).[15]

As a step toward developing such a method, we focus here on hardware and software developed, manufactured, and/or published by Nintendo that either overtly thematizes such issues, tacitly raises them, or serves as evidence for the technological, cultural, historical, and national(istic) factors that inform them. The worldwide success of a game franchise such as *Pokémon* indicates how digital games can be rooted in a specific cultural context and yet migrate freely across borders.[16] While the global influence and prestige of Nintendo's digital games is widely acknowledged, however, they have rarely been considered in relation either to (inter)national contexts or to media archaeology. The labyrinthine history of the medium resists the casual ascription of cause and effect or of originality and imitativeness. Similar elements can be found in different ecosystems, and the perception of affinities and discrepancies is preliminary to assembling a relational method that can account both for local idiosyncrasies and for the transnational logic of capitalism and control that has driven interactions within, among, and beyond East Asian and Western nations since World War II.[17] This process is made more complex by the rhetoric of exceptionalism that often infiltrates national discourses, which can itself be understood to respond to the dynamics of globalization.[18] By recognizing this, we wish to avoid essentializing Japanese and Western approaches to the design, reception, and representational attributes of digital games without reifying the differences between them. While not discounting paradigms derived from Western perspectives on games, we thus propose that supplementary discursive strategies will be necessary to explain how gaming experiences have been configured by Nintendo's employees.

In pursuit of a "Japanese way of playing," Rupert Cox concludes that those who play "accept the context which constrains their action and the ludic structure which frees it."[19] Along similar lines, digital game scholar and former Nintendo developer Akihiro Saito has observed that the perception of affordances where others see constraints is characteristic of a playful mindset that pervades Japanese visual and literary culture.[20] Art historian Nobuo Tsuji claims that a playful shuttling between the childlike and the orderly, the artistic and the artisanal, and the decorative and the functional has distinguished Japanese culture for centuries.[21] In considering the question of how relatively simple devices (such as the Game Boy) can sustain complex phenomena (such as *Pokémon Red* gameplay), Saito invokes the refinement, precision, and ambiguity wrought via the relatively crude technology of Edo-era woodblock prints (*ukiyo-e*) and the intricacies that emerge from the rigorous compression of the *haiku*.[22] Saito maintains that the carefully designed interfaces of Nintendo's games draw on the spaces and rituals of *motenashi* (hospitality), such as the artful arrangement of flowers in the *chashitsu* (tea ceremony room): for him, it is no coincidence that "the birthplace of Japan's hospitality culture" is Kyoto, where Nintendo was founded in 1889.[23]

A related facet of play that is global in scope and yet holds distinct significance within Japan is the concept of miniaturization.[24] From rock gardens and *bonsai* to cars and transistor radios, the operations of shrinkage, compression, and folding, often related to portability, on the one hand, and microcosmic consolidation, on the other, have been central to Japanese aesthetics and cultural practice.[25] Akin to Johan Huizinga's notion of the "magic circle" in which play takes place, tightly circumscribed spaces such as the *chashitsu* are understood to be separate from the everyday world.[26] The strict protocol that governs behavior there nonetheless gives rise to extraordinary and unrepeatable events.[27] In such contexts, miniaturization concentrates the magical qualities of objects: by making them "manageable [and] accessible to handling," as Rolf A. Stein writes of East Asian miniature gardens, "magical instruments share the nature of the work of art; the work of art shares that of a toy."[28]

Stein's formulation encapsulates the nexus of qualities that we identify in Nintendo's systems. From the Game & Watch (1980) to the Wii U (2012), portability, scale, instrumentality, and illusions of magic wrought by the manipulation of technology have been of central importance to Nintendo's playful enterprises. While portability and scale might appear to apply primarily to handheld devices, Nintendo has applied the same philosophy to its home consoles: the GameCube was furnished with a handle, while both the Wii and Wii U consoles that succeeded it are markedly smaller than their direct competitors. This indicates an attentiveness to gamespace that redefines the role of the screen: rather than taking place on the screen, Nintendian gameplay takes place through, between, and beyond screens. This idea, articulated independently by Nintendo's celebrated game designers Gunpei Yokoi and Shigeru Miyamoto, indicates how the screen need not operate as a cinematic or televisual fixture, but can function simultaneously as an interface, a reflective plane, and a barrier.[29] In different configurations, the screens of the DS and Wii U systems are portable, multiple, foldable (in the case of the DS), touchable, and usable as a surface for writing, drawing, and painting. In all these regards, they are closer to *byōbu* (Japanese folding screens), such as those painted by Edo-period artist Ito Jakuchu, than to the silver screen.[30] As such, they help define a space analogous to the *chashitsu* in which unexpected and delightful encounters may take place.[31]

Ludomusical Instruments

As for audio, the paradigm of high-fidelity musical reproduction associated with the home theater and even the compressed formats and mobile listening practices associated with Sony's Walkman and Apple's iPod are perhaps less relevant here than the idea that the Nintendian gaming device is itself akin to a musical instrument such as the harmonica or melodica, both of which were widely used in post-World War II Japanese music education programs.[32] Like the harmonica, Nintendo's Game Boy (released in 1989) offers a distinctive timbre, located mainly in the upper portion of the audible frequency spectrum, that has been modified, extended, and repurposed by dedicated users to perform musical feats that far exceed its capacity as defined in its original design specification; like the melodica, the 3DS system (released in 2011) affords digital, gestural, and pneumatic input and can be played in different orientations.[33] Nintendo's controllers and handheld systems are not mere representational systems, computers, prosthetic extensions of the body, modes of communication, or vehicles of fantasy (although they are all those things). As objects that are played, they also form loci of performance; as technological nodes in historico-cultural networks, they embody the concept of instrumentality both in a specifically musical sense and within a broad Heideggerian framework.[34] Music informs the playing of games just as games enable the playing of music.

Examples of this duplex configuration are strewn across Nintendo's output. Within the mythos of the *Legend of Zelda* franchise, musical instruments (such as the eponymous Ocarina of Time from the N64 game) perform super-natural functions such as warping through time and space, unlocking sealed gateways, and healing physical and psychic trauma.[35] These functions are activated through the reproduction of sequences of notes imparted to the player after the fashion of memory games such as Milton Bradley's iconic *Simon* (1978).[36] Music is thus instrumental as an agent that helps the player accomplish gameplay objectives. Conversely, however, the Ocarina of Time can be played as an instrument for its own sake; beyond the five notes required for gameplay purposes, the player can produce a chromatic scale by means of button combinations, and can even add vibrato. This facilitates a strictly musical performance by way of the N64 controller. In this sense, perhaps the most obviously instrumental among Nintendo's products is *Wii Music*, an improvisatory music "game" offering 66 instruments sounded by mimetic motions and techniques that players enact via the Wii remote and nunchuk controllers.[37] Miyamoto, who coproduced the software, encouraged people to think of it "as a new kind of instrument . . . that allows you to become a creator . . . and a performer of music."[38]

Across a broad array of genres and titles, the instrumentality of Nintendian gameplay can, in our view, be described as ludomusical, a term that indicates the playfulness to be found at the manifold intersections between music, toys, and games. Reflecting on the ways in which such ludomusical relationships are structured, Koji Kondo, the composer for *The Legend of Zelda* and *Super Mario Bros.* for the Famicom/Nintendo Entertainment System, has observed that both characters' movements and sequenced music in digital games are synchronized to the CPU's clock.[39] Kondo wrote the music for *Super Mario*

Bros. after playing the game repeatedly to gauge how Mario ran and jumped, identifying the character's unique "rhythm" in order to create a satisfying counterpoint between music and gameplay. While the music was initially "inspired by the game's controls," it ultimately creates a positive feedback loop by choreographing the player's digital performance.[40] While working on *New Super Mario Bros.* for the Nintendo DS more than two decades later, Kondo, in his role as music director, went a step further by choreographing the behavior of non-player characters.[41] As they dance and jump in time to the music, they directly affect gameplay mechanics and make rhythm a strategic resource for players; at the same time, their "performance" breaks the fourth wall, foregrounding a playful theatricality redolent of *kabuki*.[42] Tellingly, the theater serves as the master trope for Nintendo's poetics of play, as revealed by *WarioWare: D.I.Y.* for the DS, which enables players to create games by producing and combining graphics, cel animation, sequenced music, and scripted artificial intelligence.[43]

Toys & Time, Game & Watch

When questioned by a journalist as to whether *Wii Music*'s main mode qualified as a game given its lack of an overarching goal, intermediate objectives, quantifiable progress, and fail states, Miyamoto acknowledged that the software was indeed not a typical game: it was "more interesting" in that it was more akin to a musical toy box.[44] Miyamoto's retort prompted consternation from Western critics wary of the rhetoric of infantilization that has long dogged the digital game medium.[45] The analogy need not be interpreted in derogatory terms, however. For Giorgio Agamben, the toy performs an invaluable and unique cultural function: it "makes present and renders tangible human temporality in itself, the pure differential margin between the 'once' and the 'no longer'."[46] Crucially, it does so along both diachronic and synchronic axes by either "dismembering and distorting the past or miniaturizing the present." For Agamben, toys materialize the historicity of objects by subjecting them to "a particular manipulation." On the one hand, this manipulation foregrounds the contingency of the past by reducing previously functional objects to iconic symbols; on the other, it reveals the absurdity and ephemerality of the present by shrinking its most significant artifacts to the Lilliputian scale that they will assume in the future as triggers of nostalgia.

Agamben has traditional toys such as dolls, pistols, spinning tops, and hobby horses in mind, but his quasi-anthropological musings on the historical narratives that toys simultaneously evoke and conceal have special relevance for what Brian Sutton-Smith dubbed the "machine toy concept."[47] Nintendo's technologies entail not only miniaturization, but also retrogression. This is one reason why their games possess a potent affective charge that, as Woodrow Phoenix writes of Japanese toys, not only triggers "a cascade of forgotten or inaccessible memories," but can also function as a direct "link back to intense personal experience."[48] Supplementing the national predilection for smallness, Nintendo's approach to technology can thus be seen to emerge from its long history as a toy company. Unlike Microsoft and Sony, Nintendo's past is not defined solely by electronics; established as a playing card manufacturer in 1889, Nintendo made products ranging from board games to dollhouses prior to the Japanese release of the Famicom in 1983. Many of Nintendo's most successful toys were created under the supervision of Yokoi, who joined the company in 1965 and quickly established himself as an ingenious designer.

Nintendo's Game & Watch systems, manufactured between 1980 and 1991, are commonly perceived to mark the company's definitive transition from toys to digital games. Competition between Sharp and Casio in the digital calculator market had flooded the market with liquid crystal displays (LCDs), and Yokoi reputedly came up with the idea of a handheld game when he saw a salaryman playing with a calculator on a bullet train.[49] Using LCD technology, he devised games in which characters and objects could be depicted using the same techniques by which numbers were assembled from segments on a calculator display. To make the games more functional and appealing to adults, he added a clock function by incorporating a crystal oscillator.

When they entered the marketplace, Game & Watch systems exhibited a peculiar mixture of cutting-edge and antiquated technologies, reflecting a philosophy that Yokoi termed "*kareta gijutsu no suihei shikō*," which can be translated as "lateral thinking with withered/seasoned technology." He believed that novelty and fun were more easily attainable through the radical repurposing of mature, inexpensive technology than by the adoption of the latest technical innovation for its own sake.[50] Yokoi's approach thus maps onto Agamben's synchronic axis by deploying familiar technologies in economical, unexpected, and playful ways. At the same time, Yokoi claimed that his ideal of play harked back to children's games such as tag and hide-and-seek, in which delight emerges from the unpredictable ebb and flow of improvised engagement rather than from the strict observance of rules and investment in a victorious outcome.[51] This type of play unfolds within Agamben's "differential margin between the 'once' and the 'no longer'." For Yokoi, "lateral thinking with withered/seasoned technology" thus assumes a dialectical relation to the principle of "making old things possible with current technology."

In visual terms, Game & Watch systems operate on the principles of hand-drawn stop-go animation rather than on the projection or modeling of an image; they are thus closer to flip books, *manga*, and *anime* than they are to film or CGI. Their rudimentary audio output consists of simple beeps, the function of which is more important than their timbral quality: as developer Hirokazu Tanaka observed, since Game & Watch gameplay is defined by a reliance on rhythm, the beeps are necessary "so the player can have timing indications."[52] Like all of Nintendo's digital systems, the Game & Watch invites players to test and refine their abilities to perform with precise rhythm and synchronization. Both functions of the Game & Watch, the "trivial" game and the "serious" timepiece, are predicated on timing and calculated according to the pressing of buttons, on the one hand, and the oscillations of quartz, on the other. It might be tempting to conceive of the former as human and the second as mechanical, but the distinction is hard to maintain. As Claus Pias argues, an electronic clock's display is a concession to human perception while, conversely, a player's button presses must be measured and converted into machine code to be processed; if communication is to occur, the human must become "machine shaped," and vice versa.[53]

By yoking play to a metronomic clock, the Game & Watch foregrounded not only ludomusical rhythm but also what Pias describes in Kantian terms as "the game player's duty."[54] Pias cites Nietzsche's observation that rhythm is "a compulsion" that produces "an insatiable desire to give in, to comply."[55] Digital game players thus twist the continuum posited by Roger Caillois from *ludus* (which entails voluntary submission to the arbitrary and intransigent conditions of the CPU) to *paidia* (associated with a childlike or contrarian delight in disregarding or defying rules) into a Möbius strip: rather than being opposed, the two terms are supplementary.[56] Nintendo's *Rhythm Tengoku* for the Game Boy Advance takes advantage of this property by demanding the synchronization of musical events with ludicrous or fantastical animated imagery.[57] The comic and surreal discrepancy between the game's cheerily syncopated musical idioms, overseen by pop music producer and composer Tsunku, and their quirky visual counterparts is characteristic of *paidia*, but the game's measurement of the player's button presses to within 1/60th of a second demands *ludus* in the form of metronomic precision if progress through the game is to be optimally achieved.[58] The minimal input bandwidth (usually restricted to a single button) and quick-fire iconographic juxtapositions that distinguish both *Rhythm Tengoku* and its direct antecedent, *WarioWare, Inc.: Mega Microgame$!*, support Pias's contention that "the discourse elements of the computer game are not called 'killing people' or 'catching gold nuggets' but timeliness, rhythm, or control."[59]

After the young Toshio Iwai had familiarized himself with the ludic systems of *Super Mario Bros.*, he started playing the game in a manner that responded to Kondo's methods of choreographing music and action: "I started playing around and producing sounds by making Mario jump, which made me feel like I was playing instruments while playing the game."[60] Iwai had a similar experience "shooting along to the background music" of Namco's *Xevious*, released as an arcade game in 1983 and ported to the Famicom the following year.[61] The game features invulnerable spinning tiles known as Bacura, which emit a high-pitched metallic sound when struck by the player's blaster. This sound was adopted as a musical element in the track "Xevious" produced by Haruomi Hosono (a member of the electronic music band Yellow Magic Orchestra) as part of his pioneering album *Video Game Music* (1984). In turn, Hosono's track inspired players in arcades to try to reproduce its catchy rhythms by shooting Bacura despite (or owing to) the futility of doing so.[62] Here, again, we perceive *ludus* and *paidia* brought together by, and as, music. Shooting Bacura for the sonorous effect could be interpreted as whimsical, contrarian, masochistic, or virtuosic; in any case, it flies in the face of the self-interest and relentless pursuit of optimal strategy associated with game theory. In terms of both score and utility, it is pointless.

The "pointlessness" of this kind of ludomusical play echoes Stein's conflation of the toy with artistic creation, pointing toward an aesthetic that Iwai's media art has consistently exhibited. The influence of *Xevious* can be clearly perceived in *Otocky* (1987), an improvisatory music-themed shoot-'em-up with a procedurally generated soundtrack developed by Iwai for the Famicom Disk System.[63] Although *Otocky* was in many respects structured as a traditional game that tallied the player's score as he or she navigates a succession of levels, dealt with patterned enemy attacks, and fights "bosses" in the form of notes, Yoshikazu Tozuka reports that players perceived the game as "a kind of children's toy that produces sounds."[64] For its part, *Electroplankton*, which has been described as both "touchable media art" and a "set of 10 small musical toys," presents the player with biological and physical metaphors that invite the kinesthetic (re)actions of touching, scribbling, drawing, blowing, speaking, and singing.[65] In creating the software, Iwai drew on his audiovisual media installations *Music Insects* (1990–1992) and *Composition on the Table* (1998–1999), as well as the experience of his ludomusical toying with *Super Mario Bros.*[66]

As a media artist, Iwai possesses formidable credentials: his avowed influences include pioneering figures in the domains of experimental film, video, music, and multimedia such as Norman McLaren and Nam June Paik and he has collaborated with Hosono's Yellow Magic Orchestra bandmate Ryuchi Sakamoto.[67] One might thus be tempted to align Iwai's intermedial and ludic sensibility with that of the Fluxus movement, which became a cultural force in Tokyo and Osaka in the early 1960s. Iwai has chosen, however, to situate himself closer to Yokoi's toy-like aesthetic than to the art world proper.[68] Upon being awarded a prize by the Multimedia Content Association of Japan, Iwai revealed the Proustian imperative that motivated him: "I've been longing for the feeling of my childhood in the digital world."[69] Iwai's pursuit of *paidia* via digital channels is matched by Yokoi's commitment to recreating the pleasures of childhood through the misappropriation of "serious" electronics, "making old things possible with current technology." Whether framed as "toys," "games," or "art," the creations of Iwai and Yokoi share the nostalgic orientation of Agamben's diachronic axis. Beyond that, however, their material forms index a common media-archaeological heritage that informs the ludomusical experiences they afford. The task of plotting the genealogical nexus that connects these objects and their ontologies is beyond the scope of this chapter, but we will conclude with a preliminary attempt to situate a handful of them in relation to one another.

Congas, Buttons, Barrels, and Hammers

In recent years, the emphasis on the gritty verismo characteristic of many big-budget Western digital games has extended across the audiovisual continuum. A particular set of modelling, lighting, and animation techniques has been naturalized and coupled to the recording and digital manipulation of acoustic and electric instruments in order to represent the "real": "immediacy" is mediated via cutting-edge technology that strives to render itself imperceptible. In contrast, the sprite-based artwork and overtly sequenced sound of many Japanese games, both classic and contemporary, embraces technological limitations by making them visible and audible rather than seeking to transcend them. To account for this state of affairs, Yokoi's philosophy of "lateral thinking with withered/seasoned technology" might be considered within the broader context of Japan's volatile cultural and economic status in the aftermath of World War II, which forced artists and designers to operate within tight constraints. At first, there was a reliance on North American resources: legendary *manga* and *anime* artist and producer Osamu Tezuka pared down Walt Disney's filmic animation techniques for television in order to save time and money, and Nintendo adopted Disney characters to destigmatize playing cards and bring them into family homes. In both cases, however, imitative measures taken at least in part for expediency's sake had unintended and far-reaching consequences: Tezuka developed a repertoire of limited animation techniques that defined the nascent medium of *anime*, while Nintendo gained access to a broad demographic that would sustain Yokoi's innovations in the world of toys.[70]

In the late 1970s and early 1980s, the material conditions of the digital game demanded the manipulation of two-dimensional sprites, which (as Space Invaders demonstrated) were easily and effectively adapted from *manga* and *anime* tropes. Meanwhile, the proliferation of inexpensive musical instruments such as the Casiotone keyboard reflected an approach to composition and arrangement that was attuned to sequencing, modularity, and automation, all of which were integral to the production of digital game soundtracks by Japanese composers. The technological restrictions of hardware—or, rather, the discipline they impose and the ingenuity they foster—have encouraged many Japanese developers to eschew the pursuit of verisimilitude in favor of creating compelling gameplay from robust mechanics, manifested audiovisually by minimalistic or abstract semiotic strategies.

As Takuya Mori observed of anime (and as the invocation of abstraction and minimalism implies), the stripped-down, miniaturized aesthetic of games such as *Rhythm Tengoku* and the quantization of image, sound, and haptic input that drives their digital gameplay confound distinctions between the mainstream and the avant-garde, commercialism and experimentalism, and toys and art.[71] A genealogical approach to Japanese digital games must therefore take account both of correspondences between technological formations and of the political and economic forces that shape their material manifestations and cultural functions in any given context. To illustrate how such an investigation might proceed, let us briefly consider a material object manufactured by Nintendo that is at once a musical instrument, a digital device, a locus of play, and the materialization of an epistemological concept.

In 1972, Nintendo released a product, billed as "a new kind of instrument from the electronic age," that constitutes an intriguing point of contact between Nintendo's history as an "analog" toy company, its future as a digital game company, and the musical technologies that connect the two.[72] Ostensibly inspired by Yamaha's popular Electone series of electronic organs and the popularity of Latin music in Japan, the Ele-Conga was effectively a battery-powered drum machine featuring five buttons that triggered the sounds of a snare drum, maracas, claps, and, of course, congas (see Figure 3.1).[73] The Ele-Conga was a toy insofar as its membranophonic form was a mere skeuomorph, but at the same time it was a serious instrument that could be connected to an external amplifier for live performance. It was accompanied by sheet music featuring patterns that instructed players how to recreate familiar dance rhythms, and an optional accessory known as the Autoplayer could be programmed to reproduce such patterns by way of the hand-cranked revolution of paper discs punched with holes corresponding to the five triggers.

Figure 3.1 Nintendo's Ele-Conga and Autoplayer (1972); photograph reproduced with the permission of Erik Voskuil (beforemario.com)

At first glance, the Ele-Conga might be dismissed as an oddity that has little bearing on Nintendo's hugely successful digital game enterprises of the 1980s, and yet its attributes are significant in light of subsequent developments of ludomusical instrumentality. On the one hand, the notion of grafting such a digital interface onto a toy-like drum can be understood to presage Namco's *Taiko no Tatsujin*, a successful series of rhythm-action games that made its arcade debut in 2001.[74] In 2003, Namco adapted *Taiko no Tatsujin* for Nintendo's domestic audience by developing *Donkey Konga*, a rhythm-action game for the GameCube that was bundled with a pair of barrel-shaped bongos. As well as riffing on the iconography of the original *Donkey Kong* arcade game created by Miyamoto alongside Yokoi in 1981, *Donkey Konga* and its bongos could be interpreted as a punning tribute to the Ele-Conga.[75] On the other hand, the particular configuration of the Ele-Conga's keyboard-like interface, which takes the form of the five adjacent buttons designed to be played with one hand, resembles the layout and function of Harmonix and Red Octane's *Guitar Hero* controller, which made its debut in 2005 (Figure 3.2).[76]

For its part, the Autoplayer (which Yokoi added as a concession to players who, born to early to have devoted themselves to *Guitar Hero*, lacked the dexterity to produce complex rhythms manually) harks back to the distant past even as it looks forward to the flourishing of rhythm-action games at the turn of the millennium. Most immediately, its hand-cranked operation and circular discs evoke the phonograph; in contrast to the analog and pits and grooves of vinyl records, however, the Autoplayer's paper discs sequence playback by digital means. The archaeology of this reproductive method can be traced via nineteenth-century technologies of musical automation associated with music boxes, fairground organs, and player pianos—including an analogous "music disk" devised by Claude-Félix Seytre (Figure 3.3a)—to water organs such as the famous sixteenth-century instrument at the Villa d'Este in Tivoli.[77]

At this juncture, we might recall that Iwai was inspired by a "hand-cranked antique music box" that used "paper cards, punched like the rolls on a player piano."[78] He considered it revelatory for the way it transduced music into visible and kinetic form, and it is no coincidence that the same mode of encoding sound via marks on a moving surface was adopted by rhythm-action games such as *Taiko no Tatsujin* and *Guitar Hero* in order to instruct players in lieu of conventional music notation. The Ele-Conga and its Autoplayer thus combine the hardware and software elements necessary for the mechanical reproduction of sequenced musical data.

As Iwai indicated, and Kondo demonstrated in *New Super Mario Bros.*, such data can easily be transduced into synchronized kinesis via centuries-old technology. In 1650, Athanasius Kircher published a design for a water-powered organ (Figure 3.4), inspired by the Villa d'Este instrument, which demonstrates how digital data could choreograph both musical

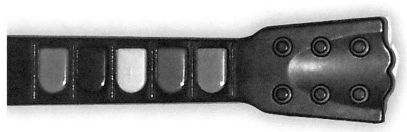

Figure 3.2 (*a*) The Ele-Conga's buttons; photograph reproduced with the permission of Erik Voskuil (beforemario.com); (*b*) Gibson SG controller for *Guitar Hero* (Sony PlayStation 2), developed by Harmonix (Mountain View, CA: RedOctane, 2005)

performance and movement.[79] The four blacksmiths on the left constitute a tribute to Pythagoras, who reputedly stumbled upon the principles of tuning while listening to the relative pitches of hammers ringing out from a forge. As it revolves, the pinned barrel of Kircher's organ programs three of the blacksmiths to hammer out a never-ending pattern, just as Jumpman's acquisition of a hammer in *Donkey Kong* triggers a looping triadic ostinato. Barrels, hammers, and bodies in repetitive motion: these elements are embedded in Kircher's organ as they are in *Donkey Kong*.[80]

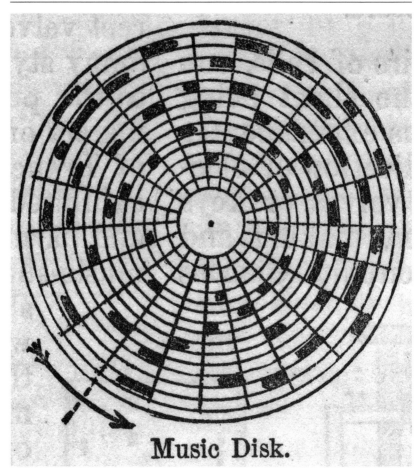

Music Disk.

Figure 3.3 (a) Claude-Félix Seytre's "music disk" (1842), reproduced from Charles R. Brainard et al., *Appletons' Annual Cyclopaedia and Register of Important Events of the Year 1885* (New York: D. Appleton & Co., 1886), 615

A more direct morphological relationship can be perceived between Kircher's organ and the music creation mode in Nintendo's *WarioWare: D.I.Y.* (Figure 3.5). As well as featuring a keyboard and animated humanoids, *WarioWare: D.I.Y.* allows the player to pin his or her virtual barrel (which performs a complete revolution every eight measures) with note markers, just as Yokoi had provided purchasers of the Ele-Conga's Autoplayer with the "withered technology" of blank paper disks (also capable of storing eight measures of data) and a hole punch.

As the Autoplayer's hole punch suggests, the digital epistemology that underpins the sounding motion of Kircher's pinned barrels and Seytre's

Figure 3.3 (b) Paper disk for the Ele-Conga's Autoplayer; photograph reproduced with the permission of Erik Voskuil (beforemario.com)

revolving disks also had significant ramifications in the realms of material and visual culture: it enabled the automation of textile production via punch cards, a technique pioneered by Basile Bouchon and Jean-Baptiste Falcon and substantially refined by Joseph Marie Jacquard in 1801. The mosaic-like arrangement of information on these cards can be seen as a "prophetic relic," to adopt Alan Liu's formulation, of the grid of pixels that configured the sprite designs of raster-based digital games such as *Space Invaders* and *Donkey Kong*.[81] Moreover, Jacquard's innovation played an important role in the history of computing itself: from Charles Babbage's Analytical Engine (conceived under Jacquard's influence in nineteenth-century London), via IBM's electric accounting machines (mass produced in the United States throughout the 1950s and 1960s), to the globally ubiquitous optical drives of today's machines, generations of computing devices have been designed to process data stored on punch cards and their disk-shaped successors.

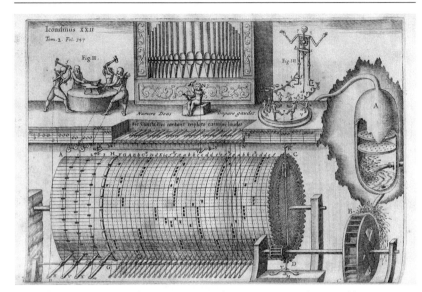

Figure 3.4 Athanasius Kircher, illustration of a water-powered organ, *Musurgia universalis, sive Ars magna consoni et dissoni*, 2 vols. (Rome: Corbelletti, 1650), 2: plate between pp. 346 and 347

While it might therefore be possible to posit tenuous connections between Kircher (a prominent member of the Society of Jesus), the music boxes brought to Japan by Jesuit missionaries in 1549, the global dissemination of computer technology in the latter half of the twentieth century, the young Iwai's formative encounters with digital media, and Yokoi's aesthetics of ludo-musical play, such links need not take the form of unidirectional vectors of transmission from Europe and North America to Asia.[81] Rather than betokening causal relationships and replication, the migration of these technologies across time and space can facilitate and represent ideas, beliefs, and practices that are quite distinct. Unlike the Ele-Conga, *Donkey Kong*, and *WarioWare: D.I.Y.*, Kircher's organ was far from a vehicle of play: the macabre figure of the skeleton, serving as a *memento mori*, reveals a deadly serious theological agenda.[83] Like many of Kircher's spectacular and sometimes outlandish inventions, the organ was conceived to arouse awe, fear, and piety rather than frivolous delight.[84] Conversely, while Japanese sprite designers may have had to accommodate the same technological affordances and constraints as their North American and European counterparts, they could also draw on the rich representational traditions of artists such as Jakuchu, as well as the immediate context provided by *manga* and *anime*.

Placing the Ele-Conga in musical, ludic, and technological relief reveals that the foundational attributes of digital games are intimately bound up with how sound has been conceived, captured, stored, organized, transmitted,

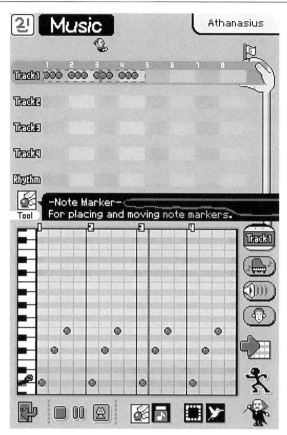

Figure 3.5 Screenshot of music creation mode from Nintendo's *WarioWare: D.I.Y.*
[Made in Ore] (Nintendo DS), developed by Nintendo and Intelligent
Systems (Kyoto: Nintendo, 2009–2010)

recreated, and transduced by mechanical means. This ontological latticework
provides an archaeological basis for paying careful attention to the sonic and
musical aspects of digital gameplay. In Foucauldian terms, it can be analyzed
as a digital *dispositif* that functions, as Hiroki Azuma has written of *otaku*
culture in Japan, as a database of elements assembled from within Japanese
culture and far beyond.[85] When these elements have been arrayed by
Nintendo's developers into ludic programs, they have shown themselves to
be capable of sustaining diverse yet distinctive forms of playful engagement.
Recognizing the importance of digitization and mediation, however, need not
overdetermine the outcomes of historical and cultural analysis. From the flip
book to *anime*, from toys to works of art, and from congas to taiko drums, the
course of each element that plays into Nintendo's ludomusicality can be traced
along paths that wind through space and time.[86] To take full measure of a

phenomenon as complex and multifarious as Nintendo's art of musical play, we believe it necessary to bring diverse discursive modes into productive contact at the points where these paths cross.

Notes

All websites were accessed November 4, 2013.

1   Gunpei Yokoi, *Monozukuri no inobēshon: "Kareta gijutsu no suihei shikō" towa nani ka?*, ed. Yohei Kusanagi and Yuki Kageyama (Tokyo: P-Vine Books, 2012), 44. Translations from the Japanese are our own unless otherwise indicated.
2   See, for instance, Sacha A. Howells, "Watching a Game, Playing a Movie: When Media Collide," in *ScreenPlay: Cinema/Videogames/Interfaces*, ed. Geoff King and Tanya Krzywinska (London and New York: Wallflower Press, 2002), 110–121.
3   *Gears of War* (Microsoft Xbox 360), developed by Epic Games (Redmond: Microsoft Studios, 2006). Convergence between digital games and films has been manifested by the central role played by ludic tropes and techniques in films such as *eXistenZ* and *Gamer*, not to mention the substantial takings of films based on the *Tomb Raider*, *Prince of Persia*, and *Resident Evil* franchises, their uniformly negative critical reception notwithstanding. While televisual correspondences might be less conspicuous, episodic adventures such as *CSI: Fatal Conspiracy* (Microsoft Xbox 360 and Windows, Sony PlayStation 3, and Nintendo Wii), developed by Telltale Games (Montreuil: Ubisoft, 2010), rely heavily on narrative structures and devices specific to the medium.
4   The trope's dissemination is monitored on http://thecitizenkaneofvideogames. tumblr.com.
5   *Space Invaders* (arcade cabinet), developed by Taito (Tokyo: Taito, 1978); *Space Invaders* (Atari VCS/2600), developed by Atari (Sunnyvale, CA: Atari, 1980); *Pac-Man* (arcade cabinet), developed by Namco (Tokyo: Namco, 1980); *Pac-Man* (Atari VCS/2600), developed by Atari (Sunnyvale, CA: Atari, 1982). The VCS and its faux-teak veneer might be considered alongside the VCR, which achieved mass market success soon after its release in 1975: while both machines could provide compromised approximations of media adapted from the arcade and the cinema, respectively, both were closer to the technologies, aesthetics, and social functions of video and television. The legal definition of the term "video game," as determined through litigation involving Ralph H. Baer, one of its pioneers, in the 1970s, stipulates that a television be involved (as opposed to a non-raster-scan display). For an account of how this came to be from Baer's perspective, see Ralph H. Baer, *Videogames: In the Beginning* (Springfield, NJ: Rolenta Press, 2005), 5–17.
6   *Heavy Rain* (Sony PlayStation 3), developed by Quantic Dream (Tokyo: Sony Computer Entertainment, 2010); *Alan Wake* (Microsoft Xbox 360), developed by Remedy Entertainment (Redmond: Microsoft Game Studios, 2010).
7   Lev Manovich, *The Language of New Media* (Cambridge, MA and London: MIT Press, 2001), 180.
8   Marshall McLuhan, *Understanding Media: The Extensions of Man* (New York: McGraw-Hill, 1964), 8; Jay David Bolter and Richard Grusin, *Remediation: Understanding New Media* (Cambridge, MA: MIT Press, 1999).
9   Consider, for instance, the perspective of renowned Japanese game producer Keiji Inafune: "I think Western designers have a much stronger . . . influence from film . . . Now that technology has advanced, Western designers view it as [an] opportunity to branch even further [toward] the idea of film scoring, while Japanese

designer continue [with their] approach to instrumentation that developed during the 8-bit era." Quoted in Kurt Kalata, "Clash of the Cultures," *1UP* (January 18, 2007), available online at www.1up.com/features/clash-cultures?pager.offset=5.

10 Manovich, *The Language of New Media*, 49–61.

11 *Electroplankton* (Nintendo DS), developed by indieszero (Kyoto: Nintendo, 2005).

12 Toshio Iwai, *Iwai Toshio no shigoto to shūhen* (Tokyo: Rikuyosha, 2000), 64.

13 Iwai, *Iwai Toshio no shigoto to shūhen*, 70.

14 "For me, the existential meaning of the flip book and the digital game are directly connected, bypassing the history of film and television. For example, I thought that the Game Boy was an electronic flip book when it was released. It could be carried around easily and played anywhere. The touch of one's fingers was directly registered via moving images and sound. I think the Game Boy restored the value of the flip book, which had been dormant for more than a century, by returning it to our hands in electronic form." Iwai, *Iwai Toshio no shigoto to shūhen*, 64.

15 On the concept of genealogy, see Michel Foucault, "Nietzsche, Genealogy, History," in *Language, Counter-Memory, Practice: Selected Essays and Interviews*, ed. and trans. Donald F. Bouchard (Ithaca, NY: Cornell University Press, 1980), 139–164. On media archaeology, see Erkki Huhtamo and Jussi Parikka, *Media Archaeology: Approaches, Applications, and Implications* (Berkeley and Los Angeles: University of California Press, 2011).

16 On *Pokémon*, see Joseph Tobin, *Pikachu's Global Adventure: The Rise and Fall of Pokémon* (Durham, NC and London: Duke University Press, 2004); and David Surman, "*Pokémon* 151: Complicating *Kawaii*," in *Gaming Cultures and Place in Asia-Pacific*, ed. Larissa Hjorth and Dean Chan (New York and London: Routledge, 2009), 158–178.

17 In this regard, digital games might instructively be set alongside Zen Buddhism and the complex history of its remediation between Japan and the West. See Shoji Yamada, *Shots in the Dark: Japan, Zen, and the West*, trans. Earl Hartman (Chicago and London: University of Chicago Press, 2009). For further perspectives on issues of authenticity and reproduction, see Rupert Cox, *The Culture of Copying in Japan: Critical and Historical Perspectives* (Abingdon and New York: Routledge, 2008).

18 Examples of such rhetoric in Japan include the concepts of *nihonjinron* (theories and discourses on "Japaneseness," which became especially influential in the years following World War II) and, more recently, *Garapagosu-ka* ("Galápagos syndrome," used to refer to a specialized and geographically isolated evolutionary "branch" of a global product).

19 Rupert Cox, "Is There a Japanese Way of Playing?," in *Japan at Play: The Ludic and the Logic of Power*, ed. Joy Hendry and Massimo Raveri (London and New York: Routledge, 2002), 169–183.

20 Akihiro Saito, *Gēmunikusu to wa nani ka: Nihon-hatsu, sekaikijun no monozukuri-hōsoku* (Tokyo: Gentosha, 2007), 204–207.

21 Nobuo Tsuji, *Playfulness in Japanese Art* (Lawrence: Spencer Museum of Art, University of Kansas, 1986), 9–14.

22 *Pokémon: Red* [*Pocket Monsters: Red*] (Nintendo Game Boy), developed by Game Freak (Kyoto: Nintendo, 1996); Saito, *Gēmunikusu to wa nani ka: Nihon-hatsu, sekaikijun no monozukuri-hōsoku*, 204–207. On the playfulness, wit, and humor that characterize *ukiyo-e*, see Donald Jenkins et al., *The Floating World Revisited* (Honolulu: Portland Art Museum and University of Hawaii Press, 1993).

23 Kenji Ono, "'Gamenics' and its Potential: Interview with Akihiro Saito," in *Game Usability: Advice from the Experts for Advancing the Player Experience*, eds. Katherine Isbister and Noah Schaffer (Burlington, MA: Morgan Kaufmann, 2008), 357–379.

24 On miniaturization in Japan, see O-Young Lee, *The Compact Culture: The Japanese Tradition of "Smaller is Better"*, trans. Robert N. Huey (Tokyo and New York: Kodansha International, 1984); and Mitsukuni Yoshida, Ikko Tanaka, and Tsune Sesoko, *The Compact Culture: The Ethos of Japanese Life* (Hiroshima: Toyo Kogyo, 1982).

25 See Yoshida, Tanaka, and Sesoko, *The Compact Culture: The Ethos of Japanese Life*, 26–31.

26 Johan Huizinga, *Homo Ludens: A Study of the Play Element in Culture* (Boston: Beacon Press, 1955), 10.

27 Although Huizinga claims that "there is no formal difference between play and ritual" (p. 10), Émile Benveniste drew a chiastic distinction between them: while rites transform events into structures, play transforms structures into events. Émile Benveniste, "Le jeu comme structure," *Deucalion* 2 (1947), 161–167. This latter formulation might be applied to the notion that the tea ceremony is a form of play that depends upon strict rules in order to create singular and unrepeatable experiences (summed up by the maxim *ichi-go ichi-e*, commonly attributed to sixteenth-century tea master Sen no Rikyu).

28 Rolf A. Stein, *The World in Miniature: Container Gardens and Dwellings in Far Eastern Religious Thought*, trans. Phyllis Brooks (Palo Alto, CA: Stanford University Press, 1990), 52.

29 Yokoi was interested in digital gameplay that could break through the frame of the television screen, as manifested by several accessories that he designed for the Famicom, known in the West as the Nintendo Entertainment System. See Takefumi Makino, *Gēmu no chichi, Yokoi Gunpei den: Nintendo no DNA o sōzō shita otoko* (Tokyo: Kadokawa Shoten, 2010), 183–185. More than 20 years after the appearance of the Famicom, Miyamoto expressed a similar outlook: "I've always thought that games would eventually break free of the confines of a TV screen to fill an entire room." Kenji Hall, "Online Extra: Meet Mario's Papa," *Business Week* (November 6, 2005), available online at www.businessweek.com/stories/2005-11-06/online-extra-meet-marios-papa).

30 See, for instance, Ito Jakuchu's late eighteenth-century *Birds, Animals, and Flowering Plants in Imaginary Scene*, a pair of six-panel folding screens composed of more than 86,000 pixel-like squares. (For comparison's sake, the two screens of the DS incorporate 98,304 pixels.) On Jakuchu, see Nobuo Tsuji, *Playfulness in Japanese Art* (Lawrence: Spencer Museum of Art, University of Kansas, 1986), 63–74.

31 On the multiple functions of the folding screen in Japanese culture, see Oliver Impey, *The Art of the Japanese Folding Screen* (Oxford: Ashmolean Museum, 1997).

32 See Junko Kitagawa, "Music Culture," in *The Cambridge Companion to Modern Japanese Culture*, ed. Yoshio Sugimoto (Cambridge: Cambridge University Press, 2009), 261–280. The melodica, or keyboard harmonica, is a portable, mass produced instrument that has a rectangular body with a keyboard interface and a mouthpiece through which one blows in order to produce sound. A short mouthpiece is used when the instrument is held horizontally and another with an extension tube when it is played vertically.

33 Nintendo's DS and 3DS systems respond to the player's breath via their built-in microphone, while the 3DS also contains a gyroscope and accelerometer that recognize gestural input. On the Game Boy's important role for circuit benders and on the chiptune scene, see Karen Collins, *Playing with Sound: A Theory of Interacting with Sound and Music in Video Games* (Cambridge, MA and London: MIT Press, 2013), 108–120.

34 On Heidegger's concept of instrumentality, see Martin Heidegger, "The Question Concerning Technology," in *The Question Concerning Technology and Other Essays*, trans. William Lovitt (New York: Harper & Row, 1977), 3–35.

35 *The Legend of Zelda: The Ocarina of Time* [*Zeruda no Densetsu: Toki no Okarina*] (Nintendo 64), developed by Nintendo (Kyoto: Nintendo, 1998). The Ocarina of Time can be placed in an organological context provided by the Magic Flute from Mozart and Schikaneder's eponymous opera, which similarly acts as a charm, a summons, and an agent of transformation and protection. On instrumentality, mechanization, and mediation in *Die Zauberflöte*, see Carolyn Abbate, "Magic Flute, Nocturnal Sun," in *In Search of Opera* (Princeton, NJ and Oxford: Princeton University Press, 2001), 55–106.

36 *Simon* (portable electronic game), developed by Ralph H. Baer and Howard J. Morrison (East Longmeadow, MA: Milton Bradley, 1978).

37 *Wii Music* (Nintendo Wii), developed by Nintendo (Kyoto: Nintendo, 2008). For more details on *Wii Music*, see Steven E. Jones and George K. Thiruvathukal, *Codename Revolution: The Nintendo Wii Platform* (Cambridge, MA, and London: MIT Press, 2012), 134–137. *Wii Music*'s emphasis on multiplayer musical performance can be placed in a Nintendian lineage that includes *Daigasso! Band Brothers* for the DS (Kyoto: Nintendo, 2004) and its sequel, released with a "DX" suffix in Japan (2005) and retitled as *Jam with the Band* for its European release (2008). Means of producing, performing, and recording music are supplied by many of Nintendo's games and products, including *Mario Paint* (Nintendo Super Famicom [Super Nintendo Entertainment System]), developed by Nintendo (Kyoto: Nintendo, 1992), and even the inbuilt camera and sound applications for Nintendo's DSi handheld system.

38 Quoted in Daniel Terdiman, "Video game legend Miyamoto talks *Wii Music*," *CNET* (October 27, 2008), available online at http://news.cnet.com/8301-13772_3-10075394-52.html.

39 *The Legend of Zelda* [*The Hyrule Fantasy: Zeruda no Densetsu*] (Nintendo Famicom/Famicom Disk System), developed by Nintendo (Kyoto: Nintendo, 1986 [FDS]/1987 [Famicom]); *Super Mario Bros.* (Nintendo Famicom/Famicom Disk System and arcade cabinet), developed by Nintendo (Kyoto: Nintendo, 1985 [Famicom]/1986 [FDS and arcade]); Koji Kondo, "Painting an Interactive Musical Landscape," presentation at the Game Developers Conference 2007, summarized in English by Vincent Diamante (March 8, 2007), available online at www.gamasutra.com/php-bin/news_index.php?story=104002. In his presentation, Kondo invoked synchronization between game and music via the CPU clock as a factor in his preference for sequenced sounds over recorded musical performances.

40 Quoted in Chris Kohler, "VGL: Koji Kondo Interview," *Wired* (March 11, 2007), available online at www.wired.com/gamelife/2007/03/vgl_koji_kondo_/.

41 *New Super Mario Bros.* (Nintendo DS), developed by Nintendo (Kyoto: Nintendo, 2006).

42 According to Adam L. Kern, *kabuki* "routinely breaks the fourth wall, closing the gap between stage and audience for a variety of calculated reasons: playfulness; a bid for authority or authenticity; dramatic effect, and so on." Adam L. Kern, "*Kabuki* Plays on Page—and Comicbook Pictures on Stage—in Edo-Period Japan," in *Publishing the Stage: Print and Performance in Early Modern Japan*, ed. Keller Kimbrough and Satoko Shimazaki (Boulder, CO: Center for Asian Studies, University of Colorado, 2011), 163–189. In *Super Mario Bros.* and many subsequent games, Mario breaks the fourth wall at the moment of "death," which is treated as a comic event: he turns to face the audience before detaching himself from the ludic plane of action.

43 *WarioWare: D.I.Y.* [*Made in Ore*] (Nintendo DS), developed by Nintendo and Intelligent Systems (Kyoto: Nintendo, 2009–2010). The explicit theatricality of *New Super Mario Bros.* and *WarioWare: D.I.Y.* can be traced back to *Super Mario Bros. 3* (Nintendo Famicom), developed by Nintendo (Kyoto: Nintendo, 1988), which features paraphernalia such as curtains, stage machinery, and costumes. Kabuki-style theatricality was also foregrounded in *Paper Mario RPG* [*Paper Mario: The Thousand-Year Door*] (Nintendo GameCube), developed by Intelligent Systems (Kyoto: Nintendo, 2004), in which battles take place on a stage before a rowdy audience.

44 Miyamoto made his comments in response to an unidentified journalist's question at the E3 Nintendo Developer Roundtable event in 2008; they were reported by Michael McWhertor, "Miyamoto: *Wii Music* is 'More Interesting than a Video Game'," *Kotaku* (July 17, 2008), available online at http://kotaku.com/5026431/miyamoto-wii-music-is-more-interesting-than-a-video-game.

45 See, for instance, Alan Kim's review, posted October 30, 2008 (www.gamesradar.com/wii-music-review/). *Wii Music* has its share of devoted and eloquent apologists, however, such as Jacob Crites, "The Brilliance of *Wii Music*," *Game Observer* (February 16, 2010), available online at www.gameobserver.com/features/inside/all-platforms/the-brilliance-of-wii-music-part-1-220/.

46 Giorgio Agamben, "In Playland: Reflections on History and Play," in *Infancy and History: The Destruction of Experience*, trans. Liz Heron (London and New York: Verso, 1993), 73–96.

47 Brian Sutton-Smith, *Toys as Culture* (New York and London: Gardner Press, 1986), 58; see also Susan Stewart, *On Longing: Narratives of the Miniature, the Gigantic, the Souvenir, the Collection* (Baltimore: Johns Hopkins University Press, 1984), 57–60.

48 Woodrow Phoenix, *Plastic Culture: How Japanese Toys Conquered the World* (Tokyo and New York: Kodansha International, 2006), 9. In an interview, Miyamoto acknowledged these qualities of Nintendo's games: "What's really important is viewing Nintendo almost like a toy company where we're making these things for people to play with. As a consumer, you want to be able to . . . have those things from your youth that you can go back to and experience again." Quoted in Tom Phillips, "Miyamoto: Nintendo's game ownership policy should operate 'like a toy company'," *Eurogamer* (June 13, 2013), available online at www.eurogamer.net/articles/2013-06-13-miyamoto-nintendos-game-ownership-policy-should-operate-like-a-toy-company.

49 Gunpei Yokoi and Takefumi Makino, *Yokoi Gunpei Gēmukan Returns: Game Boy o unda hassōnyoko* (Tokyo: Film Art, 2010), 101. This was not an isolated occurrence: the ludic potential of calculators was explored in publications such as Koichi Kishida's *Dentaku de asobu hon* [*Book for Playing with the Calculator*] (Tokyo: Subaru Shobō, 1977), and the calculator provided current Nintendo president Satoru Iwata with his point of entry into the gaming world. Megan Farokhmanesh, "Iwata joined gaming because computers 'were going to change the world'," *Polygon* (October 28, 2012), available online at www.polygon.com/2012/10/28/3567254/iwata-joined-gaming-because-computers-were-going-to-change-the-world.

50 Yokoi and Makino, *Yokoi Gunpei Gēmukan Returns*, 199–200. Nintendo continued to espouse Yokoi's philosophy after his departure from the company in 1996 and his untimely death the subsequent year; in particular, the DS and Wii systems bear his hallmarks. See Osamu Inoue, *Nintendo Magic: Winning the Videogame Wars*, trans. Paul Tuttle Starr (New York: Vertical, 2010), 122–145.

51 Makino, *Gēmu no chichi, Yokoi Gunpei den: Nintendo no DNA o sōzō shita otoko*, 130.

52 Quoted in Florent Gorges and Isao Yamazaki, *The History of Nintendo 1980–1991: The Game & Watch Games, An Amazing Invention* (Triel-sur-Seine: Pix'n Love Publishing, 2012), 23. The beeps were deemed so integral to gameplay that they could not be silenced by the player (despite any annoyance they caused to others in the vicinity).

53 Claus Pias, "The Game Player's Duty: The User as the Gestalt of the Ports," in *Media Archaeology*, ed. Erkki Huhtamo and Jussi Parikka, 164–183.

54 Pias, "The Game Player's Duty: The User as the Gestalt of the Ports," in *Media Archaeology*, ed. Erkki Huhtamo and Jussi Parikka, 179–180.

55 Friedrich Nietzsche, *Werke in drei Bänden* (Munich: Carl Hanser, 1954), 2: 93.

56 Roger Caillois, *Man, Play, and Games*, trans. Meyer Barash (Urbana and Chicago: University of Illinois Press, 1961), 27–35. For a summary of Caillois's taxonomy of play and its applicability to music, see Roger Moseley, "Playing Games with Music (and Vice Versa): Ludomusicological Perspectives on *Guitar Hero* and *Rock Band*," in *Taking It to the Bridge: Music as Performance*, ed. Nicholas Cook and Richard Pettengill (Ann Arbor: University of Michigan Press, 2013), 279–318. Nintendo's longtime president Hiroshi Yamauchi, who ran the company from 1949 until 2002, approvingly cited Caillois's taxonomy in terms of its relevance for digital games in general and *Space Invaders* in particular. Quoted in Gorges and Yamazaki, *The History of Nintendo 1889–1980: From Playing Cards to Game & Watch*, 189.

57 *Rhythm Tengoku* (Nintendo Game Boy Advance and arcade cabinet), developed by Nintendo with J.P ROOM (GBA) and Sega (arcade) (Kyoto: Nintendo, 2006 [GBA]/2007 [arcade]). Three examples will serve to illustrate the whimsical variety of the game's scenarios: in one, the player plucks "facial" hairs from an onion that stares back at him or her with small round eyes; in another, the player assumes the role of a monkey who must clap hands in response to a pop singer's performance along with other monkey fans; in a third, the player participates in a call-and-response love duet with a fellow moai. Additional gameplay modes include a set of "Rhythm Toys" whose lack of rules, points, time limits, and purpose is characteristic of *paidia*.

58 In developing *Rhythm Tengoku*, Tsunku (whose real name is Mitsuo Terada) espoused the didactic goal of "improving Japanese people's sense of rhythm," and he approached Nintendo with the project specifically because he thought of them as a "play" company rather than a "game" company. Quoted in "Shachō ga kiku *Rhythm Tengoku Gold*," *Nintendo*, available online at www.nintendo.co.jp/ds/interview/ylzj/vol2/index.html. He has asserted that "there's a clear link between music, rhythm and play, and these things conspire together to draw the player into the game world naturally." Quoted in Chris Kohler, "J-Pop Producer Tsunku Perfects Music Games With *Rhythm Heaven*," *Wired* (April 10, 2009), available online at www.wired.com/gamelife/2009/04/qa-japans-pop-i/.

59 *WarioWare, Inc.: Mega Microgame$!* [Made in Wario] (Nintendo Game Boy Advance), developed by Nintendo (Kyoto: Nintendo, 2003); Pias, "The Game Player's Duty: The User as the Gestalt of the Ports," in *Media Archaeology*, ed. Erkki Huhtamo and Jussi Parikka, 180.

60 Iwai, *Iwai Toshio no shigoto to shūhen*, 64.

61 Iwai, *Iwai Toshio no shigoto to shūhen*, 64; *Xevious* (arcade cabinet and Nintendo Famicom/Famicom Disk System), developed by Namco (Tokyo: Namco, 1983 [arcade]/1984 [Famicom]/1990 [FDS]).

62 Yoshikazu Tozuka, foreword to Chapter 6, in *Gēmu Ongaku*, ed. Yoshikazu Tozuka (Tokyo: Exceed Press, 1999), 136.

63 *Otocky* (Nintendo Famicom Disk System), developed by Scitron & Art and SEDIC (Tokyo: ASCII Corporation, 1987). For more information on *Otocky*, see Bruno de Figueiredo's encomium to the game (August 2009), available online at www.hardcoregaming101.net/otocky/otocky.htm.

64 Tozuka, foreword to Chapter 6, in *Gēmu Ongaku*, 136–137. It is telling that Ikinari Myūjishan [Instant Musician] (Nintendo Famicom), developed by Tokyo Shoseki, and Doremikko (Nintendo Famicom Disk System), developed by Konami, were released alongside Otocky in 1987: both games foreground music-driven improvisatory play, but whereas the former features an onscreen keyboard activated by the regular Famicom controller, the latter can also be played with a special keyboard-shaped controller (one of the earliest of its kind). In different ways, all three games blur the distinctions between gameplay and musical performance.

65 The first quote is cited in James Burns, "Inside *Electroplankton*," *N-Sider* (July 24, 2005), available online at www.n-sider.com/contentview.php?contentid=317&page=1. The second is taken from Fares Kayali, "Playing Music: Design, Theory, and Practice of Music-Based Games," Ph.D. dissertation (Technische Universität Wien, 2008), 66. On *Electroplankton* as an "art game," see Martin Pichlmair, "*Electroplankton* Revisited: A Meta-Review," *Eludamos* 1/1 (2007), available online at www.eludamos.org/index.php/eludamos/article/view/vol1no1-8; and Axel Stock-burger, "Sound-Image Relations in Video and Computer Games," in *See This Sound: Audiovisuology Compendium*, ed. Dieter Daniels, Sandra Naumann, and Jan Thoben (Cologne: Walther König, 2010), 129–139. *Electroplankton*'s two modes, dubbed "performance" and "audience," suggest musical roles for the player instead of enforcing ludic rules.

66 Iwai adapted the concepts and mechanics behind *Music Insects* in the form of *Sound Fantasy* (Nintendo Super Famicom), developed by Nintendo (unpublished, 1994); the game was canceled by Nintendo, but reworked for the PC and published as *SimTunes* (Microsoft Windows), developed by Maxis (Emeryville, CA: Maxis, 1996). In *Electroplankton*, the influence of *Music Insects* can be perceived in "Tracy," Composition on the Table appears as "Luminaria," and Kondo's "invincibility" music from *Super Mario Bros.* is featured in "Beatnes."

67 Most prominently, Iwai and Sakamoto collaborated on *Music Plays Images X Images Play Music*, a multimedia performance staged in Mito in 1996 and Tokyo the following year, where it was billed as *MPIXIPM*. The program included *Ongaku no chesu* [Music Chess], an apparent homage to John Cage and Marcel Duchamp's *Reunion* (1968) featuring a "game board" that functioned as a real-time step sequencer. (In strictly morphological terms, the "game" played by Iwai and Sakamoto in Tokyo was closer to peg solitaire than chess.) In association with Yamaha, Iwai proceeded to develop the Tenori-on (2007), a portable electronic instrument that operates along similar lines.

68 Yokoi was the executive producer of *Sound Fantasy*. Although the game was canceled, Iwai was struck by Yokoi's receptiveness to its facilitation of a "play with sounds" rather than normative gameplay or composition. Iwai describes himself as in sympathy with Yokoi's ideas, which he came to appreciate fully after his death in 1997: "I thought maybe my job is much closer to the work that Mr. Yokoi had been doing than to art." Iwai, *Iwai Toshio no shigoto to shūhen*, 67.

69 The quote was cited in Iwai's online profile as winner of the Multimedia Content Association of Japan's Multimedia Grand Prix in 1997; the profile is no longer accessible.

70 On the "modernity" of limited animation, see Thomas Lamarre, *The Anime Machine: A Media Theory of Animation* (Minneapolis, MN and London: University of Minnesota Press, 2009), 184–206.

71 Cited in Lamarre, *The Anime Machine: A Media Theory of Animation*, 188. A discussion between Iwata and the developers of *Minna no Rhythm Tengoku* [*Rhythm Heaven Fever/Beat the Beat: Rhythm Paradise*] (Nintendo Wii), developed by Nintendo and TNX (Kyoto: Nintendo, 2011), is revealing in this regard: it emerges that eliminating intermediate frames of animation (just as Tezuka had done) improves the synchronization of image, sound, and button-pressing, yielding superior results to those obtained from the use of three-dimensional models and "realistic" graphics. "*Shachō ga kiku Minna no Rhythm Tengoku*," *Nintendo*, available online at www.nintendo.co.jp/wii/interview/somj/vol1/index.html.

72 Quoted in Gorges and Yamazaki, *The History of Nintendo 1980–1991: The Game & Watch Games, An Amazing Invention*, 146.

73 The genesis of the Ele-Conga is briefly described in Gunpei Yokoi and Takefumi Makino, *Yokoi Gunpei Gēmukan Returns: Game Boy o unda hassōryoku*, 40–43.

74 *Taiko no Tatsujin* (arcade cabinet), developed by Namco (Tokyo: Namco, 2001).

75 *Donkey Konga* (Nintendo GameCube), developed by Namco (Kyoto: Nintendo, 2003); *Donkey Kong* (arcade cabinet), developed by Nintendo (Kyoto: Nintendo, 1981). The appearance of the *Donkey Konga* bongos might also reflect the fact that Cuban congas were often made from salvaged barrels. The bongos were subsequently repurposed by Nintendo's *Donkey Kong: Jungle Beat* (Nintendo GameCube), developed by Nintendo (Kyoto: Nintendo, 2004), a platform game in which players control Donkey Kong's movements by striking the bongos and clapping their hands (an action registered by the bongos' built-in microphone). *Donkey Kong: Jungle Beat* thus approaches the ludomusical fusion of rhythm and gameplay described by Kondo in relation to *Super Mario Bros.*, but from an angle that explicitly foregrounds instrumentality and performance.

76 *Guitar Hero* (Sony PlayStation 2), developed by Harmonix (Mountain View, CA: RedOctane, 2005). On *Guitar Hero*'s controller, see Kiri Miller, *Playing Along: Digital Games, YouTube, and Virtual Performance* (Oxford and New York: Oxford University Press, 2012), 86–93.

77 On the relationship of this technological lineage to digital games, see Moseley, "Playing Games with Music (and Vice Versa): Ludomusicological Perspectives on *Guitar Hero* and *Rock Band*," 297–300.

78 Deanna Morse, "Pre-Cinema Toys Inspire Multimedia Artist Toshio Iwai," *Animation World Magazine* 3/11 (1999), available online at www.awn.com/mag/issue3.11/3.11pages/morseiwai.php3.

79 As Jessica Riskin points out, Kircher's organ can be placed in a long tradition of mechanical clocks and organs that animated doves, roosters, biblical figures, angels, devils, and skeletons, among other things; the earliest documentation of such devices dates from the mid fourteenth century. Jessica Riskin, "Machines in the Garden," *Republics of Letters* 1/2 (2010), 16–43.

80 The most direct manifestation of Donkey Kong's ludomusicality was never released. *Donkī Kongu no Ongaku Asobi* [*Donkey Kong's Musical Play*], developed by Nintendo and announced for the Famicom in 1983, was to feature Jumpman and Pauline hammering piano keys while Donkey Kong strummed the bass; a collaborative karaoke mode was also planned. On other aspects of Donkey Kong's lineage, see Neil Lerner's essay in this volume, 1–29.

81 Alan Liu, "Transcendental Data: Toward a Cultural History and Aesthetics of the New Encoded Discourse," *Critical Inquiry* 31 (2004), 49–81.

82 See John W. O'Malley, *The First Jesuits* (Cambridge, MA: Harvard University Press, 1993), 76–77.

83 Despite its allusions to Pythagoras and Virgil, the organ's Christian symbology is made evident by the musical ubiquity of the number three and the Latin text directly above the keyboard.

84 On the proselytizing motives behind Kircher's media techniques, see Friedrich Kittler, *Optical Media*, trans. Anthony Enns (Cambridge, MA and Malden, MA: Polity Press, 2010), 76–81.

85 Hiroki Azuma, Otaku: *Japan's Database Animals*, trans. Jonathan E. Abel and Shion Kono (Minneapolis, MN and London: University of Minnesota Press, 2009). On Foucault's concept of the *dispositif*, which has been variously translated as "apparatus," "ensemble," and "system of relations," see Foucault et al., "Le jeu de Michel Foucault," *Ornicar?* 10 (July 1977), 62–93.

86 On the relationship between layering in *anime* and calligraphy, see Miho Nakagawa, "Mamoru Oshii's Production of Multi-Layered Space in 2D Anime," *Animation* 8/1 (2013), 65–83.

Chapter 4

Transcribing Musical Worlds; or, Is *L.A. Noire* a Music Game?

Steven Beverburg Reale

In many video games, the musical score functions in the manner of typical film scores: once finished, or mostly finished, a game world is adorned with a soundtrack designed to amplify, heighten the intensity of, or provide emotional or ironic commentary on a narrative unfolding in a pre-constructed tableau. Even in games with highly dynamic audio design, interactive audio cues are often intended to respond to decisions or actions originating in the narrative. For this reason, much scholarship on video game music advances strategies for composing accompaniments to branching or indeterminate scenarios in what is traditionally a fairly linear medium—hence, Jesper Kaae's observation that the challenge for modern game composers is essentially the same one faced by early film composers: "the problem of not knowing when things happen."[1] Framing the video game score in this way asserts a primacy on a game's narrative to which music is applied, *ex post facto*; even in light of Kristine Jørgensen's conclusions that video games played without sound suffer a marked decrease in usability, it seems obvious that games keep their ontological status *qua* game when lacking a soundtrack, the same not being true in the case of game music absent gameplay.[2] Thus, the release of video game soundtracks, or their arrangement for orchestral performance (such as by the Video Games Live Orchestra), necessarily flatten out the interactive element in the video games, removing the uncertainty of when things happen; the music, notwithstanding its origins, ceases to be "video game music" and becomes "music from a video game." We could therefore read the emergence of the music game genre as an attempt to grapple with this problematic, unidirectional relationship between games and their soundtracks; the creation of game spaces intimately tied to their audio can be understood as a reaction against the assumption of ludic primacy and musical supplementarity.

The *Guitar Hero* phenomenon seems to be at ground zero for studies of interactive music gameplay.[3] Dominic Arsenault explains how the game's notation abstracts (with surprising fidelity) guitarists' facility within a system of frets and strings to a simplified representation among five buttons on the *Guitar Hero* controller.[4] In the same journal issue, Henry Adam Svec submits the process of converting *Guitar Hero*'s notation into button presses and strums to a Marxist critique of virtual production and immaterial labor.[5] Peter Shultz's study argues that the games' metaphorical tablature notation exists in four states of varying affinity to the music it represents, which, in a quasi-Schenkerian manner, serves to familiarize the players with varying levels of the musical structure as they progress from Easy to Expert mode.[6] Kiri Miller uses the term "schizophrenic performance" to describe the friction between the rhetoric of live musical creation in *Guitar Hero* players' simulated performance and the prerecorded audio that is "realized" through it.[7]

Because of the numerous writings on *Guitar Hero* within the ludomusi-cological discourse, detailed discussion of its core gameplay mechanics is not necessary here, but certain key features of the game can serve as a framework for understanding music and gameplay interactions in other titles. As is well described in the works referenced, *Guitar Hero* features a notational system that resembles, and is metaphorically based on, guitar tablature. As a pre-recorded song plays, graphical noteheads, represented by cropped cones that correspond both in location and color to five fret buttons on a guitar-shaped controller, move toward the bottom of the screen on an endlessly approaching guitar neck (often called the "highway") (Figure 4.1). If the player presses the corresponding fret button and strums (by means of a switch on the body of the controller) just as the note reaches the bottom of the screen, the soundtrack plays the associated note or group of notes in the song; failing to correctly respond to the note results either in a screech (as though the guitar were mis-strummed) or the melody dropping out of the recording.

Since one purpose of *Guitar Hero* is to simulate the act of performing music, it makes sense that its graphic design, while abstracted, is intended to simulate

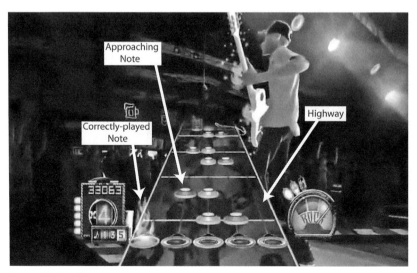

Figure 4.1 Still from *Guitar Hero III: Legends of Rock* (Activision, 2007)

a real-world musical notation. Nonetheless, the underlying process is not limited to representations of guitar performance, and I distill it to four abstract features. In *Guitar Hero*, there exists: (1) an ideal musical object (here, a prerecorded rock song); (2) a visual representation of the ideal musical object (the highway tablature); (3) a means by which the player can interact with the visual representation of the musical object (buttons on the guitar controller correspond to oncoming notes in the highway tablature); and (4) a means by which the game communicates success or failure in realizing the ideal musical object (the soundtrack either plays or omits notes from the prerecorded song). These features provide a starting point for exploring how other games, even ones that are not, strictly speaking, music games, allow their players to interact with their soundtracks.

*   *   *

The *BIT.TRIP* series of music games, released on the Nintendo Wii but later ported to PC, makes a good launching point to abstract the concept of performance in music games. The six games tell a story about the creation and life of a superhero figure, "Commander Video"; *BIT.TRIP BEAT* (Gaijin Games, 2009), the first game of the series, represents his genesis. The player controls a paddle on the left side of the screen that may be moved up and down; the game's titular "bits," imitated low-resolution pixels, hurtle from the right and must be deflected using the paddle. The game's retro aesthetic, with an archaic graphical style and chiptune soundtrack, self-consciously references early video game titles, particularly *Pong* (Atari, 1972) and *Breakout* (Atari, 1976), both of which are given explicit homage in two of the game's boss sequences. But while there is a degree of randomness in those games (indeed, the heart of their challenge is to both anticipate where the ball [actually a square] will be as it returns to the paddle, as well as to choose where on the paddle the ball will strike so as to manipulate its direction and speed as it hurtles back across the field), the patterns of bits in *BIT.TRIP BEAT* are predetermined by the game designer and are exactly the same on each playthrough (the only exception to this is, notably, during the *Pong* and *Breakout* homage sequences). The bits are what Fares Kayali calls "sound agents," or "playful widgets that exist aurally and also visually as interactive gameplay elements."[8] Deflecting a bit sounds a melodic note in the level's soundtrack, while missing one sounds a tone resembling a tennis ball being struck.

BIT.TRIP's designer, Alex Neuse, describes his intention for *BIT.TRIP BEAT* as to suggest that no person (or superhero) can always perform optimally, but that all agents need to rest; the idea is implemented through *BIT.TRIP BEAT*'s three modes: "Nether," "Hyper," and "Mega."[9] Levels begin in Hyper mode by default (Figure 4.2a), and by successfully deflecting enough bits, the player can move into Mega mode (Figure 4.2b), where the timbre of the cues of deflected bits changes to a smoother, square-wave sound as contrasted with

Hyper mode's sawtooth, and successive combinations of accurately deflected bits is rewarded with score multipliers. Mega mode also features an increase in visual effects: explosive particle effects accompany deflected bits, the word "Great" appears each time a deflected bit reaches the opposite side of the screen, and the text indicating the accumulated score and current multiplier, listed in the upper and lower borders of the screen, bleeds into the game field. While the player has the opportunity to earn more points in Mega mode, the game's visual design increases the likelihood that the player will miss too many bits, returning the mode to Hyper.

When the player misses too many bits in Hyper mode, the game descends to Nether mode (Figure 4.2c). Resembling Jørgensen's "degraded usability" of muted gameplay, in Nether mode most of the visuals drop out (the paddle, bits, and meters are the only things that remain), the color palette flattens to a white foreground with black background, and the music ceases playing; the sole sound in Nether mode is a flat, monotone beep when the paddle deflects a bit. Nether mode makes *BIT.TRIP BEAT*'s homage to early Atari gaming most clear; its simulation of the limited audio and graphical capabilities of early video games provide the strongest resemblance to *Pong*. Neuse intends Nether mode not so much as a punishment for poor performance in Hyper mode (although the removal of color and the ongoing soundtrack seems to have that effect), but as an opportunity for the player to rest and recuperate while playing the game with no audio or visual distractions. Should the player miss too many bits in Nether mode, though, the game ends.

The simple, predictable bit patterns with which the game begins give way to complicated and disorienting ones: one pattern, approximately two-thirds through the game's second level, sends the bits toward the player in an incredibly confusing pattern that deceptively suggests that the paddle should move in the wrong direction (Neuse refers to this pattern as "the gates of hell"). In actuality, the correct paddle motions are much smaller and simpler than the wild bit oscillations imply. At the same time, as the game progresses, visual design in the stage backgrounds become more graphically intensive, their colorful images distracting the eyes away from the onslaught of bits. Once the player learns the correct motions and begins to ignore the visual distractions, the passage becomes simpler to complete. Through practice, muscle memory, and memorization, the player learns how to respond to (or to ignore!) the on-screen stimuli, and what emerges is a realization that this is not a game of *Pong* at all, but an abstracted—and problematized—version of the *Guitar Hero* experience: an abstracted bit notation accompanies a pre-composed soundtrack, and the game rewards successful deflections with a kind of rhythmic descant to the ongoing score. But whereas *Guitar Hero* provides a predictable, if challenging, notation for the player, whose goal (tweaked by the use of Star Power) is ideally the perfect realization of its tablature, *BIT.TRIP BEAT*'s notation provides distracting, disorienting visual disturbances that the player must learn to negate in order to perform well.

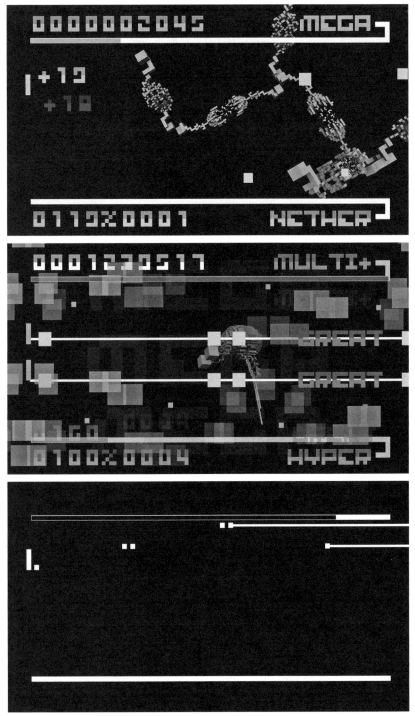

Figure 4.2 *BIT.TRIP BEAT* stills. (*a*) is Hyper mode, (*b*) is Mega mode, and (*c*) is Nether mode

The fourth game in the series, *BIT.TRIP RUNNER* (Gaijin Games, 2010) is a rail platformer; Commander Video constantly runs to the right of the screen, accompanied by a prerecorded soundtrack, and the player can make him jump, duck, kick, or block to avoid oncoming obstacles; musical cues reward successful actions while a failure to avoid an obstacle resets the level.[10] Additionally, Commander Video can collect gold and power-up items. As an additional reward for collecting all gold pieces in a single level, the game offers a retro bonus level, and by collecting the power-up items, the level's mode increases by one step (in this game, the modes are "Hyper," "Mega," "Super," "Ultra," and "Extra"—each of the various *BIT.TRIP* games draws from the same set of modes, all of which have spondaic names), the player earns a score bonus, and, more importantly for our purposes, the music's orchestration intensifies.[11]

In contrast to the abstract level design of *BIT.TRIP BEAT*, *BIT.TRIP RUNNER*'s platforming levels have a more concrete geography to them. The levels are pre-constructed collections of what might be thought of as "obstacle motives," by which I mean recurring patterns of groups of obstacles, such as steps to be ascended, gaps to be leapt over, and narrow squeezes to duck beneath (see Figure 4.3). Not only do individual levels feature returns of these motives, but they are developed and recapitulated, so to speak, in later ones as well. Each obstacle is associated with a particular kind of audio cue; therefore, recurring sets of audio cues accompany recurring obstacle motives. The return and variation of each of these obstacles serve as formal markers, a role amplified by the audio reiterating the corresponding cue motives.

To clarify how this works, see the transcription of Level 1-9, "Beat Deposits," in Example 4.1 The bottom three staves represent the ongoing soundtrack, while the upper staff represents cues that sound when Commander Video either collects gold (the grace note cues) or successfully negotiates an obstacle. Occasional ossia measures appear when Commander Video collects an upgrade, and the transcription here assumes that all upgrades are collected, meaning that the texture and accompaniments in the lower three staves change at the point where the upgrades are collected. If the upgrade is not collected, the musical texture would remain as it is in the preceding measures, introducing a degree of indeterminacy not reflected in the transcription.[12] Vertically aligned with the transcription is a map of the level (since musical notation is not to temporal scale, neither is the map; in-game, each beat occupies a fixed horizontal distance while, here, beats in the level design are shifted in coordination with those in the notation).

Aligning the map with the score transcription helps to clarify how obstacles combine to create obstacle motives, how the repetitions of obstacle motives combine to create obstacle phrases, and how the phrases combine to create larger formal structures, complete with a kind of motivic return and development we might expect in a musical passage. The opening of the level (mm. 1–9) repeats an obstacle motive four times: Commander Video must

Figure 4.3 Stills from *BIT.TRIP RUNNER*. In (*a*), Commander Video approaches the obstacle motive in m. 5 of the transcription in Example 4.1. In (*b*), Commander Video has just collected the power-up item in m. 13, whose explosive remnants still shimmer on the screen. In (*c*), Commander Video leaps from the springboard in m. 30.

leap to collect a piece of gold, kick through a crystal, and then leap onto a raised platform and over a pile of rubble; at the same time, the audio repeats an accompanying musical motive. Then, the level introduces a new motive: Commander Video leaps over a pile of rubble, ducks through a narrow passage, then leaps to collect gold (mm. 11–14). The music changes to a new motive, but in the second iteration, Commander Video must also collect a power-up item, necessarily modulating the orchestration. After skipping up a staircase (m. 15), the paths branch: to follow the upper path, Commander Video must leap from platform to platform (collecting gold on each one), while following the lower one requires ducking under a UFO and leaping over an obstacle (mm. 16–20). The next section (mm. 21–30) involves leaping over gaps in the ground and ducking under UFOs to arrive at a springboard that the player uses to leap over a very large gap and collect a gold piece. This passage repeats a second time but with new orchestration, as Commander Video collects another power-up positioned at the first springboard. The level next reiterates its opening motive and then fragments the preceding passage, sounding only the springboard motive in a rapid, threefold succession, the last of which is rewarded by a cascade of gold collection (mm. 31–37).

As a text, *BEAT.TRIP RUNNER* offers complex, seemingly contradictory implications with respect to the issue of ludic versus musical primacy. On the one hand, as Alex Neuse, the principal game designer, remarked to me: "Ideally, we would get the music first, and then we would design the levels to basically dance with that music." Sometimes real-world logistics did not always make that possible, but even in situations where the gameplay was designed first, it was always subject to revision in order to better fit the musical score. On the other hand, the game's visual cues (represented by level geography) is probably more immediate to the player's success than are its audio cues, and since the obstacle motives are associated with musical cues, it seems that the obstacles themselves function as formal generators for a coherent passage of music: indeed, gameplay is not excessively hampered when the sound is turned off, but it would be nearly impossible to play relying on the audio alone. We can therefore conclude that the level design here features a musically organized geography rather than a geographically organized music.

*   *   *

Dyad (right square bracket left square bracket, 2012) resembles cylindrical shooters such as *Tempest* (Atari, 1981) and *Gyruss* (Konami, 1983), although enemies are not merely obstacles to be avoided or destroyed, but require various kinds of interaction to meet the disparate goals of each level. For example, in an early level, racing on the lowermost surface of a cylinder, which can be rotated clockwise or counterclockwise, the player creates eponymous dyads by "hooking" (selecting) two enemies of a matching color, thereby earning a speed boost that both shortens the time it takes to reach the goal and increases the risk of colliding with the enemies. Music plays an important

Example 4.1 Transcription plus map of *BIT.TRIP RUNNER*, "Beat Deposits"

Example 4.1 continued

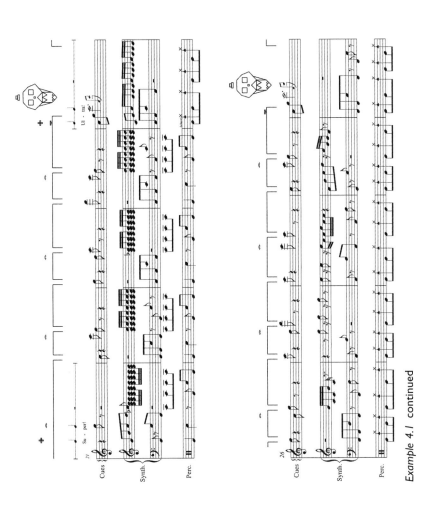

Example 4.1 continued

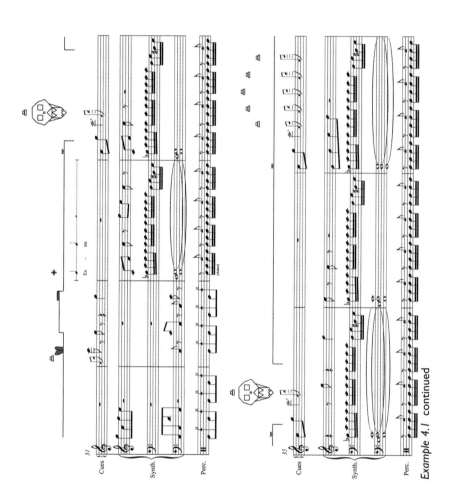

Example 4.1 continued

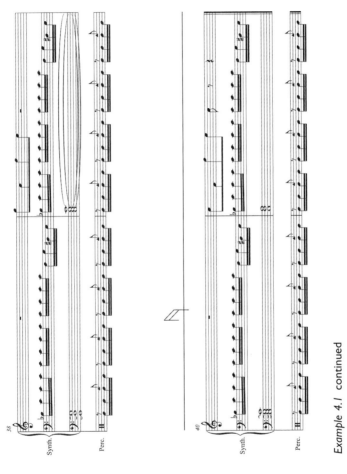

Example 4.1 continued

role in *Dyad*, as the levels are examples of what Fares Kayali calls "active scores, [which] are a dynamic form of representation that can be modified in real time by a player, who consequently triggers musical change" (p. 120). Different interactions within the level are associated with specific audio cues—hooking enemies creates a tone, collecting a power-up item adds a musical layer, striking obstacles causes the soundtrack to stop and play in reverse, and acceleration increases the tempo. The specific ordering of the level's events, which are unique to each playthrough and virtually unrepeatable, realize its dynamic soundtrack; the game's composer, David Kanaga, cited the aleatoric compositional philosophies of John Cage's student Christian Woolf as highly influential on the game's musical aesthetic.[13]

In one of the game's later levels, "A Subliminal Reprise" (the title puns on that of an earlier level with a similar conceit, "Observations on the Beautiful and the Sublime"), a depleting "life energy" meter limits play time; when the meter reaches zero, the level ends. At the start of the level, life energy depletes by about one percent per second but the rate slowly increases over time. To survive, the player must collect invincibility power-ups—through the duration of invincibility, the rate of life energy depletion is halved, and the player can replenish some life energy (beginning at about 20 percent, but decreasing as the level progresses) by colliding with an enemy. The game designer, Shawn McGrath, described the level as a metaphor for the inevitability of death through the implementation of a "swarm mechanic," and offered *Pac-Man* and *Asteroids* as examples, where a prototypical survivor must keep at bay hordes of attackers (be they zombies, insects, or aliens) for as long as possible, even though the swarm will eventually overtake the protagonist.[14]

The level incorporates three mechanics: first, hooking (read: selecting) a pair of enemies creates a "zip line" between them, which the racer can ride to increase its speed. Second, by selecting an enemy and navigating closely enough to it, the player can charge a "lance" that, when used, gives a short speed boost and allows the player to lance through enemies, replenishing some life energy in the process. Third, by collecting the invincibility power-up, the player can slow the depletion of life energy and, as with the lance, allow collisions with enemies to replenish it. The level consists of a randomly generated collection of four kinds of items: yellow enemies, pink enemies, green "lance-extender" enemies, and invincibility power-ups. Figure 4.4 is a still taken during a period of non-immunity. The racer (in purple near the bottom-middle of the screen) has hooked two yellow enemies, creating a dyad between them, and is riding along the created zip line. Zooming past at the upper-left is a lance-extender, and in the distance, several yellow and pink enemies approach. The player, unable to interact with all of the presented items, must choose, quickly and strategically, which will confer the highest benefit, and the level generates its music procedurally on the basis of those choices.

The level's audio, which is dynamic and changes adaptively based on the level conditions, can be divided into two parameters: score and cues.[15]

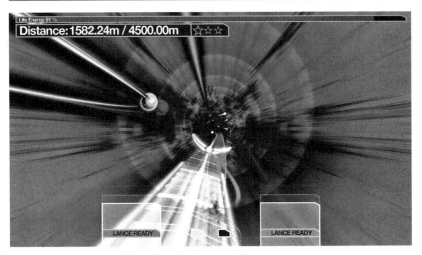

Figure 4.4 Still from *Dyad*, "A Subliminal Reprise"

The cues are feedback responses to the player's interactions with the level's sound agents—some of these are listed in Table 4.1—while the score is the ongoing musical accompaniment for a particular level condition—Table 4.2 lists some possible conditions with their associated scoring loops. Notice, in particular, that the loop signaling impending death is both atonal and irregular in meter; these aspects intrude upon the soundtrack's stable A-minor tonality and the regular 4/4 groupings of all of the other loops and cues, intensifying the affect of impending death. The level's limited raw materials offer the possibility for combination and recombination in nearly limitless ways: it would be virtually impossible for a player to exactly recreate a playthrough, and so it is concomitantly unlikely that the level's audio could ever be realized in the same way on multiple occasions. Still, some characteristics are likely to occur in various playthroughs: a relatively quiet, though fast-paced beat begins the level punctuated by chirps, flutes, and reeds; over time, distorted tones occupy a pronounced position in the texture, which are replaced by a ringing motive and cessation of the bass beat during sections of invincibility. A crescendoing snare drum signals the impending end of invincibility, which is articulated by a reverberating cymbal crash and return of the bass drum beats. Over time, cacophonous, distorted strings in irregular meters swell, reminiscent of The Beatles' "A Day in the Life." The stop-time chimes of invincibility temporarily keep these at bay, but eventually they overtake the entire texture. The screen goes white and the noisy strings loop until the player presses a button to either retry the level or quit. Example 4.2 represents the audio that would accompany a (highly simplified) hypothetical playthrough, and is annotated with the specific player actions that trigger musical changes.

Table 4.1 Some events and their associated cues in "A Subliminal Reprise"

Event	Cue	
Hook a yellow enemy	Chirp	
Create yellow dyad	Chirp	
Hook a pink enemy	Synth Flute	
Create pink dyad	Synth Flute	
Hook lance-extender	Synth Reed	
Create lance-extender dyad	Synth Reed	
Graze an enemy	Square wave with reverb	
Strike an enemy while invincible	Distorted cymbal	
Lance an enemy	An Aeolian scale beginning on B4, each additional enemy steps up the scale	

Zip line between enemies

Table 4.2 Some conditions and their accompaniments in the score of "A Subliminal Reprise"

Condition	Score Loops
Persistent (this loop is always present); loops beneath are added as needed	
Not invincible	
Invincible	
Invincibility about to end (sixteenth notes loop as long as needed; cymbal crashes at end of invincibility)	
Impending death (volume and distortion inversely proportional to remaining life force)	

Example 4.2 is somewhat unsatisfying, as it is unable to really capture the indeterminacy of the gameplay; it is also rather short and notates a spectacularly bad performance on the part of the player. Yet, systematically transcribing one playthrough, such as occurs in Example 4.1, would hardly be much better, even though it would be longer and more detailed, because it would still fail to capture the sense that the score is unfolding dynamically. This is precisely why, when I explained the present project to McGrath, he objected to the very idea of transcribing the game's music into musical notation, and insisted that "the notation for *Dyad*'s music . . . is its game"; I am inclined to agree with him on this point, only appending Tables 4.1 and 4.2 to serve as a symbolic key, much like the graphic notation that Penderecki supplies for his score to *Threnody for the Victims of Hiroshima* (1960).

*   *   *

The previous analyses have begun from the standpoint that certain games reward skillful play with audio signals. By assigning certain cues to success

Example 4.2 Hypothetical audio to a playthrough of *Dyad*, "A Subliminal Reprise"

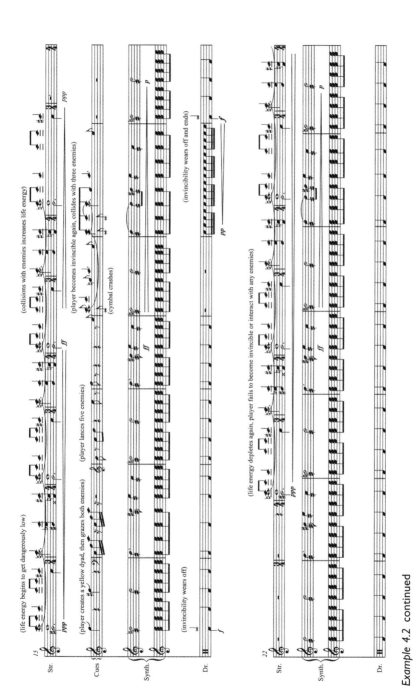

Example 4.2 continued

Example 4.2 continued

and others to failure, the players can either recreate an ideal musical object, as occurs in *Guitar Hero* and *BIT.TRIP*, or, through judicious decision-making in *Dyad*, realize an aleatoric musical composition. What these examples have in common is the suggestion that the levels themselves become a form of abstracted musical notation. When the player correctly responds to the game stimulus, the correct musical cues sound; when the player fails to correctly respond to the stimulus, incorrect, or less ideal, musical cues result. By skillfully reading the game world "score," the player performs the intended composition.

What happens if we apply this schema—game world as musical score—to a title that few people would consider a music game? Rockstar Games's *L.A. Noire* (2011) adopts the open-world sandbox formula used in their well-known *Grand Theft Auto* series for their take on the cinematic mode of *film noir*.

The game's protagonist is Cole Phelps, a World War II veteran turned police officer making his way through the detective ranks at the L.A.P.D. During a typical case, Cole drives through an open-world representation of Los Angeles to investigate crime scenes for clues and to interrogate any persons of interest; the goal of each mission is to either solicit a confession or uncover enough information to charge a suspect. Both Cole's investigations and interrogations make ludic use of musical cues. During an investigation, a moody, atonal theme on piano, muted brass, string bass, and vibraphone—resembling modernist tropes in some 1950s, second-wave *noir* scores—plays as Cole walks through the crime scene.[16] When he approaches a potential clue, a three-note chime sounds on the piano to attract the player's attention (Example 4.3). When the investigation is complete and Cole has found all the relevant clues, or when Cole walks too far from the crime scene, the investigation theme ceases playing, signaling to the player to either return to the area or to move on with the case.

During the interrogation sequences, Cole can select avenues for questioning based on the clues found at the crime scene, and must decide whether he believes the suspect's answer to be true, doubtful, or, if he has collected contradictory evidence, a lie. The musical cues in the interrogation sequences have a tremendous impact on the experience of playing *L.A. Noire*. There are several elements: first, strings play a droning C♯-major triad throughout the entire interrogation; each time Cole chooses a correct response, the drone increases in volume. Second, each time Cole makes a response, one of two brief atonal cues sound, depending on whether the response was correct: the first features two ascending fifths, with the last note "harmonized" as part of an [014], while the second begins with the same ascending fifth, but is followed

Example 4.3 Cue in *L.A. Noire* investigation sequences signaling that Cole is near a potential clue

by a major third and a descending semitone, while strings enter the texture with tritones and a major seventh (Example 4.4).

It is significant that both cues open with the same two tones. The player, having been trained throughout the game as to which is the correct motive, must wait for the third pitch in order to know whether he or she has selected correctly; this anticipation heightens the tension of the encounter in a way that mere textual feedback would not. At the same time, the C♯-major drone has a symbolic role: amid an angst-ridden, atonal score, the persistence of a major triad suggests that the light of truth is emerging from the darkness and corruption of Cole's cases. The effect on the player is pronounced: in a successful interrogation, the chord even begins to drown out the dialogue.

Because the goal of the interrogation encounters is to respond correctly to each of the suspect's statements, and because doing so has a particular musical result, for which the player has been trained throughout to listen, we can understand the interrogation sequences themselves as containing an ideal musical composition, which the player, through correctly responding to the suspect's statements, performs. The musical score for a generic three-question interrogation is given in Example 4.5. While Cole deliberates about the response he will give, the strings drone on their C♯-major chord. Each time Cole provides a correct response, the score takes the lower branch, and the game sounds both the "correct" cue and increases the dynamics of the string drone. Each time Cole provides an incorrect response, the score takes the top branch, cuing the "incorrect" motive without affecting the volume of the string drone. Simply put, the ideal musical performance of the interrogation sequence is represented by the lower branches of Example 4.5, while a non-ideal performance will make a detour along at least one upper branch.

*   *   *

It should be clear that the existence of an ideal musical object in its interrogation sequences does not somehow make *L.A. Noire* a music game. However, the sound design of these sequences shares the same musical logic with the other games in this study, albeit in a very abstracted manner. We can now return to the model advanced at the outset of this essay to explore

Example 4.4 Cues when Cole responds to suspect's statements (*a*) correctly and (*b*) incorrectly

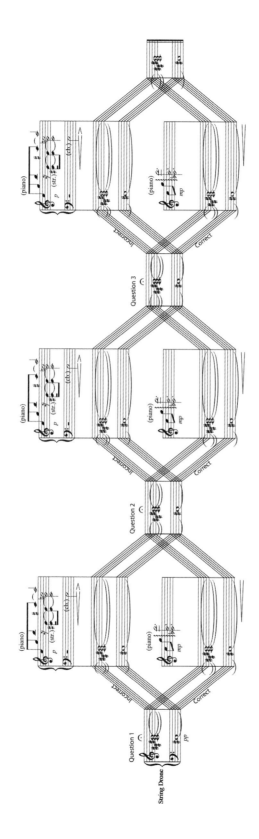

Example 4.5 Branching score for a hypothetical investigation in *LA. Noire*

how these disparate games relate (see Table 4.3). Perhaps not surprisingly, BIT.TRIP BEAT and BIT.TRIP RUNNER fit the Guitar Hero model best. Both games feature ideal musical objects (even if Neuse does not necessarily intend for the player to realize them perfectly); visual representations of the ideal musical object (a near one-to-one correspondence between obstacle structure and musical structure in BIT.TRIP RUNNER, or anti-representations, in the case of BIT.TRIP BEAT's fiendishly deceptive bit patterns); a means of interacting with the visual representations (deflecting bits in BIT.TRIP BEAT; negotiating obstacles in BIT.TRIP RUNNER); and a means by which the games communicate success or failure in realizing the musical object (collision with an obstacle in BIT.TRIP RUNNER triggers the level to reset; missing too many bits in BIT.TRIP BEAT decrements the mode until the game ends when Nether is failed).

More surprising, though, is that L.A. Noire is also a very close fit: the level design, in this case the interrogation sequences, features an ideal musical object, a visual representation of the ideal musical object (the interrogation dialogue and Cole's detective notebook, his log of all clues and locations pertinent to the case, which help the player decide which option is correct); a means by which the player can interact with the visual representation of the musical object (buttons mapped to the options "Truth," "Doubt," and "Lie"); and a means by which the game communicates success or failure in realizing the ideal musical object: failure follows the upper path and success the lower. The subject's statements create the musical score for the interrogations; Cole's responses to them create the performance.

By contrast, Dyad departs tremendously from the Guitar Hero model: there is no ideal musical object, but rather a multiplicity of acceptable musical objects, and therefore the game visually represents (and offers a means of interacting with) not an ideal musical object, but rather the possibility of all acceptable musical objects. Moreover, since the goal of "A Subliminal Reprise" is to play for as long as possible without allowing life energy to reach zero, success or failure in the level hinges not on how the musical object is realized, but only on its duration.

Guitar-shaped peripherals are not required for a game's music to be intractable from its gameplay; it probably does not even need an active score or a foregrounded soundtrack. Even in the most ostensibly cinematic video games, the interaction of the game world with its audio invites the possibility that playing the game is playing its music. This way of thinking would allow us to consider the skilled, practiced gamer as a kind of virtuoso; or the practice of making tool-assisted videos, where a sequence of keystrokes is fed into an emulator to create inhumanly perfect—and often stunningly beautiful—playthroughs, or their opposites in the fan-created levels of Super Mario World that send the title character careening through a precisely arranged course of blocks, enemies, and power-ups and compose their reactive audio cues into extended musical compositions as examples of the kind of machinic virtuosity

Table 4.3 Performative comparison of Guitar Hero, BIT.TRIP BEAT, BIT.TRIP RUNNER, L.A. Noire, and Dyad

Parameter	Guitar Hero	BIT.TRIP BEAT	BIT.TRIP RUNNER	L.A. Noire	Dyad
Existence of an ideal musical object (IMO)	Yes	Yes	Yes, but subject to minor variation	Yes	No
Visual representation of IMO	Yes	Yes, although sometimes purposefully misleading	Yes	Yes, but also relies on spoken dialogue	No, but there is a visual representation of a multiplicity of acceptable musical objects
Means of interacting with IMO	Yes	Yes	Yes	Yes	No, but there is a means of interacting with the multiplicity of acceptable musical objects
Means of communicating success or failure in realizing IMO	Yes	Yes	Yes	Yes	No, success and failure hinges solely on maintaining a nonzero amount of "life energy"

(to borrow Svec's term) implemented by Conlon Nancarrow in his compositions for player piano.[17] Games keep score by tabulating and evaluating a player's ability to accomplish its tasks, but when game scores and musical scores collide, we might consider player performance literally: that the playthrough becomes—more than a measure of skill—a kind of expression to be judged aesthetically.

Notes

All websites were accessed November 4, 2013.

1   Jesper Kaae, "Theoretical Approaches for Composing Dynamic Music for Video Games," in *From Pac-Man to Pop Music: Interactive Audio in Games and New Media*, ed. Karen Collins (Hampshire, UK: Ashgate, 2008), 85.
2   Kristine Jørgensen, "Left in the Dark: Playing Computer Games with the Sound Turned Off," in *From Pac-Man to Pop Music: Interactive Audio in Games and New Media*, ed. Karen Collins (Hampshire, UK: Ashgate, 2008), 175.
3   *Guitar Hero* (Harmonix Music Systems, 2005) saw several sequels and a spin-off in *Rock Band* (when the development company split from its publisher). For simplicity, I use the title *Guitar Hero* as a catch-all for its later incarnations.
4   Dominic Arsenault, "Guitar Hero: 'Not Like Playing Guitar At All'?" *Loading . . . Journal of the Canadian Gaming Studies Association* 2/2 (2008), available online at http://journals.sfu.ca/loading/index.php/loading/article/view/32/29.
5   Henry Adam Svec, "Becoming Machinic Virtuosos: *Guitar Hero*, *Rez*, and Multitudinous Aesthetics," *Loading . . . Journal of the Canadian Gaming Studies Association* 2/2 (2008), available online at http://journals.sfu.ca/loading/index.php/loading/article/view/30/28.
6   Peter Shultz, "Music Theory in Music Games," in *From Pac-Man to Pop Music: Interactive Audio in Games and New Media*, ed. Karen Collins (Hampshire, UK: Ashgate, 2008), 177–188.
7   Kiri Miller, "Schizophrenic Performance: *Guitar Hero*, *Rock Band*, and Virtual Virtuosity," *Journal of the Society for American Music* 3 (November 2009), 395–429.
8   Fares Kayali, "Playing Music: Design, Theory, and Practice of Music-based Games," Ph.D. dissertation (Technische Universität Wien, 2008), 102.
9   Interview with author, September 21, 2012.
10 In this respect, *BIT.TRIP RUNNER* references modern "endless runner" games such as *Canabalt* (Adam Saltsman, 2009), as well as older side-scrollers, such as the famous "Turbo Tunnel" sequence in the NES game *Battletoads* (Rare, 1991).
11 Much like in *BIT.TRIP BEAT*'s Nether mode, the retro bonus levels preserve the basic game mechanics but degrade the graphics in an homage to the classic Atari 2600 title *Pitfall!* (Activision, 1982), while monotone bleeps replace the rich musical accompaniment of the regular levels.
12 Two additional features of indeterminacy: there is no penalty if Commander Video misses a piece of gold, which would result in an omission of the associated cue (the transcription assumes all gold is collected), and the cues for successfully negotiated obstacles (as opposed to the collection of power-ups or gold, and excepting the springboard, which always sounds C5-G5-C6) are actually randomly selected from a set of pitches: F4, G4, A4, C5, E5, F5, G5, A5, E6, F6. Therefore, this transcription represents only one of a very large set of possible successful playthroughs.

13 Interview with the author (August 8, 2012). In this respect, *Dyad* resembles *Rez* (Sega, 2001), a game that has attracted some scholarly attention, and Svec's description of the latter's gameplay describes the former rather well: "[O]stensibly, the primary objective in *Rez* is to defend the avatar, not to execute digital paradiddles or flans. Still, an infinitely complex, improvisatory musical work develops as one plays the game." Similarly, in a paper presented at the 2012 meeting of the American Musicological Society (and later published in *The Oxford Handbook of Film Music Studies*, Neil Lerner observes "an aleatoric and minimalistic quality to the rhythmic surprises of *Pong*'s [(Atari, 1972)] severely limited pitch collection" of "a B♭ each time the paddle (represented on screen with a rectangle) hits the ball (a small square), a B♭ an octave lower each time the ball strikes the wall, and a B a half step higher each time the ball makes it past a paddle and scores a point." See Neil Lerner, "The Origins of Musical Style in Video Games, 1977–1983" in *The Oxford Handbook of Film Music Studies*, ed. David Neumeyer (Oxford: Oxford University Press, 2014), 321–322.

14 Interview with the author (August 8, 2012).

15 See Karen Collins, *Game Sound: An Introduction to the History, Theory, and Practice of Video Game Music and Sound Design* (Cambridge, MA: MIT Press, 2008), 4 for discussion of dynamic, nondynamic, interactive, and adaptive music in video games.

16 The author is grateful to Christopher Coady for assistance locating *L.A. Noire*'s score within the musical traditions of *film noir*.

17 One classic, and highly impressive, example of the practice was a simultaneous playthrough of *Mega Man X* and *Mega Man X2* using the exact same set of keystrokes (DeHackEd, "SNES Mega Man X & X2 (USA v1.1) in 41:41.43," TASVideos, http://tasvideos.org/380M.html). The video hilariously amplifies reviews that criticized *Mega Man X2* for being too similar to *Mega Man X*. User "agwawaf" upped the ante by adding *Mega Man X3* to the mix. agwawaf, "SNES Mega Man X & Mega Man X2 & Mega Man X3 (USA) '300%' in 43:51.02," *TASVideos*, available online at http://tasvideos.org/1894M.html.

Chapter 5

Meaningful Modular Combinations

Simultaneous Harp and Environmental Music in Two *Legend of Zelda* Games

Elizabeth Medina-Gray

As video games and game hardware become increasingly technologically advanced, so too do the musical possibilities of games expand. Freed from the stricter technological constraints of early gaming systems, more recent games have access not only to a higher sonic quality, but also to a wider scope, variety, and flexibility of musical material. With such freedom, game soundtracks frequently produce more than one musical element at once, and it is the sum of this musical material—not only the individual elements in themselves, but also the sonic interactions between them—that may convey important meaning and information to the player. Such a multilayered soundtrack has the potential to influence the player's experience in powerful ways, including providing information related to actions in the game, a critical role that Kristine Jørgensen has identified as game audio's *usability* function.[1]

This chapter explores several emergent effects in two examples of multi-layered game soundtracks, and consequently illustrates the importance of analytical attention to such simultaneous musical combinations. The two examples in this chapter come from Nintendo's *The Legend of Zelda* series of games: the first from the Nintendo GameCube's *The Legend of Zelda: The Wind Waker* (2003), and the second from *The Legend of Zelda: Skyward Sword* (2011) on the Nintendo Wii (hereafter *Wind Waker* and *Skyward Sword*).[2] These two examples are intriguing case studies, first because they are similar in context: each example features an in-game character who plays a harp while the game's normal environmental music—that is, the continuous score that accompanies gameplay in a particular area—also sounds. The two examples diverge drastically, however, in the actual sounds of these musical combinations, and in the information this provides for the player. Each musical example, moreover, is uniquely appropriate and useful for its own specific game situation. In short, the harp music of *Wind Waker* and *Skyward Sword* yields a brief yet diverse sample of multilayered game soundtracks and provides an entry point into broader analytical questions. Before we examine these two examples in detail, however, we must first establish some basic concepts and methods.

Modularity, Smoothness, and Analytical Methods

Modularity provides a useful way to conceptualize the multiple elements of any given video game soundtrack. In a modular system, a collection of modules—discrete chunks of music—goes through a process of assembly to yield the overall sounding result, following specific rules for how those modules may combine.[3] When we play a video game, the soundtrack's musical content arises mainly from modules (often distinct digital files) triggered in real time according to rules programmed into the game. Through modularity—and sometimes also through modifications to modules—game soundtracks therefore become unique to every playthrough of a game, and are able to reflect and affect a player's individualized gameplay experiences. This music becomes, in other words, *dynamic*.[4]

When two musical modules combine during gameplay, an element of *smoothness* may result. Smoothness is an intuitively familiar concept in situations where one module switches to another; indeed, authors often refer to smooth transitions between segments of music.[5] Such smoothness hinges, most clearly, on a sense that two modules fit together well, and that the second module sounds believably like a continuation of the first. In situations where two modules sound at the same time (as, for instance, in the examples in this chapter), smoothness is still a sense that the modules fit together well, but now in the vertical dimension. Two modules in a smooth simultaneous combination seem to agree with each other, even to work together to yield a denser whole, similar to the way simultaneous instruments may work together to yield a single piece of music. By contrast, a lack of smoothness in simultaneous combinations yields a sense of non-merging, or even conflict, between the two modules, a situation that I term *disjunction*, which closely resembles Albert Bregman's concept of segregation between simultaneous (yet perceptually distinct) auditory streams.[6]

Smoothness is often an aesthetic goal in video game music because it yields cohesion and continuity among modules in real-time game soundtracks, and it avoids producing sounds that might be jarring or unpleasant (such as dissonance).[7] Disjunction, however, is also appropriate in certain situations precisely because the modules remain distinct, and because their jarring combinations can serve dramatic and/or usability functions.[8] Neither smoothness nor disjunction is therefore inherently better than its opposite, but rather each quality—and the degree to which it occurs—has the potential to contribute significant effects to a gameplay experience. The two examples in this chapter highlight some of the interpretive benefits that we stand to gain when we focus analytical attention on smoothness and disjunction as equally valuable aspects of modular combinations.

Since smoothness and modularity are unusual topics for music analysis, we will require some new tools to explore this material. First, we need a way to examine smoothness and disjunction when two modules sound simultaneously, and we can do this by focusing especially on the modules' timbre, meter, and pitch.[9] Critically, a single modular combination may contain elements of both smoothness *and* disjunction, depending on how these various aspects of the music interact. Two modules will combine smoothly in terms of *timbre* if they each contain the same instruments, whereas different instrumentation produces disjunction. The *meters* of two simultaneously sounding modules will yield smoothness if they are similar and aligned, which is to say, if they each have the same underlying pulse and placement of strong beats. If these metric properties do not agree, then disjunction results instead. Finally, the *pitches* of two simultaneous modules will fit together best if their combination creates only consonance.[10] In general, the harsher the dissonance produced by two simultaneous modules, the more disjunct that combination will be. Other aspects of the music may also contribute to smoothness or disjunction, but timbre, meter, and pitch are some of the most consistent and significant components.

The above discussion assumes that we are examining a fixed simultaneous combination, which would indeed be the case if we were to analyze the soundtrack from one player's individualized gameplay session. However, the particular modular combination in one player's session represents only one instance of the game's dynamic soundtrack out of many (potentially infinite) realizations for just as many players. In order to treat the soundtrack during every possible instance of gameplay equally—and to not treat one player's soundtrack over another's—we will need to consider the modules in all of their possible combinations, given their behavior in the game. This analytical approach consequently produces *likelihoods* of degrees of smoothness and/or disjunction when these modules combine.[11]

This chapter's analytical methodology thus comprises first, an attention to smoothness and disjunction through comparison of the individual modules' musical content, and second, a view of these systems in terms of the probabilities of such smoothness and disjunction over all possible modular combinations. With this framework, we can now turn to this chapter's two main analyses, each of which highlights certain critical results of simultaneous musical modules within a game's soundtrack.

Medli's Harp

In *Wind Waker*, the player controls the young hero, Link, as he explores islands in a vast ocean on a quest to save the world. In later portions of this quest, the player learns that he or she must recruit two specific characters to aid Link on his journey. One of these characters is Medli, a young girl whom Link befriended earlier in the game, and who possesses a harp.[12]

On Headstone Island, near a large stone that blocks Link's way, Link meets the spirit of an ancient temple guardian, a sage, who carries a harp identical to Medli's. The sage tells Link: "You must find the one who carries on my bloodline … The one who holds this sacred instrument …". With this information, Link sets off to find the owner of the harp: Medli, although the game never makes this explicit. Fortunately for Link—and the player—Medli has, at this point in the game, begun to play her harp publicly, and the music she produces is readily audible, provided that Link is near enough to hear it. This harp music provides critical meaning and usability information by itself, but even more so when it sounds in combination with concurrent environmental music.

Medli has a repertoire of five major chords, which she practices incessantly, day and night, from a high cliff on Dragon Roost Island, one of the main locations in the game. While Link is almost anywhere on the island, Medli's music plays in the game's soundtrack. Her chords always come in patterns of threefold repetition: she chooses a single chord at random from among the five chords she knows, plays that chord three times in a row at a slow tempo, then plays another random chord (the same chord or a different one) three times, and so on. These five chords are each transpositions of the same major triad, with roots on A, B, D-flat, E-flat, and E, respectively. Each threefold repetition of a chord behaves in the game as a single module, yielding five different 2.25-second modules in all.[13] Example 5.1 provides transcriptions for each of these modules.

The player can derive ample meaning just from Medli's harp music by itself. Indeed, if the player arrives on Dragon Roost Island at nighttime in the game world, the island's normally looping environmental music is silent, making Medli's chords the only music the player hears. From her constant and highly patterned music-making, we can understand certain (true) aspects of Medli's character: she is diligent in her drive to practice and improve at her instrument, but not (yet) a very skilled musician—her constrained and repetitive chord selection, her slow tempo, and her slightly faltering rhythm

Example 5.1 Medli's five harp modules

all reinforce this fact. She will eventually awaken to her full potential as a sage and musician with Link's help, but for now, she is very much a novice, albeit a dedicated one.

Medli's harp music also provides several important pieces of information related to usability. Just the fact that there is harp music on Dragon Roost Island at all confirms that: (1) there is something new and interesting going on here (because this music never sounded during previous visits to this island); and (2) this is the right place to be (once the player has visited the sage and knows that he or she must find someone with a harp). The game also applies a special dynamic process to Medli's harp modules—they get louder as Link moves closer to Medli's location, and quieter as he moves farther away—allowing the player to intuit that (3) following the increasing amplitude of the harp sounds will lead Link to Medli. Finally, while the player always begins exploration of Dragon Roost Island at sea level, Medli stands on a high ledge and well out of sight. The player may therefore also benefit from (4) the acousmatic aspect of the music, and an associated curiosity to find the source of the sound.[14] This last component is a useful motivator, since it takes a fair bit of exploration before Medli (and her harp) finally comes into view.

The harp music alone thus supplies character-related meaning and gives the player more than enough information to locate Medli and progress the game's story. Daytime on Dragon Roost Island, however, brings a 1'15"-long looping module as the environment's normal musical accompaniment. This looping music is upbeat and dance-like, with a tuneful melody on panpipes and support from rhythmically active acoustic guitar. If the player explores Dragon Roost Island during the day, Medli's harp music sounds at the same time as this looping module, and the simultaneous combination of harp and environmental music yields further effects. Example 5.2 shows a reduced transcription of the environmental music from Dragon Roost Island by itself.

Together, the harp and environmental music—despite the flexibility of timing and five different possible harp modules—will almost always be extremely disjunct. The harp modules promote a $\frac{3}{4}$ meter at 80 bpm, which disagrees strongly with the 170 bpm $\frac{3}{4}$ meter of the environmental module: the two simultaneous streams of music do not even share an underlying pulse, and cannot reconcile into a relatable metric organization. In terms of pitch content, the disjunction is likely to be similarly extreme. Of the harp's five major triads, only the E-flat major chord has any chance of combining with the primarily G-natural minor environmental music without creating dissonance, and then only rarely—the rest of the time, it will produce varying amounts of dissonance. Each of the remaining four harp chords is so far removed from the pitch content of the environmental music that it will almost always yield multiple harsh dissonances (major sevenths, minor seconds, and tritones), regardless of when it sounds.

Pitch and meter are thus especially strong and likely indicators of disjunction in this modular combination. The harp's timbre also helps set it apart from the looping environmental music simply because this instrument does not appear in the island's normal musical accompaniment. (The harp's timbre is, however, related to the environmental music's guitar, so this source of disjunction is mild at most. In other words, the harp's sound quality is not especially jarring or foreign in the context of the environmental music's instrumentation, but it is still unique.) Even the harp's volume contributes to disjunction, since the two types of simultaneous music operate under separate auditory rules: the harp music gets louder and softer as Link moves around the island, while the environmental music remains at a constant volume throughout.

Overall, whenever a harp module sounds simultaneously with Dragon Roost Island's environmental music, chances are very high that the combination will be extremely disjunct. Moreover, since the harp music is continuous, this strong disjunction is virtually guaranteed in any given playthrough of the game (provided the player visits Dragon Roost Island during daytime in the game world). The harp and environmental modules reliably sound like they do *not* fit together, and they most clearly belong to two entirely different (albeit simultaneous) musical streams.

The above analysis opens the way for several additional pieces of information that may emerge from these disjunct modular combinations. First, within this larger sonic context, Medli's character becomes not only dedicated, but also oblivious: she is entirely absorbed in her own music as she practices, and is somehow not in tune (both musically and metaphorically) with the environment in which she stands. Additionally, perhaps Medli is an even worse musician than her repetitive and faltering performance by itself suggests. The player is likely to blame Medli for any unpleasant aspects of the overall soundtrack—including its incongruence, disorganization, and harsh tonal and metric dissonance, all of which are part of the extreme disjunction— since her music is new in comparison to the island's familiar environmental music. In this larger sonic context, in other words, Medli's music becomes especially bad.[15]

The disjunction also means that the harp modules stand out as strongly distinct from the environmental loop, thereby ensuring that they can still serve the various usability functions outlined previously—including direction-finding and acousmatic functions—even set as these harp sounds now are within the denser soundtrack. It will be difficult, in other words, for the player to mistake the harp sounds for part of the island's normal environmental music, and just as difficult for the player to miss the harp entirely. Finally, the player might reasonably find him or herself not only curious about where the harp sounds are coming from, but also possessed of a need to locate the source of the grating sound and *make it stop*. Even worse, if one has gained a particular affinity for Dragon Roost Island's environmental music by this point

Example 5.2 Dragon Roost Island's environmental music

Example 5.2 continued

in the game (after previous lengthy visits to the island), this new musical overlay might even be heard as offensive, and as forcefully preventing the player from enjoying the island's typically tuneful and consonant musical atmosphere. For such a musically sensitive player/listener, what better motivation could there be to find Medli, lead her to realize her latent skills as a (good) musician, and help her to break out of her practicing rut?[16]

Link's Harp

In *Skyward Sword*, the player controls Link in a world where islands float in the sky. In this game, it is Link who possesses and plays a harp, and these sounds often occur, as with the harp in *Wind Waker*, in simultaneous combination with environmental music. There the similarities between the two examples end, however, as *Skyward Sword*'s close control over which harp modules may sound at any given moment reliably yields smoothness rather than disjunction, and this smoothness—together with the player's own limited control over the instrument—produces several unique effects.

The harp in *Skyward Sword*—which characters in the game call the "Goddess's Harp"—is an instrument imbued with special powers. Link must play this harp (usually accompanying a singer) at particular points in the game to affect the game world and progress the story, but the player can also choose to have Link play the harp during normal exploration, with or without any additional game world effects. I will focus here on the latter type of situation, in which the game imposes no rules on the player's performance, and where there are no performance-based rewards or repercussions. To control Link as he plays the harp, the player uses the motion-sensing Wii controller as a real-world stand-in for Link's virtual hand: as the player swings the controller to the left and right, Link replicates these motions with his right hand across the harp in the game world, producing the sounds of plucked strings. The game determines the actual notes that sound; all the player must do to play the instrument is make this physical strumming gesture.

Each harp note is its own module, and *Skyward Sword* uses a finely detailed system to determine which single-note module to sound at any given instant— and therefore what pitch will sound on top of any concurrent environmental music. First, the game establishes a set of 12 different single-note modules and maps each of these modules spatially to the 12 strings of the virtual instrument.[17] Figure 5.1 shows one such 12-string arrangement. The 12 modules ascend in register from left to right, and the player triggers each module individually by moving the controller across the virtual strings. The player may, for example, make a broad sweeping gesture that triggers each of the 12 modules in a row, or, with more constrained motions, activate only a few strings in one small area of the instrument's range. The player dictates the speed and breadth of these motions, but the result is always an arpeggiated or scalar sound: there is no way for the player to pluck two strings simul- taneously (although the resonating sounds may overlap), nor can he or she activate two strings in a row without also running through all of the other notes in between.

Starting from this basic one-to-one, module-to-string mapping, *Skyward Sword* next incorporates many *different* sets of these 12 mapped modules, one set for each underlying harmony in the given location's environmental music, and mainly using pitches drawn from that harmony. When Link plays the harp, the game continuously repopulates the instrument's virtual strings with single-note modules according to the current position in the environmental music's harmonic progression. For instance, Example 5.3 shows the harp system for the looping environmental music on Skyloft, Link's home island and the main hub of the game's world. Skyloft's environmental music is in a major key and moderate tempo, with a gently lilting melody that shifts between

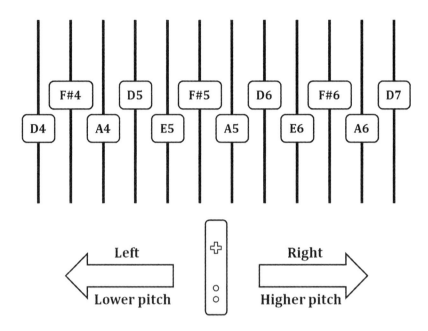

Figure 5.1 Link's virtual harp, with a sample set of 12 modules

flute, accordion, trumpet, and strings, and with steady accompaniment from acoustic guitar, marimba, and bass. (This music is significantly reduced in Example 5.3's transcription.)[18] The system from Figure 5.1 comprises the first measure of Example 5.3, and the 12-string mapping pattern continues from there. *Skyward Sword* contains equally complex systems tailored to nearly every looping environmental module in every location where it is possible for Link to play his harp—including dungeons as well as safer areas—as many as 20 (or more) systems in all. Overall, the specific pitches that the harp produces depend both on the player's actions (for the timing and identity of the module within a 12-module set) and on the concurrent musical material in the rest of the game's soundtrack (for the 12-module set itself).[19]

Skyloft's modular system serves as a reasonable representative of the harp music across *Skyward Sword*, since other systems in the game behave in similar ways and with similar probabilities of smoothness. There are a few brief instances in which the game prompts Link to play the harp on Skyloft, but the player can also choose to play the harp here at any time, and for however long he or she wants. There are no in-game benefits for the latter behavior, however, which leaves only one likely reason why the player might want to play the harp on Skyloft for any great length of time: to have fun.

At night in the game world, Skyloft's environmental music is silent, but the harp's modular system still applies, and the 12-module sets change over

Example 5.3 Skyloft's environmental music (reduced), with available harp modules

time according to the (silent) harmonic progression of this music. In other words, the harp exhibits the same behavior at night as it does during the day. Even alone, the harp modules provide important usability information: these sounds audibly confirm for the player that he or she is successfully playing the harp. Although basic, such feedback is essential for the player to be able to engage with this unusual (and sometimes difficult-to-control) interface.

Example 5.3 continued

The harp modules also provide some information about the harp itself: we already know that the harp is a special instrument because characters in the game say as much, but we now get an expanded sense of the harp's magical properties, first in its ability to produce many more pitches than it visibly has strings. (The same was true of Medli's harp, for that matter.) The harp also demonstrates a magical ability to change collections of pitches on its own,

Example 5.3 continued

that is, without provocation from the player, or, apparently, from Link, who makes no visible changes to his handling of the instrument. Finally, a run through the harp's strings produces patterns of only a few notes repeated at different octaves, rather than random pitches, and this audible organization suggests a basic musicality in the harp's output. The harp's sounds by themselves thus allow the player to feel that he or she is interacting with a versatile and powerful musical instrument.

As in *Wind Waker*, the full extent of this harp music's meaning and effects becomes apparent only when it sounds in simultaneous combination with the environmental music. Unlike Medli's harp, however, most of the effects in *Skyward Sword* come from the combined modules' high likelihood of strong smoothness, especially in terms of pitch.

Each set of 12 harp modules consists of four pitch classes that are very unlikely to create harsh dissonance against the environmental music, and are often already present in their associated sections of the environmental loop— see, for example, the D, E, F-sharp, and A harp pitches available during the D-major tonic harmony in the first measure of Skyloft's environmental music.

In terms of pitch, then, the combination of the two musical layers is likely to be very smooth, and as long as the player strums through multiple harp strings, smoothness will dominate in nearly every gameplay session. At the same time, the harp's timbre provides mild disjunction, since this instrument is not present in (but also not strongly foreign to) the instrumentation of Skyloft's environmental music.

The individual harp modules (single pitches) contain no meter by themselves, but they string together through the player's actions to yield a theoretically infinite variety of temporal organization. Regardless of the player's intent and motor skills, however, the game imposes a subtle—but consistent—meter on the sequences of harp pitches through the regular change of 12-note sets already built into the system. Because these changes align precisely with the harmonic rhythm of the concurrent environmental music, metric qualities can contribute at least a small degree of smoothness in almost every instance of gameplay, even if the onsets of the individual harp pitches do not actually align with the environmental music's pulse. These player-determined onsets will often produce disjunction against the environmental music, while the game-controlled harmonic organization yields consistent mild smoothness in terms of meter.

Link's harp is thus likely to create both smoothness and disjunction with the simultaneous environmental music through different musical aspects, and each of these qualities contributes important usability and interpretive meaning to these modules in the game. Mild disjunction in timbre and rhythmic onsets helps the harp's sounds to remain distinguishable from the richer environmental music, so that the player may still hear the results of his or her actions (and gain auditory feedback) even among so many other concurrent musical sounds. The very likely strong smoothness in pitch content and subtle metric support, however, yields some new and special effects. There is no indication that Link has ever played a harp before receiving this instrument, nor that he has had any musical training, yet the harp's special abilities ensure that the plucked strings' pitches predominantly agree with the game's other concurrent music. In this larger sonic context, the harp's control over its musical output is thus extraordinary (and magical) not only in the fact that it moves through a wide range of pitches and pitch collections on its own, but also in its ability to reliably produce pitches that sound *correct* in the sonic environment of the game. Through the harp, Link gains some musical ability, as well as a special (audible) connection to his environment.

By extension, this magical quality of the harp allows the *player*—without necessarily possessing any preexisting musical knowledge or expertise—to consistently produce streams of pitches that sound as if they belong in the game's musical context.[20] The player may thus feel that his or her output is a productive and fitting component of the soundtrack, and indeed of the virtual environment in which his or her character stands. In other words, the player may feel that he or she is engaging in the creation of real music, even contributing to the very musical essence of the game's virtual world. Other *Legend of Zelda* games (e.g. *The Legend of Zelda: Ocarina of Time* [1998]) also feature powerful interactions between player-created music and environmental music, but *Skyward Sword* brings an extra layer of engagement by framing this interaction as simultaneous musical combination, and in real time.[21]

This brings us back to the possibility that the player might play the harp for fun—without necessarily fulfilling gameplay goals or affecting the game's world—a behavior that the game implicitly encourages through reliable simultaneous smoothness. The player may, on one level, have a positive experience with this virtual instrument that automatically produces a wide variety of sounds without requiring any special effort or musical knowledge. The instrument's smoothness with the environmental music promotes an even stronger positive impression of its output, just as Medli's harp music promotes negative judgments through disjunction. In this way, *Skyward Sword*'s player can enjoy the music-making act—a form of experimentation, or play—without fear of aural reprimand.

Conclusion

The two examples from *Wind Waker* and *Skyward Sword* point to smoothness and disjunction as widely divergent—but equally important—functional aspects of a game's soundtrack, and highlight the importance of modular combinations as a focus of musical analysis. In both examples, some basic elements of disjunction (especially through timbre) help to distinguish the special musical sounds of an in-game character from the simultaneous normal music of the game's environment. At the same time, additional likely qualities—strong smoothness in the case of *Skyward Sword* and extreme disjunction in *Wind Waker*—provide further critical function and interpretive meaning, to the extent that the player may even cast value judgments on the instruments' sounds and the person producing them (an in-game character or even the player him or herself). The soundtrack obtains a unique position of contribution to the game, since these powerful effects are available only through this multilayered dynamic music.

A final consideration for the two examples in this chapter relates to the different sources of this simultaneous music. The harp music is diegetic (issuing from a source within the game world) while the environmental music is non-diegetic (with a source outside of the game world). This binary distinction comes from film studies and has sparked much recent debate, and the modular combinations in *Wind Waker* and *Skyward Sword* only emphasize some of the problems in this formalization.[22] In short, the diegetic and non-diegetic realms should logically be distinct, yet they interact sonically to yield emergent effects, and are even able to influence each other and gameplay. In *Wind Waker*, for example, Link and the other in-game characters (presumably) cannot hear these musical combinations, yet the player may act in response to the resulting extreme disjunction, affecting the game world (through Link) as a result. In *Skyward Sword*, the harp changes its set of available pitches to yield smoothness with the environmental music, but how is the instrument able to do this if the two types of music exist in completely separate conceptual realms?[23]

Perhaps, then, the distinction between diegetic and non-diegetic music is a false lead, at least where this music is concerned. In particular, it is less important that looping environmental music is non-diegetic (that it has no obvious source in the game world), and more important instead that this music is an integral part of the virtual environment itself. Indeed, this view has been implicit throughout this chapter's discussion. In this way, the in-game characters and their musical instruments are able to demonstrate a disconnect with their environment (as Medli does), or else an extraordinary connection to the environment and its music (as does the harp in *Skyward Sword*, as well as certain other specially powered instruments in the *Legend of Zelda* series). Through smoothness and disjunction, characters and worlds can associate and separate, and players can engage with virtual environments in unique ways. These dynamic musical effects are integral components of their respective game worlds, yielding rich avenues of interpretation for players and analysts alike.

Notes

1 Kristine Jørgensen, *A Comprehensive Study of Sound in Computer Games: How Audio Affects Player Action* (Lewiston, NY: Edwin Mellen Press, 2009), 4, 158.
2 *The Legend of Zelda: The Wind Waker*, Nintendo (2003); *The Legend of Zelda: Skyward Sword*, Nintendo (2011).
3 This view of modularity derives from James Saunders, "Modular Music," *Perspectives of New Music* 46/1 (Winter 2008), 152–193.
4 Karen Collins, *Game Sound: An Introduction to the History, Theory, and Practice of Video Game Music and Sound Design* (Cambridge, MA: MIT Press, 2008), 139.
5 See, for example, Paul Hoffert, *Music for New Media: Composing for Videogames, Web Sites, Presentations, and Other Interactive Media*, ed. Jonathan Feist (Boston: Berklee Press, 2007), 33; Collins, *Game Sound: An Introduction to the History, Theory, and Practice of Video Game Music and Sound Design*, 146.
6 For a brief discussion on the various levels of integration and segregation that might exist between simultaneously sounding musical objects, see Albert S. Bregman, *Auditory Scene Analysis: The Perceptual Organization of Sound* (Cambridge, MA: MIT Press, 1990), 460–461.
7 Some authors of game composition guides make this aesthetic goal of smoothness clear. See, for example, Aaron Marks, *The Complete Guide to Game Audio: For Composers, Musicians, Sound Designers, Game Developers*, 2nd edn. (New York: Focal Press, 2009), 234, 249; G. W. Childs, IV, *Creating Music and Sound for Games* (Boston: Thomson Course Technology PTR, 2007), 152.
8 Paul Hoffert, for example, highlights disjunction as a valuable resource in game soundtracks. Hoffert, *Music for New Media: Composing for Videogames, Web Sites, Presentations, and Other Interactive Media*, 33–35.

9 Paul Hoffert provides an important (albeit rough) precedent for judging smoothness during transitions from one module to another, in which one gauges the similarity between the modules in terms of various musical aspects such as key, volume, and tempo. Hoffert, *Music for New Media: Composing for Videogames, Web Sites, Presentations, and Other Interactive Media*, 33–42.

10 The music perception literature supports a basic connection between consonance and simultaneous smoothness. For instance, David Huron suggests that "harmonic congruence" (i.e. consonance) strongly affects listeners' judgments of how well a concurrent probe tone fits with simultaneous musical material. David Huron, *Sweet Anticipation: Music and the Psychology of Expectation* (Cambridge, MA: MIT Press, 2006), 47. Similarly, Albert Bregman proposes that consonance helps multiple simultaneous pitches to perceptually fuse into a single chord, and multiple instrumental parts to integrate into a single piece of music. Bregman, *Auditory Scene Analysis: The Perceptual Organization of Sound*, 495–496.

11 This type of probabilistic view of this modular music may also be useful from a design point of view, but the goal of the current analytical approach is to arrive at an equally weighted and end-oriented view of all of this music's possible sounding results. For further discussion of methods and calculations for examining smoothness—including additional details for the two examples in this chapter— see my forthcoming dissertation: Elizabeth Medina-Gray, "Modular Structure and Function in Early 21st-Century Video Game Music," Ph.D. dissertation (Yale University, forthcoming).

12 The game refers to this instrument as a harp, but based on its appearance it may be more accurately described as a lyre.

13 Each individual chord deviates slightly (and apparently at random) in its onset and duration from the average tempo—thereby contributing to the sonic impression of a real/human/live performance—and so this musical system more accurately comprises many single-chord modules. The close approximation of five different three-chord modules is, however, accurate enough for our present purposes.

14 Acousmatic sounds are those that come from an unseen source. For more on the effects of acousmatic sound in film, see Michel Chion, *Audio-Vision: Sound on Screen*, trans. and ed. Claudia Gorbman (New York: Columbia University Press, 1994), 71–73, 85–86.

15 In direct contrast to a player's potentially negative experience of Medli's music, a nearby in-game character comments on her music's beauty: "Mmmm . . . Such beautiful tone. Medli's really gotten good." This same character then says that Medli is "a really hard worker" and "beginning to fill the shoes of her teacher." On the one hand, the larger musical context might reveal additional meaning in these words: we could read a tinge of sarcasm here, or perhaps genuine (biased) indulgence for—or support of—a beloved character. On the other hand, the in-game characters may simply not perceive the extra level of "badness" in Medli's music because they cannot hear the island's environmental music, thus leaving this additional context for the player's ears alone.

16 Interestingly, *Wind Waker* does not use a similar musical system for the second of the two characters that Link must find at this point in the game: diminutive Makar, who plays a cello-like instrument. When the player arrives on Makar's island (Forest Haven), she sees musical notes emanating from his hiding place behind a waterfall, but does not actually hear his sounds until she enters that second area. The contrast between these two similar situations in this game is intriguing, but is outside the realm of the current discussion.

17 This despite the fact that the instrument we see in the game only has eight strings.

18 When Link is in a certain area of Skyloft, most of the environmental music's melody becomes silent, although other instruments in the loop continue to play as normal. In this sparser version of the environmental music, the harp module system remains the same, and the resulting probabilities of smoothness are very similar to those with the full musical texture.

19 Certain other games from Nintendo also make use of this type of modular design. *Wii Music* (2008), for example, uses a similar system to produce the sounds of various player-controlled instruments in a musical ensemble, and *Super Mario Galaxy* (2007) uses this system to synchronize tones produced by a player's actions (not related to a virtual musical instrument) with the harmonic progression of environmental music. *Skyward Sword*'s system is unique among these other games in that it involves a player-controlled instrument as well as environmental music in an expansive game world.

20 This virtual instrument bears some parallels with real-life harps: A harp's pedals fix a collection of pitches (often a diatonic collection) on the strings, so that even a non-musician might strum a harp and produce a stream of organized pitches that can sound like they belong (to various degrees) in the context of simultaneous music. In this view, *Skyward Sword*'s harp presents a super-capable version of the instrument in that it sets only four different pitch classes at a time (greatly restricting the pitches that the player can produce) and switches frequently among many different collections of pitches.

21 In *Ocarina of Time*, the player (as Link) plays an in-game ocarina by pressing buttons on the controller to trigger specific pitches, which he or she then strings together to yield brief melodies. Certain melodies that the player performs (following the game's instructions and yielding special effects in the game world) also appear in the game's environmental music, thus tying the player's musical output to particular environments in the game.

22 For discussions on the problems with the diegetic/non-diegetic binary, and suggestions of ways to nuance and mediate this view in video game audio, see Jørgensen, *A Comprehensive Study of Sound in Computer Games: How Audio Affects Player Action*, 97–116; Kristine Jørgensen, "Time for New Terminology? Diegetic and Non-Diegetic Sounds in Computer Games Revisited," in *Game Sound Technology and Player Interaction: Concepts and Developments*, ed. Mark Grimshaw (Hershey, PA: Information Science Reference, 2011), 78–97; Isabella van Elferen, "¡Un Forastero! Issues of Virtuality and Diegesis in Videogame Music," *Music and the Moving Image* 4/2 (Summer 2011), 30–39.

23 Karen Collins discusses a similar example in another game, in which the player can have her character sing or play an instrument "along with" the non-diegetic background music, presumably in a very smooth combination of musical modules. Collins argues that in this instance, the formerly non-diegetic music actually becomes diegetic. Collins, *Game Sound: An Introduction to the History, Theory, and Practice of Video Game Music and Sound Design*, 125. Although this view logically explains how music made by characters in the game world could coordinate smoothly with this other music, the suggestion that Skyloft's environmental music might be diegetic only raises more questions, not least of which is the question of this orchestral music's possible game world source.

Chapter 6

Wandering Tonalities

Silence, Sound, and Morality in *Shadow of the Colossus*

William Gibbons

Riding through the desert on my way to kill a Colossus, I listen to the sounds of wind and hoof beats.[1] At some point in the near future, I will arrive at my destination and begin a fight with a hulking behemoth that probably wants nothing more than to be left alone. Not for the first time, I question my actions. Is this really the only way to achieve my goals? Is this thing really my enemy? Why am I doing this? I have no easy answers to these questions, and no one is there to offer either solace or affirmation. With the exception of the horse I am riding and a few scattered wild animals eager to stay out of my way, I am unmistakably alone. There are no helpful townspeople providing directions or quests, no shopkeepers peddling their wares, not even any dangerous monsters in need of slaying. As I make my way through the wilderness—a period that might last anywhere from several minutes to several hours, depending on my choices and skills—I can do nothing but embrace this solitude and consider the meaning of my journey, reflecting on the past and anticipating the future.

This sense of isolation and moral ambiguity is at the heart of the PlayStation 2 game *Shadow of the Colossus* (Sony Computer Entertainment, 2005), a title that often arises in discussions of "art" games due to both its moral complexity and its minimalist approach to plot and gameplay.[2] Though its story bears some similarity to other action-adventure games—most obviously Nintendo's *Legend of Zelda* series—here, the archetypical plot is pared down to its bare essence. The protagonist—known only as the Wanderer, or "Wander"—enters the Forbidden Land seeking the help of a godlike being to resurrect Mono, a young girl whose cause of death is never revealed, nor is her relationship to the Wanderer ever explained. The entity he seeks, Dormin, agrees to help only if the Wanderer defeats the 16 Colossi that limit his power too much to restore Mono to life.[3] As a critic for the video game webzine *Eurogamer* sums up:

> [*Shadow of the Colossus*'s] boldly retrograde stance strips away many of the conventions of video games that we've come to take for granted over the decades . . . You don't even meet anyone (apart from the Colossi, of

course) on your extensive travels. It's just you, your horse, a bow and arrow, a sword, a jump button, a grab button, and the occasional unseen voice from the ether.[4]

What remains is an atypically streamlined fantasy/adventure game, an aspect of the game that players have been as quick to note as critics. In the words of one reviewer on the user-contributed website *GameFAQs*:

> The real trick of the story is that it is like haiku. Minimalist but effective and open to interpretation. It matches the barren land you will be stalking the Colossi in. Leaving you wondering as you pursue your goal what it is all about and what it all means. The story isn't much but it just fits everything else in the game.[5]

This sense of "wondering . . . what it is all about" is a recurring theme in players' experiences with this game, and significantly, *Shadow of the Colossus* relies entirely on the player to raise these moral questions; nothing in the game world ever explicitly forces us to confront them.

In his analysis of the game's narrative, literary critic David Ciccoricco finds that this signature ambiguity stems, at least in part, from the sense of isolation created during the often lengthy travel times, when the game

> makes time and space for a reflective response . . . that is, it makes you think about what you've done after you've done it while, experientially, it may seem as though you're not *doing* anything in terms of a material outcome in the game world.[6]

In other words, without direct technical challenges occupying their thoughts, players are given an unusual opportunity to consider the impact of their actions (via the protagonist) on this fictional world.[7] While many games focus on the single-minded pursuit of a goal (e.g. saving the princess, preventing world destruction, or perhaps just attaining the next batch of loot), *Shadow of the Colossus* demands introspection. Players must face their own role in the Wanderer's morally ambiguous quest—a journey in which music and silence alike play major roles.

Composer Kow Otani's symphonic score punctuates moments of action and plot development, most prominently the battles with the 16 Colossi. The symphonic score is one of the most frequently praised elements of the game, and understandably so: it contributes greatly to both the sense of urgency underlying each confrontation with the game's titular titans and to the player's sense of achievement at discovering the correct method for slaying each beast. Much of the game, however, including the moment I described above, takes place in diegetic musical silence—that is, with only sounds emerging from the diegetic game world (wind, hoof beats, waterfalls, etc.).[8] This aspect of its design runs counter to prevailing trends regarding music placement in interactive media, yet as we will see, the interplay of silence and music is central to the moral ambiguity that pervades *Shadow of the Colossus*. Moreover, the game offers a case study for this type of sound design and its effects, highlighting the role that music—and its absence—play in shaping player involvement.

Silence and Solitude

Moments of silence are relatively uncommon in video games—or, at least, moments of extended and unavoidable silence.[9] For technical reasons, the earliest games—such as *Computer Space* (1971) or *Pong* (1972)—contained no music, but by the end of the 1970s, hardware had overcome these severe limitations on memory and processing power, allowing for rapid improvements in both quality and quantity of music in games.[10] In fact, once the "looping" of musical segments became a prominent technique around 1984, game designers and composers went to great lengths to fill every possible moment with music. There was music for the title screen, for every different level, for when players won a level, for when they lost, for end credits, and so on— most often composed in loops that allowed hardly a moment of silence.[11] These trends likely derived, at least to some extent, from arcade machines, where constant loud music and sound effects were important both for drawing in players and for keeping them playing.[12] As game consoles moved into the home, they imported these musical tropes, generally eschewing silence in favor of wall-to-wall sound. Despite enormous technological advances and increasingly cinematic narratives, this predilection for more or less constant music has proved remarkably hardy, though certainly the music itself has gotten more complex.[13] In sum, to quote sound designer Rob Bridgett (writing in 2008), "from an aesthetic standpoint, a competent use of subtlety and silence is distinctly missing from video game audio."[14]

The aesthetic justification for this musical overabundance is that music is a crucial element for keeping players immersed in the game world. Artist and game audio theorist Axel Stockburger, for example, opined in 2003 that "generally the score has a huge emotional impact on the player and it can enhance the feeling of immersion. This means there should not be too many gaps within the musical score of a game as this would threaten the immersive bond with the player."[15] In this mindset, every moment of silence endangers the fragile sense of immersion so crucial to players' enjoyment. It is worth clarifying here that Stockburger (and other critics) seem chiefly concerned with what we might call "diegetic immersion" (being immersed in the game world—roughly interchangeable with the idea of "presence") as separate from "non-diegetic immersion" (that is, a player's enjoyment of playing the game).[16] In other words, music was crucial for keeping players involved in a game's narrative rather than focused on its rules or construction. We might draw parallels here to "silent" film, where music sometimes counterbalanced issues of technology and immersion in the new medium. Although silent films often did contain periods with no music, by the end of the era, a number of films did feature wall-to-wall scores.[17] "Silent film," in film music scholar Kathryn Kalinak's words, "faced a greater threat to a perpetuation of the illusion than sound film [and so] balanced its greater threat of disruption with a greater proportion of music."[18] Though speaking (not unproblematically) of silent film accompanied by live musicians, Kalinak's description echoes issues in early game design. As film technology improved, the balance gradually shifted, and many genres of film began to include less music. Games followed the same pattern: as soon as it was possible, many games featured near-constant music in an effort to keep gamers immersed despite their narrative or technological limitations. Once these limitations were removed (or minimized), the amount of music—or, at least, its ubiquity—could be reduced.

This turning point occurred in the early 2000s, at which point more cinematically oriented games began to move away from the wall-to-wall music ideal.[19] Borrowing narrative techniques from other screen media—particularly film—many recent games strive to create what we might think of as "interactive cinema."[20] To that end, they often map film-scoring techniques onto games, including both style and placement. Yet, the underlying attitude regarding music and diegetic immersion has remained fairly consistent. As a result, even in narrative-based games in which significant portions of the game do not include music, these moments are often treated as "the absence of music" rather than being aesthetic objects in themselves. Considered in this way, silence may best be understood as (in Michel Chion's words) "the negative of sound we've heard beforehand or imagined; it is the production of a contrast."[21] A typical example of this silence as negative musical space would be the popular *Halo* games (first-person shooters with a complex space opera plot), which feature extended silences between action set pieces. Composer Martin O'Donnell approached silence in the original *Halo* (Bungie, 2001) as a way to avoid musical oversaturation:

> Music is best used in a game to quicken the emotional state of the player and it works best when used least. If music is constantly playing it tends to become sonic wallpaper and loses its impact when it is needed to truly enhance some dramatic component of game play . . . Therefore, much of the time no music is present.[22]

Too much music might cheapen players' experiences, or (possibly even worse) remove them from their immersion. Silence provides the negative space to ensure the music's emotional effect, but it is not in itself aesthetically significant.

In fact, if anything, silence functions as something of a deterrent here; if players remain in one location too long without advancing the action, the music fades out "to avoid getting annoying," as one critic noted regarding

Halo 2 (Bungie, 2004).[23] This fading out undesirably interrupts the action (standing at odds with the tension-filled narrative), encouraging players to move on to the next area. The Halo series is a typical example of silence as a deterrent, but we may also look at the other side of this coin: music as reward. The Grand Theft Auto series offers a clear example of this trend. Recent entries in the series take place in diegetic silence except during cutscenes and when in a vehicle. Music is thus a reward for following the path the game designers have chosen—hijacking a car—despite the fact that many of the games' tasks can be accomplished just as well on foot.[24] Music is a reward for entering into the game's world and playing by its rules—it is both crucial to, and a result of, diegetic immersion. Silence thus plays important roles in both the Halo and Grand Theft Auto games, yet in both cases it is avoidable, a tool to discourage players from deviating from the developer's intentions. Viewed in this light, silence functions as a kind of invisible fence that keeps players from wandering too far from the safety of the game's narrative structure—a role that fundamentally limits its potential for narrative effect. Players can, of course, individually choose to construct meaning from these optional and discouraged moments of silence. We are free, for example, to wander through Halo, contemplating the meaning of humanity and warfare and projecting those thoughts onto our avatar. But such behavior is akin to pausing a film; while it may provide a moment of reflection, the narrative cannot continue until we hit "play" again. And while it is theoretically possible to wander through Halo's environment in silence for hours, I would question whether the player is actually "playing Halo" at that point, or simply enacting a user-created narrative using the Halo game engine. In Shadow of the Colossus, by contrast, the silence is a mandatory aspect of continuing the narrative (at least barring players turning on their own music during that time, which is a possibility beyond the scope of analysis).

To find a model for Shadow of the Colossus's meaningful silence, we must look outside games, since, in this respect, it has more in common with other screen media. Film sound designers have been exploring the emotional (and disorienting) uses of silence since the early days of cinema, with television following closely thereafter. Like game players, film audiences are made uncomfortable by silence—not only by total silence (the lack of either diegetic or non-diegetic sound, which is quite rare in any medium), but also by extended musical silences with no dialogue or loud sound effects. Audience members in theaters become alienated from the film, forcibly reminded of their position outside the diegetic world. They may become consciously aware of their environment: of the sounds of rustling in nearby theater seats, of people eating popcorn and drinking soda, of the tiny lights of cell phone screens, of the uncomfortable temperature of the theatre. At home—a setting with more in common with video games—viewers may be reminded equally strongly of their surroundings, the anonymity of the theater giving way to the solitude or small-group ambiance of the living room.

This alienation has been an effective, if fairly uncommon, tool for filmmakers seeking to create a sense of anxiety in the viewer.[25] One notable example is Hitchcock's repeated use of "almost silence" in *The Birds* (1963), in which, as Elisabeth Weis notes, "the silence of the birds can be more terrifying than their shrieks."[26] Without clearly identifiable "music" in several scenes, audiences are left confused, repeatedly shocked by the brutality, suddenness, and apparent randomness of the bird attacks. Hitchcock nearly employed the same technique in *Psycho*; he initially wanted the infamous shower scene to take place in diegetic silence. Although composer Bernard Herrmann eventually changed the director's mind, Hitchcock clearly thought the lack of music would be more brutal and shockingly alienating to the audience than any music could be.[27] More recently, the near-complete absence of music in the Coen brothers' *No Country for Old Men* (2009) contributes significantly to the film's minimalist aesthetic and, like *The Birds*, increases tension while less overtly shaping the audience's emotional state.[28] An even closer analog to *Shadow of the Colossus* may be *Cast Away* (2000). The lengthy portion of the film in which the protagonist finds himself marooned on a desert island occurs in diegetic silence, conveying his solitude to the audience and intensifying their own feelings of isolation and confusion.

Television programs have used the same techniques to unsettle audiences, occasionally using silence to great effects for moments of great emotional impact or as semiotic shorthand. The cult favorite *Buffy the Vampire Slayer* (1997–2003) offers one particularly clear example. As Gerry Bloustien has observed, in *Buffy*, silence represents "the protagonists' fears along a continuum of unease—from small niggling doubts to full-blown anxiety."[29] In the episode "The Body" (Season 5, Episode 16), the teenage Buffy and her friends, accustomed to all manner of supernatural threats and casualties, react to the natural death of Buffy's mother Joyce. Unique in the series (and extremely uncommon in television), the entire episode takes place in a diegetic silence unbroken by musical cues (excepting the title and end credits). The effect is startling. Without Joyce's reassuring presence, the normally (super)heroic cast of characters is unsure how to act or feel, overwhelmed by self-doubt and impotence; without the generally stabilizing presence of the music giving them aural clues, the audience feels much the same way. Without musical signifiers to help guide their emotions, viewers are forced to come to their own conclusions and turn to self-reflection for answers.

Silence in media can thus open spaces for unencumbered individualistic audience reflection and self-discovery. In film and television, these uses of silence draw spectators inward by removing them from their privileged quasi-omniscient position of insight into characters' mental states and by forcing them to confront their own feelings and draw their own conclusions about the unfolding events. As alienating as this experience may be in earlier screen media, however, in games, the situation becomes even more complex. While in film and television the audience bears no responsibility, in games, the line between player and avatar is often quite thin; filtered through these alter egos, events are, in a sense, not happening to other people, but to ourselves.[30] The absence of music in games is thus even more frustrating, since it has potentially serious effects on our interpretation of the game's events—and thus our responses (via our avatars). What, then, happens when a story-based game deliberately makes use of extended musical silences? This question brings us back, finally, to *Shadow of the Colossus*. Rather than treating silence as a void, the game embraces all its effects in a more cinematic fashion, turning the absence of music into a critical part of its aesthetic.

Extended silences in single-player, story-driven video games such as *Shadow of the Colossus* can be as alienating to players as those in film and television are to viewers—but with markedly different results given the nature of games as interactive media. Most often played at home alone, games of this kind carry little of the sense of community that is (or was) an inherent part of the theatrical film experience. Faced with extended situations of musical silence, and thus at least partially deprived of a complete sense of diegetic immersion, players can become acutely aware of their own solitude—something that, as we have already heard, game designers generally go to great lengths to avoid.[31] Yet, reinforcing players' sense of solitude is precisely what *Shadow of the Colossus* consistently does. There are two related results to this loss of diegetic immersion: players create a strong bond with the Wanderer, and they are given space to question the ethical ramifications of their actions.

Each time players leave Dormin's Temple in search of the next Colossus, they travel in diegetic silence, the exact duration of which depends on two factors, one immanent in the game and the other varying from player to player. First, the amount of virtual distance the player must traverse to get to the next encounter varies significantly from colossus—something over which the player has no control. Players may choose, however, to also engage in optional exploration, creating a self-imposed time for reflection. These semi-silent periods may remove players from the game world to some extent, but even if they are limited in their diegetic immersion, they can remain fully immersed in the game itself. Far from reducing their enjoyment of the game, the feelings of alienation and solitude that accompany this transition to non-diegetic immersion can paradoxically bring players into closer identification with the game's protagonist, immersing them in an atypically affective way.[32]

Narrative-based games generally create a bond between players and their avatars (or "playable characters") through traditionally cinematic means, such as plot, dialogue, and music. We care about *Halo*'s Master Chief, *Tomb Raider*'s Lara Croft, or *Mass Effect*'s Commander Shepard (to name only three examples) because we understand them, and make their goals our own. As the avatars progress through the game—with our help, of course—we empathize with them, resulting in a sense of emotional satisfaction from completing the game. In *Shadow of the Colossus*, by contrast, nearly the entire plot is laid out from the beginning; there are no major developments until the game's final moments. The Wanderer speaks only a few times, has no backstory, and has unclear motivations and relationships to all other characters; without even a name, he is a complete enigma. For players to connect with this atypical protagonist, they have to have a sense of common experience—in this case, through a powerful, if counterintuitive, shared isolation.[33] The Wanderer is as alone in his world as we are in ours, and thus we understand him, and share his goal: saving his beloved Mono, thus winning the game. Essentially, in the absence of plot developments or musical cues providing clues to the Wanderer's mindset, players project their own thoughts and emotions onto him, particularly the sense of moral ambiguity that players often experience.[34] We, the players, are ourselves the Wanderers, and thus take on an enhanced sense of responsibility for the events of the game, particularly the Colossus battles.

Shadow of the Colossus's bare-bones narrative is thus complicated through our assumption—despite no evidence in the game itself—that the inscrutable Wanderer shares the sense of confusion and uncertainty that players have developed over the course of these diegetic silences. The silences become, then, about questioning—players question the value of what they are doing. As Ciccoricco points out, what we do during these moments is think:

> You think about the fact that you are about to bring down another one of these awe-inspiring creatures even though you know that they have not wronged you in any way, and they are definitely not expecting you and your sword. All you know . . . is that you must kill them in order to complete your quest.[35]

This point brings us to a discussion of the music in *Shadow of the Colossus*. The music becomes a kind of foil for the self-questioning afforded by the game's extended silences, interjecting moments that are simultaneously more like the familiar underscores of action-adventure games and shockingly alienating.

Sound and Ambiguity

The effects of silence in *Shadow of the Colossus* are dependent on juxtaposition with music, and vice versa. The musical strategies at work in the game become evident even in the introductory cutscene, a cinematic montage in which the Wanderer travels through mountains and verdant forests before finally reaching the Forbidden Lands, where the game's action takes place. As this prologue begins, only music is audible (synthesized voices along with what sound like koto, shakuhachi, and organ, joined by string orchestra after approximately 90 seconds). Diegetic audio is entirely absent until the protagonist enters a long stone bridge leading to the desolate Forbidden Lands, at which point the music reaches a melodic and dynamic climax and then quickly fades out, replaced by the sound of the wind. There is no joyous, epic, or ominous music to reveal the character of this mysterious realm to players—after having been lulled into a sense of familiarity and comfort by the orchestral introduction, they are left alone. This introduction quickly and effectively establishes the connection between the isolation of the Forbidden Land and musical silence. The Wanderer and the player have both left the familiar and comfortable for the unknown.

From this point on, musical cues are fairly sparse throughout *Shadow of the Colossus*, making them all the more potent for their rarity. Figure 6.1 details the cyclic appearance of music in the game. There is Dormin's church-like music—featuring the religiously suggestive timbres of wordless voices and organ—that accompanies each interaction with this mysterious being, reinforcing his godlike status and adding religious overtones to the idea of Mono's resurrection. Additionally, a cue indicating arrival in the general area where the next Colossus can be found presages each battle, setting the stage for upcoming battle and confirming that players have found the right place. Both the church music and the arrival music are fairly short, linear (i.e. not looped)

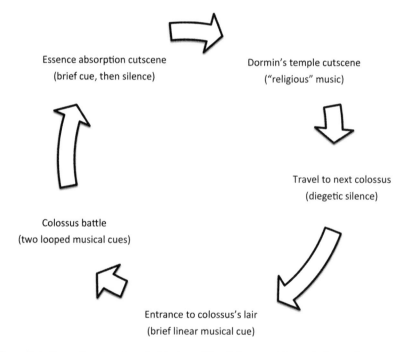

Essence absorption cutscene
(brief cue, then silence)

Dormin's temple cutscene
("religious" music)

Travel to next colossus
(diegetic silence)

Colossus battle
(two looped musical cues)

Entrance to colossus's lair
(brief linear musical cue)

Figure 6.1 Gameplay structure in *Shadow of the Colossus*, with musical cues in parentheses. Length of arrows indicates relative length of gameplay segments

transitional cues; the former is the starting/ending point for the cyclic structure of the game, and the latter transitions between the silence of travel and the combat music to come. This combat music, underscoring the 16 Colossus battles, is by far the most prominent music in the game, and it is at these moments that we find the close bond between protagonist and player—developed over the game's silences—most powerfully in effect.

For gamers such as myself, at least, the music comes as a welcome relief from the extended diegetic silences: something is finally happening, allowing me (and presumptively the Wanderer) to focus on an external threat rather than internal doubts. The game's 16 Colossus battles share the same basic musical structure, mainly consisting of two looped tracks, described here as the caution music and the combat music. The caution music—which can vary widely in tone depending on how violent (or not) this particular Colossus is—typically begins when the battle begins or when a Colossus becomes visible. At some point, this track transitions (via direct cut or cross-fade) into a second, more triumphant loop when players discover the special maneuver required to tackle the creature, usually associated with successfully climbing onto the Colossus. Though each player's emotional response to the game might be somewhat different, the intended trajectory seems clear: initially apprehensive, players are swept away in the moment, any lingering doubts about their quest silenced by a need to focus on overcoming the mental and technical challenge at hand. Hesitation, confusion, and self-reflexivity give way to survival instinct and, frankly, fun (at least for many players).

Yet this exultation is short-lived. Just when a triumphal fanfare seems most called for, upon killing a Colossus, the music abruptly fades into a short and ambiguously victorious track followed by silence. A few seconds later, the Wanderer absorbs some kind of power released by the Colossus's death, passes out, and awakens in Dormin's temple, beginning the cycle anew. With the immediate danger passed, doubts and self-reflection quickly take the place of adrenaline; in the words of one critic, "Battling the Colossi rewards you with a rich sense of accomplishment that bleeds into guilt."[36] Game designer and critic Nick Fortugno in fact cites *Shadow of the Colossus* as an exceptional example of game as interactive tragedy—in essence, a massacre perpetrated by the player:

> The more Colossi Wander finds, the clearer it is that they are all sequestered away from anything they could harm, so that Wander's mission feels a great deal more like a whale hunt or a safari than a world saving quest.
>
> . . . Despite the size and destructive power of the Colossi, it's hard to shake the feeling that Wander is the aggressor, and that the player is the monster, ruthlessly hunting down and killing innocent beasts in the barren wilderness.[37]

When all is said and done, players have no choice; unless they choose to abandon the game, they must kill the Colossi to progress. Fortugno goes on to describe the result of this morally dubious task:

> Ultimately, the player is continually left in a conflicted position, triumphant about the completion of the puzzles [i.e. the Colossus battles] but regretful that this puzzle-solving lead to the painful death of a largely innocent creature. In this way, the game's core challenge pushes the player to struggle, but then betrays him [sic] by poisoning the rewards of the struggle. All by itself, this ambivalent approach to the game's core objectives creates a new kind of gaming experience.[38]

This "new kind of gaming experience" involves the player's participation in morally ambiguous actions. Players, like the Wanderer, have no choice but to go along with possibly reprehensible tasks if they wish to complete their goals.

Again, the sound design is central to achieving this sense of ambivalence. The music lies to us, tricks us, forces us to forget the moral concerns we have developed over the course of the silent travels. Music in media is, as K.J. Donnelly reminds us, a "subtle medium of manipulation," designed to tell us how to feel and when to feel it.[39] Beginning with the musical cue that introduces each Colossus's lair, it slowly ratchets up the player's sense of tension and excitement, sweeping the player along in its wake—just as the Wanderer's fight-or-flight response would—telling us to defeat this monster and encouraging us to have fun while doing it. But when it sneaks out without so much as a climactic chord (much like the game's introduction), we are left only with regret. We recall our doubts, and the self-reflection brought on by the game's silences renders pyrrhic what in another game would have been a clear-cut victory. The repetition of the process 16 times intensifies this sensation; eventually, victory over a Colossus becomes a truly uncomfortable mixture of self-congratulation and self-loathing. The close alliance between the Wanderer and the player keeps us from maintaining emotional distance. We killed the Colossus as much as he did, a heavy moral burden for a player to bear. Even worse, thanks to the music's manipulative power (and clever game design), we might even have enjoyed doing it.

In the end, the music has been lying all along, abetting as players commit these acts of questionable morality, discouraging them from dwelling too long on the questions they have amassed during the diegetic silences. But this dishonest, evasive aspect of the music does not end with the Colossus battles—Dormin's church music is equally deceitful. Each time players return to his temple after slaying a Colossus, there is a brief cutscene before they set off for the next battle; each cutscene uses this quasi-sacred music to reinforce the ultimate morality of the quest. In the end, Dormin is revealed to be evil incarnate, a powerful, malevolent being sealed in the Forbidden Lands. The player has been working for him all along, deluded by his or her own hopes and the religiously coded music into thinking that Dormin might be a force for good. Again, the music breaks the trust that we subconsciously place in it. The extended silences of the game have allowed us ample time to consider the morality of our decisions and the consequences of our actions. The bond between—or perhaps the fusion of—the Wanderer and the player shows us a protagonist as deeply conflicted and ambivalent as we are. Yet—at least for those players who choose to complete the game—over and over, throughout the game, the music overcomes these doubts. We prove that Adorno was right when he wrote that music "trains the unconscious for conditioned reflexes."[40] Conditioned by game music (and by games in general) to complete the tasks ahead of us no matter what, many players—including myself—press on, moving forward because it is all we know how to do. The alternative is to leave the game uncompleted, giving up on the Wanderer's quest (or, at least, resigning ourselves to never knowing how it ends).

Shadow of the Colossus forces us to confront who we are as players, and in doing so, it encourages us to rethink our relationship with game audio in general. It calls our attention to the acts of violence we—via our avatars—perpetrate in games, and also to the ways in which we are manipulated into doing so. The game's use of silence allows space for us to ask questions; it gives us the unusual opportunity to ask questions and reflect on the meaning of our actions. The music temporarily relieves this burden. It provides us, however briefly, with a way out of our ethical quagmire. It gives us the answers, but they are the wrong ones. *Shadow of the Colossus*, in short, begs us to question what a video game soundtrack can and should be. By removing, to some extent, their diegetic immersion in the game world via silence, players are better able to understand the effects of the music when it does occur, making the entire game an effort in self-reflection. Players are able to see their own role in the game process, creating a new type of immersion, simultaneously inside and outside the game world, in which—although the game's plot is linear and unalterable—the player's motives and emotions nonetheless become critical elements of interpreting the game. Ultimately, the game offers us a glimpse of how sound and silence can create experiences that are influenced by traditional media, yet unique to the agency afforded by interactive media.

Notes

All websites were accessed November 4, 2013.

1 Portions of this chapter were presented at the 2011 Music and the Moving Image conference at New York University and as a keynote at the 2013 Ludomusicology conference at the University of Liverpool. I am grateful for the many helpful comments and suggestions I received at both meetings.

2 *Shadow of the Colossus* has since been released with updated HD (and optional 3D) visuals on the PlayStation 3 as part of *The Ico and Shadow of the Colossus Collection* (Sony Computer Entertainment, 2011). Throughout, I will be using the original PlayStation 2 version as my point of reference. I should note that I have not closely compared this rerelease to the original to verify that all music cues remain identical, but the uses of silence and sound remain apparently unchanged (with the exception of the 2011 version being updated to accommodate 7.1 surround sound).

3 Though the game's plot is set in a self-contained fantasy world, David Ciccoricco notes that "Dormin" is "Nimrod" in reverse, and that the godlike being's condition reflects the fate of that ancient king, widely reviled by biblical scholars as the creator of the Tower of Babel. Nimrod was cut into pieces and scattered across the kingdom; he could not be brought back to life without all pieces. Notably, in Dante's *Inferno*, Nimrod is portrayed as a giant (arguably, a Colossus) and speaks only in a nonsensical language. See David Ciccoricco, "'Play, Memory': *Shadow of the Colossus* and Cognitive Workouts," *dichtung-digital* 37 (2007), available online at www.dichtung-digital.org/2007/ciccoricco.htm.

4 Kristan Reed, "*Shadow of the Colossus* Review," *Eurogamer* (October 27, 2005), available online at www.eurogamer.net/articles/r_sotc_ps2.

5 Cabalos14, "An Experience that May Change the Way You Look at Games," *GameFAQs* (January 2, 2006), available online at www.gamefaqs.com/ps2/924364-shadow-of-the-colossus/reviews/review-96013.

6 Ciccoricco, "'Play, Memory': *Shadow of the Colossus* and Cognitive Workouts."

7 Lengthy travel time in games is typically accompanied by at least some form of music. More traditional games such as *The Legend of Zelda: Ocarina of Time* (1998)—which shares with *Shadow of the Colossus* the idea of extended travel by horse—feature upbeat, wall-to-wall music to make the travel more exciting, for example. Other games with large open worlds feature either player-selected music (via some kind of in-game radio) or occasional clips of music to avoid the possibility of player boredom. A case in point would be Bethesda's open-world role-playing games *Fallout 3* (2008) and *Fallout: New Vegas* (2010), which include extended periods of exploration. Players have the option of listening to in-game radio stations; if they choose not to, the game provides sporadic orchestral cues during travel.

8 My use of the term "diegetic musical silence" follows Claudia Gorbman, *Unheard Melodies: Narrative Film Music* (Bloomington: Indiana University Press, 1987), 18. Diegetic musical silence is separate from non-diegetic silence, which is the total absence of any sound whatsoever, which is extremely uncommon in games (or film, for that matter).

9 Players have the option, of course, of creating their own silences. In most recent games, for example, there is the option of simply turning off the music and/or sound, a method of playing common in genres such as puzzle games, or for mobile platforms in which sound (at least without headphones) would create a distraction. K.J. Donnelly raises this point in his study of *Plants vs. Zombies* contained in this volume, "Lawn of the Dead: The Indifference of Musical Destiny in *Plants vs. Zombies*."

10 Neil Lerner points to 1977's *Circus* as one of the first games to include melodic material in addition to sound effects. Neil Lerner, "The Origins of Musical Style in Video Games, 1977–1983," in *The Oxford Handbook of Film Music Studies*, ed. David Neumeyer (Oxford and New York: Oxford University Press, 2014), 319–347. For technical details on the development of music in early games, see Karen Collins, *Game Sound: An Introduction to the History, Theory, and Practice of Video Game Music and Sound Design* (Cambridge, MA: MIT Press, 2008), Chapter 2.

11 Collins notes a drastic increase of looping in game music around 1984, particularly on the ColecoVision and Nintendo Entertainment System (NES) consoles. Collins, *Game Sound: An Introduction to the History, Theory, and Practice of Video Game Music and Sound Design*, 19.

12 Lerner, "The Origins of Musical Style in Video Games, 1977–1983," 322. On the lack of dynamic variety in game music, as well as the use of constant music, see Rob Bridgett, "Dynamic Range: Subtlety and Silence in Video Game Sound," in *From Pac-Man to Pop Music: Interactive Audio in Games and New Media*, ed. Karen Collins (Aldershot, UK and Burlington, VT: Ashgate, 2008), 127–134.

13 Aside from the aesthetic reasons with which I am chiefly concerned, I should note that much of this tendency toward loud music likely stems from financial considerations. Despite the billions of dollars in annual game sales, few new releases turn a profit. Successful titles thus spawn countless clones, and most developers are hesitant to innovate in areas that are not obviously "broken." Few gamers, presumably, complain about the lack of silence or dynamic range, and so large companies would naturally be hesitant to experiment. Not surprisingly, independent games by minor studios tend to experiment more with audio elements than do major studios.

14 Bridgett, "Dynamic Range: Subtlety and Silence in Video Game Sound," 127.

15 Axel Stockburger, "The Game Environment from an Auditive Perspective," in *Proceedings: Level Up: Digital Games Research Conference*, ed. Marinka Copier and Joost Raessens (Utrecht University, 2003), available online at www.audiogames. net/pics/upload/gameenvironment.htm. On immersion in games more generally, the seminal work is Janet H. Murray, *Hamlet on the Holodeck: The Future of Narrative in Cyberspace* (New York: Free Press, 1997), especially Chapter 4.

16 On the distinctions between diegetic immersion, non-diegetic immersion, and presence, see Alison McMahan, "Immersion, Engagement, and Presence: A Method for Analyzing 3-D Video Games," in *The Video Game Theory Reader*, ed. Mark J.P. Wolf and Bernard Perron (New York and London: Routledge, 2003), 67–86.

17 Lerner notes this connection as well in "The Origins of Musical Style in Video Games." On silence (or the lack thereof) in silent film, see, for example, Rick Altman, "The Silence of the Silents," *Musical Quarterly* 80 (1996), 648–718; and Rick Altman, *Silent Film Sound* (New York: Columbia University Press, 2004).

18 Kathryn Kalinak, *Settling the Score: Music and the Classical Hollywood Film* (Madison: University of Wisconsin Press, 1992), 43.

19 Several games on the short-lived but technologically advanced 1990s Atari Jaguar console made use of extended silences. Most notable among these is the first-person shooter *Alien vs. Predator* (Rebellion, 1994), which featured no music after the title screen, presumably in an effort to increase tension.

20 Cliff Bleszinski (the former design director of Epic Games), for example, wrote in the instruction manual to 2008's *Gears of War 2*: "This Video Game . . . was designed around the idea of cinematic action. We wanted the gameplay experience to feel like a summer blockbuster where you, the gamer, are the star" (p. 2).

21 Michel Chion, *Audio-Vision: Sound on Screen*, ed. and trans. Claudia Gorbman (New York: Columbia University Press, 1994), 57.

22 Marty O'Donnell, "Producing Audio for Halo," Talk given at 2002 Game Developers Conference (San Jose, California), available online at http://halo. bungie.org/misc/gdc.2002.music/.

23 Eric-Jon Waugh, "GDC 2005 Report: Audio Production on *Halo 2*," *Gamasutra* (March 14, 2005), available online at www.gamasutra.com/view/feature/130670/ gdc_2005_report_audio_production_.php.

24   On music in *Grand Theft Auto*, see Kiri Miller, *Playing Along: Digital Games, YouTube, and Virtual Performance* (Oxford and New York: Oxford University Press, 2012), Chapters 1 and 2. Miller focuses, in particular, on the interactive element of music in the games, as players can change diegetic radio stations while driving. On the relationship between music and silence in the games, she notes that music is "a significant incentive to steal a vehicle and take long drives around the gameworld" (55).

25   Paul Théberge, for example, notes that "the level of audience discomfort generated through the use of silence is quite different [from audiences' usual awareness of their surroundings], extremely powerful, and has been exploited by filmmakers only on occasion, usually in instances where intensely dramatic or violent acts are depicted." Paul Théberge, "Almost Silent: The Interplay of Sound and Silence in Contemporary Cinema and Television," in *Lowering the Boom: Critical Studies in Film Sound*, ed. Jay Beck and Tony Grajeda (Urbana and Chicago: University of Illinois Press, 2008), 53.

26   Elisabeth Weis, *The Silent Scream: Alfred Hitchcock's Sound Track* (Rutherford, NJ: Fairleigh Dickinson University Press, 1982), 140. Weis discusses the interplay of silence and loud noise throughout Chapter 8 of the book.

27   The shower scene in *Psycho* has attracted a considerable amount of attention from film music scholars. For an examination of the music and the possibilities of the silence, see, for example, James Wierzbicki, "Psycho-Analysis: Form and Function in Bernard Herrmann's Music for Hitchcock's Masterpiece," in *Terror Tracks: Music, Sound, and Horror Cinema*, ed. Philip Hayward (Oakville, CT: Equinox, 2009): 14–46.

28   In the words of the film's sound designer, Skip Lievsay: "The idea here was to remove the safety net that lets the audience feel like they know what's going to happen. I think it makes the movie much more suspenseful. You're not guided by the score and so you lose that comfort zone." Quoted in Dennis Lim, "Exploiting Sound, Exploring Silence," *New York Times* (January 6, 2008), available online at www.nytimes.com/2008/01/06/movies/awardsseason/06lim.html?pagewanted= all&_r=0.

29   Gerry Bloustien, "And the Rest is Silence: Silence and Death as Motifs in *Buffy the Vampire Slayer*," in *Music, Sound, and Silence in* Buffy the Vampire Slayer, ed. Paul Attinello, Janet K. Halfyard, and Vanessa Knights (Surrey, UK and Burlington, VT: Ashgate, 2010), 93. See pp. 103–105 for Bloustein's discussion of the episode "The Body."

30   On the complex relationship between player and avatar, see Bob Rehak, "Playing at Being: Psychoanalysis and the Avatar," in *The Video Game Theory Reader*, ed. Mark J.P. Wolf and Bernard Perron (New York and London: Routledge, 2003), 103–127. Rehak notes, in particular, that "the avatar does double duty as self and other, symbol and index. As *self*, its behavior is tied to the player's through an interface (keyboard, mouse, joystick): its literal motion, as well as its figurative triumphs and defeats, result from the player's actions. At the same time, avatars are unequivocally *other*. Both limited and freed by difference from the player, they can accomplish more than the player alone; they are supernatural ambassadors of agency" (106).

31   See Kristine Jørgensen, "Left in the Dark: Playing Computer Games with the Sound Turned Off," in *From Pac-Man to Pop Music: Interactive Audio in Games and New Media*, ed. Karen Collins (Burlington, VT: Ashgate, 2008), 163–176.

32   In the words of one *GameFAQs* user, the silence "was incredibly constructive for the feel of the game, incredible. So really, the lack of sound is kind of what boosts this game up." BulletBill22, "One of the Best," *GameFAQs* (June 29, 2009),

available online at www.gamefaqs.com/ps2/924364-shadow-of-the-colossus/reviews/review-134881.

33 One could also argue that, much like the bond between the player and the Wanderer, the silences facilitate a connection between the Wanderer (player) and Argo, his horse. In the absence of music, Argo's rhythmic hoof beats in fact create a kind of music themselves, an almost hypnotic pattern that serves as a reminder of both Argo's comforting presence and the lack of other sounds (other animals, people, etc.). Since the Wanderer and Argo are almost never separated (at least until near the game's end), I find it difficult and ultimately pointless to extricate the two from an emotional point of view; they operate as a pair, and consequently the player's bond with the Wanderer extends to both.

34 This projection of players' own characteristics and preoccupations onto virtual avatars seems fairly widespread in games where the characters lack their own strong characterizations. Thaddeus Griebel, for example, has explored the psychological tendency for players to project their personalities, value systems, and personal histories onto their avatars in *The Sims 2*. Thaddeus Griebel, "Self-Portrayal in a Simulated Life: Projecting Personality and Values in *The Sims 2*," *Game Studies* 6/1 (December 2006), available online at http://gamestudies.org/0601/articles/griebel.

35 Ciccoricco, "'Play, Memory': *Shadow of the Colossus* and Cognitive Workouts."

36 Ryan Clements, "*Ico* & *Shadow of the Colossus Collection* Review," *IGN* (September 8, 2011), available online at www.ign.com/articles/2011/09/08/ico-shadow-of-the-colossus-collection-review.

37 Nick Fortugno, "Losing Your Grip: Futility and Dramatic Necessity in *Shadow of the Colossus*," in *Well Played 1.0: Video Games, Value and Meaning*, available online at www.etc.cmu.edu/etcpress/node/278.

38 Fortugno, "Losing Your Grip: Futility and Dramatic Necessity in *Shadow of the Colossus*."

39 K.J. Donnelly, *The Spectre of Sound: Music in Film and Television* (London: BFI, 2005), 1.

40 T.W. Adorno, *Introduction to the Sociology of Music* (New York: Seabury, 1976), 53. Quoted in Donnelly, *The Spectre of Sound: Music in Film and Television*, 5. Donnelly addresses the manipulative quality of film music throughout the overview to his book.

Chapter 7

Fear of the Unknown

Music and Sound Design in Psychological Horror Games

Rebecca Roberts

Survival horror games manipulate players through their use of music and sound design to convey a range of atmospheres and engage players through deep emotional connections to the terrifying environment. Through strict audiovisual interactions, music is pushed beyond standard narrative design aspects of time and place and into a symbiotic, sensory relationship with the on-screen action. Both parts must work together in order to form one compelling product, where, in many other genres, music is not necessarily required. Music in horror settings is rarely used as incidental backing music. Instead, it is intended to convey atmospheric moods and provide sonic instructions to the players. These games not only rely on emotionally captivating and disturbing music, but also complex uses of sound design in the effects chosen and their positioning within the level design.

The survival horror genre began in the early 1990s with the first 3D horror game, *Alone in the Dark* (Infogrames, 1992), but the term was actually coined with the 1996 release of *Resident Evil* (Capcom, 1996). Among one of the pioneers of the genre was the hugely influential psychological horror *Silent Hill* (Konami, 1999). It had a "more cerebral approach due to the intricate story and emphasis on character development," which set it aside from others in the survival horror genre, namely *Resident Evil*, due to its unsettling direction.[1] It approached the concept of fear in a more mentally disturbing manner, concentrating on player immersion rather than shock tactics. Music was used as a continuous atmospheric signifier of danger, where previously it had been used to indicate sections of upcoming combat or as sonic stingers in tense, shock situations. With music continuously playing, the players have no real indicator of safety and will remain tense throughout long periods of activity. Composer Akira Yamaoka faced a difficult challenge with *Silent Hill* because he was tasked with arranging a series of tracks that could loop seamlessly, without being repetitive and monotonous, and that had the ability to arouse a sense of fear and anxiety in the players. He was able to achieve this with music that had no real structure or tonal center: a collection of dissonant melodies and mechanical rhythms, supported by a bass drone fading in and out of focus. This allows the music to repeat without becoming tedious.

It also allows for a greater textural density at any random moment when an attack is triggered. With this nondescript, ambient music, a whole cacophony of sounds can be generated and played together to create music that incessantly rises in tension, leading toward a point of climax and conflict as the players must decide whether to fight or flee.

Silent Hill is a vast, expansive space that exists within open spaces and closed labyrinth structures. The parameters are quite free in outside spaces, where Harry, the protagonist, is free to move around looking for clues and solving puzzles. When he is required to enter buildings, or claustrophobic alleyways, however, the structure becomes extremely confined, thus cleverly turning the frustrating third-person camera issues of the late 1990s into an aesthetically beneficial part of the game. In these sections, the music changes to a more distinct mechanical sound and an air-raid siren is usually heard. The siren quickly becomes recognizable to players as a terrifying signifier that causes the world around them to change from a dark, atmospheric fog into a burning, hellish dystopia, containing an abundance of enemies ready to attack. The descent into darkness is also mirrored by the dynamic change in pace of the music from relatively ambient, mechanical-based sounds, to loud, crashing noises combined with pulsating bass undertones. This has a direct emotional effect on the players. They are left feeling confused and unsure of what lies ahead, arousing a greater sense of fear that is attributable solely to the music. Confusing the players through the use of audiovisual interactions has always been a key element to the *Silent Hill* games, and it is what makes them so successful and truly terrifying. The most frightening enemy is one that remains unseen, relying on the resultant madness and fear concocted by the minds of the players.

The Endless Labyrinth

There is often a sense of linearity to the level design within games, where the path to take is the most obvious or only available one to the players. Most survival horror games adapt linear conventions by providing an illusion of choice to trick and confuse players, causing them to spend long periods of time exploring haunting atmospheres. The illusion of choice is provided by varying labyrinth models throughout open levels of gameplay. They can be as small as unlocked doors and corridors to explore, to entirely different paths leading to a variety of outcomes. It is almost always the case that only one particular choice of action will be the correct one, forcing the players to take on the confusing maze-like structure to find the right path. In *Hamlet on the Holodeck*, Janet Murray describes the conventions of navigation within electronic environments:

> The navigational pleasures are richly exploited by the many forms of labyrinths . . . All of them allow us to experience pleasures specific to

intentional navigation: orienting ourselves by landmarks, mapping a space mentally to match our experience, and admiring the juxtapositions and changes in perspective that derive from moving through an intricate environment. . . . Electronic environments offer the pleasure of orienteering in two very different configurations, each of which carries its own narrative power: the solvable maze and the tangled rhizome.[2]

The players have the freedom to walk around within these complex environments, but that sense of freedom and pleasure can quickly turn to fear and anxiety when it is discovered that they have spent long periods of time exploring the same environment without successfully progressing further. The intimate sound design of maze structures is described throughout this chapter. In order to establish the reasons for their use, however, we must turn to Greek mythology.

One of the best-known uses of labyrinths within a narrative is the story of Theseus and the Minotaur. Trapped within a labyrinth to prevent wreaking havoc on the city, the Minotaur dwelled within its darkest depths, causing no problems except for the occasional sacrificial demands. The hero, Theseus, set out to slay this evil beast with a sword given to him by the king's daughter, Ariadne. The hero's journey through the labyrinth was one of tension, anxiety, and terrifying fear. Every step he took brought him closer to the source of his terror, yet it was a necessary process for him to enter and then exit the labyrinth if he was to slay the beast and gain the affection of Ariadne. As the hero in the story, Theseus needed to face his fears, carry onward, and return triumphant in order to complete his quest. Turning away from Greek mythology, Murray also describes philosopher Deleuze's "rhizome" root structure, in which structures are connected to each other with multiple outcomes.[3] The players can spend hours wandering within this system without ever finding a particular resolution to their anxiety and fear. While the players long for a narrative end within the structure, they almost hope that the state of play continues since a resolution would mark the start of conflict and possibly the end of the game or level. When describing the two forms of navigation, Murray states:

> Both the overdetermined form of the single-path maze adventure and the underdetermined form of rhizome fiction work against the interactor's pleasure in navigation. [. . . They are] stories that are goal driven enough to guide navigation but open-ended enough to allow free exploration and that display a satisfying dramatic structure no matter how the interactor chooses to traverse the space.[4]

These models combined can be used to describe almost every game in the survival horror genre. The players are required to search for a way out by confronting horrific enemies that they have spent significant amounts of time listening to and trying to avoid.

Listening to the Unknown: Player Space and the Unseen Enemy

Music does not exist by itself. It will always accompany one or more senses to form a greater picture, whether the simulation of an idealized real-world narrative in the mind of the listener, or accompanying an autonomous entity such as film, dance, or theatre. Music creates a sonic and virtual reality around the listener that heightens emotions and engages with imaginative thought. Video games can be just as enjoyable without sound, or without the intended game soundtrack in lieu of a personal choice of music, but survival horror games cannot operate to their full potential without sound and music. Taking note from games such as *Doom 3* (id Software, 2004), *Penumbra* (Frictional Games, 2007), *Fatal Frame* (Techmo, 2002), or games in the *Silent Hill* series, the most frightening enemy is the one that is audible but unseen. It allows for individual interpretations of fear, causing tension to rise to an uncomfortable height. The sound design, combined with the music, acts as an anchor to keep the players focused within the action of the game world. Audio developers and composers must convince players that they only exist within the context of the game during play, or they risk breaking any intense, emotional connections. Players learn how to read audio clues that arise within a state of play. For example, in a typical horror game setting, players can comprehend the location of the approaching enemy through the use of directional audio, and incidental music will either increase in volume and texture, or work as dynamic audio increasing in layers of different polyphonic timbres to mount to a cacophonous climax. After the fight ends, there will be a sigh of relief as the music drops to signify safety and the players can relax.

The interpretation of spatial planes within the sound design creates another dimension for the players to exist within. Laurie Taylor discusses the idea of "telepresence" as "the subject's presence in separate simultaneous areas that are based on differing spatial domains, but not necessarily differing geographical areas."[5] The space that the players occupy is divided into different "spatial planes" such as the shared relationship between player and avatar, the existence of the players outside the diegesis (from an audience perspective, having the ability to hear non-diegetic audio), and the physical space of the players within the real world. By developing a relationship with the avatar on-screen, or even by becoming the subject in first-person settings, the players use the avatar as an embodiment or vehicle as their agent in the game world.[6] As they direct their avatar through twisting labyrinths, they begin to personify fear as if they were actually present within the game world. In musical terms, Isabella van Elferen describes a significant portion of the game audio as "*meta-diegetic*" music that extends across boundaries of diegetic and non-diegetic.[7] The players must feel a connection with their avatar to feel a full sense of telepresence and immersion, but they can still hear non-diegetic music that would be inaudible to the avatar. Van Elferen therefore refers to non-diegetic music in sections of gameplay as *meta-diegetic*, because it provides more than a narrative setting or emotional understanding to the players. It provides a set of musical instructions that are instinctively interpreted to follow a course of action throughout sequences of play.

Identification in video games can often provide problems with the relationship between player and screen: the players viewing a projection of their direct actions. If the players find difficulty in connecting with their avatar, then the immersion of the game world will be broken. Addressing the idea of identification from a psychoanalysis perspective, Taylor refers to Lacan, who explains identification as "the transformation that takes place in the subject when he assumes an image."[8] While Lacan refers to the projection of real-life subjects in a mirror, this principle can also be used to describe the mirrored embodiment of the players on-screen. Bob Rehak explores the psychoanalysis of the avatar and refers also to Lacan's views on self-projection. This embodiment comes in two forms, the "self" and the "other":

> Appearing on-screen in place of the player, the avatar does double duty as self and other, symbol and index. As self, its behavior is tied to the player's through an interface (keyboard, mouse, joystick): its literal motion, as well as its figurative triumphs and defeats, result from the player's actions. At the same time, avatars are unequivocally other. Both limited and freed by difference from the player, they can accomplish more than the player alone; they are supernatural ambassadors of agency.[9]

Turning to Perron's account of the "extended body," he explains how it becomes more difficult to address gamers as a "disembodied eye" as they are the "lived body in front of the screen."[10] The players will cease to advance their character toward danger that inevitably lies ahead due to a built-up fear of pain and death provided by the visuals and increasing musical discomfort. By surpassing any rational thought, the players fear the death of their avatar beyond on-screen boundaries that transcend into genuine emotions. Anxiety is heightened through the unseen monster, but also the body of the monster itself, when it actually arrives, often later reinforced by other unexpected enemies to bombard and panic the players. In these sections, the music will increase in tension and the players will feel part of the digesis mentally and often physically, through heightened adrenaline and blood pressure, as they cross over into the game interface.

Game sound is emergent as technology permits, with the ludic study of music following gradually behind. Rob Bridgett has described the use of over-compressed soundtracks causing a loss of dynamic range, which, unfortunately, is necessary for games to compete with all other sounds around them.[11] Video games must maintain a state of immersion while competing with extraneous sounds. Fortunately, in the current climate of high production value, players are paying more attention to music and narrative through the use of cinematic sequences and recorded orchestral soundtracks. As games have moved away from the arcade culture of repetitive melodies and basic gameplay, they are becoming increasingly more dependent on isolation where the players should devote their full attention to the game in order to experience the best possible immersive effect. Games such as *Amnesia: The Dark Descent* (Frictional Games, 2010) and even mobile games such as *Year Walk* (Simogo, 2013) start with instructions for the players to wear headphones for the best possible experience. This necessity for audio involvement differs from genre to genre; for instance, in first-person shooter (FPS) games such as *Call of Duty: Black Ops II* (Treyarch, 2012) and *Battlefield 3* (DICE/EA, 2011), incidental music is not always an essential part of the overall experience. In these war shooter settings, the players are required to partake in the repetitive activity of shooting their targets. Often, players will group together physically or online to play these types of games, which results in conversations, distractions, and often the replacement of in-game music with their own preference. The immersive capacity in multiplayer military FPS games comes from the team activity of reaching a goal, which requires concentration but still allows the players to maintain their space within the physical dimension. Other genres, by contrast, require complete silence and the undivided attention of the players in order to experience the maximum immersive potential. These are typically survival horror genres and some action-adventure role-playing games. They are rich in narrative capacity, allowing an intricate story to unravel as the game progresses, demonstrating a diverse, dynamic audio range. Bridgett discusses the idea that music and dynamics correspond to the narrative events taking place, as also discussed earlier in regard to auditory instructions. The players instinctively knows that enemies will approach or continue to attack within sections of tense music. It is that instinctive acceptance that allows game designers to break conventions and surprise the players:

> The audio aesthetics of these narrative dynamics can either play with the action game-play . . . or play against them. They can even begin to set up expectations in the matching of audio action to game-play action, and then break those rules as the narrative progresses to provide even further excitement and immersion in game-play.[12]

Dead Space (EA Redwood Shores, 2008) combines specific sound design manipulation techniques with the claustrophobic nature of the level design to provide a tense atmosphere throughout. The entire game is set on a gigantic, labyrinthine space ship with winding corridors and air vents. It is a survival horror third-person shooter, with the essential elements of tense, psychological sound design, but in contrast with traditional survival horror games, the protagonist is heavily armed with a variety of different powerful weapons and well prepared to defeat his enemies. Typically, survival horror games rely on an average, feeble protagonist to maximize player embodiment. They often begin with no weapons or armor, and the characters themselves display a bewildering sense of fear. *Dead Space* shares the shooter and soldier aspects with *Resident Evil*, but its distinct focus on sound design and psychological manipulation sets it aside from its counterparts. The enemies are called "Necromorphs," which appear in a variety of different mutations as the game progresses. Depending on the type, these enemies often cannot be killed by a single bullet, instead requiring the players to dismember their multiple limbs before continuing to kill them, usually by stamping on their crawling, disfigured torsos. This level of accuracy while playing in a tense environment causes a greater sense of anxiety as the pressure to survive rises. The developers working on *Dead Space* designed sections of the combat environments to have open, or even circular, labyrinth structures. The players remain in a constant state of tension during exploration and combat, as they are never certain which direction the enemies will attack from or whether the combat is really over. A *Gamasutra* article investigated the scariest aspects of gaming, measured by looking at players' biometric data, focusing specifically on the sequel, *Dead Space 2* (Visceral Games, 2011) as one of its studies. In one of the experiments focused on audible and unseen enemies, the study found:

> The second feature of the scene that regularly prompted a fear response was when players were knowingly pursued by enemies, but said aliens were not visible on-screen, and Isaac [the protagonist] was just out of harm's way. This "implied danger" was a key cause of scariness for the participants, with Olivia [the participant] suggesting, amongst screams, that knowing they were behind her was really scary.[13]

Sonic signifiers are usually the only real indication of approaching danger, and the audio designers frequently use these basic conventions against the players. Various sequences within the game contain sound effects coming from one direction, which the players will instinctively investigate, but the enemy will actually approach from another direction. Players will then panic as they must quickly dismember the enemy before they themselves are killed and have to go through the trauma of that level again. Players are put in a state of constant anxiety as they realize traditional rules of sound effects and music do not apply; they will feel a sense of apprehension toward their embodied avatar as they begin to doubt their instincts. When players are focused on unpredictable sound design and directional surround sound, the flow state has an all-encompassing effect. They become absorbed by the demanding amount of concentration required by the game and ignore all environments but the simulated one. After play ceases, players will often feel emotionally drained and exhausted as a result of the game's captivating and immersive power.

Diversion and directional techniques in sound design and music are not confined to the survival horror genre alone. Various action shooter titles such as *Gears of War* (Epic Games, 2006), *Resistance: Fall of Man* (Insomnia Games, 2006), and *Left 4 Dead* (Valve, 2008) incorporate directional sound manipulation alongside dynamic changes to volume levels. Despite the fact that they are primarily first- or third-person shooters,[14] which make their capacity for horror far lesser than focused survival horror titles, the audio aesthetics give the games an added level of enjoyable experience. They use dynamic volume changes to signify areas of importance within the narrative. After a sonically loud event or fight has taken place, the music and ambient effects either cut out completely or drop significantly in volume to contrast with the previous section and to enhance its narrative power. They also use music as a sonic representation of enemy type. For instance, in the two former games there are small, vicious creatures that will gather at the foot of the players and devour them unless stopped. There are faint sonic signifiers and music used to indicate their presence that build in dynamic range as the threat becomes greater, but the specific direction of the oncoming attack is always ambiguous. The players are usually distracted by this sound and will actively search for the oncoming attack, often while still being attacked by enemies further ahead. The use of sound in this case confuses the players and creates tension as they frantically attempt to find and kill the creatures before it is too late. Similarly, in *Left 4 Dead*, the players are one of four protagonists who must fight through zombies to survive a zombie apocalypse. There are five different types of special infected zombies that can attack at any given moment, and the only indication of their presence is a distinctive leitmotif unique to each special zombie infected. These motifs are mostly orchestral and include clashing piano chords, five-note double bass melodies, high-pitched violin scratching, and overwhelming orchestral blasts. Players can instantly pick out these signifiers as they sit comfortably outside of the ambient incidental soundtrack. *Left 4 Dead* is played as a multiplayer experience with friends at home or online, so these audio cues enable players to communicate quickly with their teammates about the type of approaching enemy.

The Power of a Haunted Environment

In most games, even survival horror titles, the skin and environment of a game are accepted as non-interactive visual content, existing solely for aesthetic purposes. Only certain games dedicate more time to realism and consequently program these non-interactive objects to respond to the player's actions. When this gameplay aspect appears in horror settings, a greater emotional response is usually aroused within the players because of the unexpected actions of the artificial intelligence (AI) in the game. These could be anything from a quick glimpse of a reflection in a mirror that shocks the players, to increasingly eerie piano music and completely disconnected sound effects in *Silent Hill 2*. One prominent example is from a horror role-playing game where the players embody a vampire of their choice: *Vampire the Masquerade: Bloodlines* (Troika

Games, 2004). The players must complete a series of different tasks, some more terrifying than others, to uncover a series of secrets about their society and the vampire council.

In this particular quest, the players are required to take care of a haunting spirit at the Ocean House Hotel. As the players arrive outside the hotel, they will see from the aesthetics that it is a horror set. Unsettling and largely atonal non-diegetic music also accompanies this sequence to set the tense atmosphere. Once players have found the keys, they begin their approach up the staircase to the front door. On arriving at the top of the stairs, there is a sudden crash of shattered glass as a light blows next to the door. These quick, unexpected shocks are present throughout the whole level. Once inside the hotel, they are free to experience the large space without loading screens, enabling anxiety levels to build without interruption. One of the first things to note upon entry is the dramatic lighting. It is dark, dingy, and a putrid green colour, reflecting the uncanny, decrepit, and cold nature of the building. The impact of dynamic lighting within games is often underrated. As El-Nasr et al. observe: "just like light in real space, simulated illumination in virtual space has a direct effect upon participants' emotional experiences . . . Warm and cool simulated illumination conditions have differing emotional and performance effects upon players."[15] The vast majority of horror-themed games use outlandish lighting techniques to heighten the immersive potential of the game. This particular level combines sharp flashes of light with overpoweringly loud crashes then moments of silence and darkness. About halfway through the level, when the players can choose to explore the upstairs, one of the rooms contains a particularly well designed, shocking sequence.

As players enter, the room appears reasonably normal, a typical hotel room with Victorian and Art Deco influences. Once they begin to explore, however, there is a sudden crash and the lights go out, leaving the room in almost complete darkness. A thunderclap is heard before the lights automatically switch back on about three seconds later. The players will now notice the wall above the bed, once clean, now reads, "Get Out." It has been scratched into the wall, and the typography would suggest it is no empty threat. As the players continue further toward the bed, a vase and a picture frame begin to shake, making a loud clattering noise before being launched toward the players by the paranormal energy that now exists within the room. These typical shock scares are used to frequently break the rising tension levels within the mission. When the players enter the hotel, there is no incidental music, removing any musical indication of danger. Without relying on music for narrative clues, the players must listen to sound effects around them. A typical soundscape consists of diegetic effects ranging from close-proximity whispers, screams, and moaning, to banging, glass shattering, and creaking. The entire building appears to ache with the painful events that previously occurred. As players explore, they will find newspaper cuttings reporting on the various murders and events connected with the hotel. One significant use of this extra information is down in the basement. If the players have spent time exploring and finding newspaper clippings, they will see one that contains the headline "Hotel Hell: Child's Severed Head Found in Laundry Room!" When they progresses further through the basement, they will begin to hear the faint sound of a washing machine. As the sound grows in volume to a disturbing level, it will become apparent that something large is moving around inside the washing machine as it operates. Players that have seen the article will immediately understand the origin of the sound and become reluctant to investigate. But by facing their fears, they will discover the presence of a key required at a later stage in the level. The players are continually required to head toward the known direction of danger in order to progress.

The Future of Survival Horror

The growing popularity of intellectual properties such as *Silent Hill* and *Resident Evil* have led to the production of various sequels on different platforms.[16] These sequels are often produced by entirely different teams, so their willingness to take risks decreases with each subsequent title. This has resulted in a series of spin-offs that have become more generic with each release. The most popular genre in the current climate is the first-person shooter, and popular survival horror franchises have been incorporating shooter aspects into new releases to appeal to a wider audience. This works for the casual player, but the hardcore audience are now looking elsewhere for their scares, and they have turned to independent (indie) PC games such as *Slender* (Parsec Productions, 2012), *Home* (Benjamin Rivers Inc., 2012), and *Outlast* (Red Barrels, 2013).

In 2007, independent developers Frictional Games released *Penumbra: Overture*, described primarily as a first-person adventure game, involving puzzle-solving, physical combat (without guns), and stealth. However, the emphasis on environmental changes makes this game into more than just adventure. The audiovisual manipulation techniques, the weakness of the protagonist, and the use of stealth traditionally place this game within the survival horror category. Since its release, it has been praised as one of the scariest games around, but was criticized for its poor combat system and bad graphics. After releasing two more games in the *Penumbra* series, Frictional Games started work on a purely survival horror game that would attempt to improve on the criticized elements of *Penumbra* to produce an intensely disturbing game. In September 2010, they released *Amnesia: The Dark Decent*, which, despite mediocre visuals, provides a dramatic horror experience through the use of audio.

The use of the entire stereo field within *Amnesia* is one of the game's significant strengths. The developers used the same first-person-style gameplay used in *Penumbra*, which made it much easier to include directional sounds, as the players are at the forefront of the action. Directional sound effects are useful when challenging a player with a hidden or out-of-sight enemy. To predict the location and even the distance of the enemy, players must use their ears just as they would in a real-life situation, by turning their head (the camera) and listening. Having to hide and listen during an enemy encounter, combined with the sheer helpless fact that players cannot fight their enemy leaves them in a state of terror. The bold choice of disallowing combat forces the players to plan out their actions strategically, immersing them further within the game. *Amnesia* is a game that contains highly sophisticated audio, demonstrated by winning the award for "Excellence in Audio" comprising of both music and sound design at the 2011 Independent Games Festival Awards, held at the annual Games Developer Convention in San Francisco. The focus on player immersion throughout sets this game far ahead of its competitors within the genre. The audio techniques and the gameplay introduce engaging ideas that could be adapted for other genres to help with the sonic identification between player and avatar.

A recent indie 2D platform game not necessarily intended as survival horror is the atmospheric puzzler *Limbo* (Playdead, 2010). In *Limbo*, the player occupies the body of a small boy, who is both delightfully innocent and eerily scary with a sense of loneliness and isolation. The game is left fairly open to interpretation, with the only real piece of narrative information being that the boy has entered Limbo to save his sister. The lack of cutscenes or a specific linear narrative focus the player's attention on the gameplay and their relationship with the protagonist. It is an extremely lonely game, and its minimalistic, greyscale visual aesthetics, along with the uncanny lack of ambience, emphasize the bewilderingly depressing environment. Players are motivated to continue through the series of challenging puzzles without ever being certain where they are going or for what reason; in a sense, the game hypnotizes players into their own state of "limbo." There is almost no music within the game; it exists through a series of fragments of electronic, ambient music, which has a disturbingly rich emotional capacity when combined with the visuals. The composer, Martin Stig Andersen, has focused his career to date on acousmatic music, which is heavily reflected in his score and use of sound design within the game. In an interview for IGN, Andersen commented:

> There are a lot of people who think there's no music in *Limbo*. If you read the reviews it's like there's absolutely no music in there. I think that's really interesting . . . one of Arnt's [the director] key concepts about this game was that it should be more ambiguous and each player will have their own impression. The whole concept of the visuals, the horizon is always blurred so you can project your own things into the spaces. I tried to do the same with the sound with noise and textures—you start to hear things that aren't there.[17]

Certain sounds take prominence within different sequences, most notably in the presence of loud footsteps, which work to underscore the sheer silence and emptiness of the environment. Andersen has also worked against sonic conventions by altering the way certain objects sound, or by adjusting their volume levels so they almost have no presence within the ambient soundscape. One example is the spider chase sequence. The increased kinesis of the action would suggest a loud accompanying soundtrack; however, in reality, the sound is dampened and quiet, which creates an unsettling sonic atmosphere. It could be further explained through the application of the McGurk effect, which generally applies to speech recognition; the principle idea is that sight takes precedence over sound.[18] If the audible sound effects are different from the visual content, then the brain will usually override this to complete the picture. The sound effects are often so altered in *Limbo*, however, that it is difficult for the brain to comprehend the on-screen action, creating a frantic sense of disembodiment.

Despite the tension, anxiety, and fear generated by audiovisual techniques in survival horror games, the experiences players receive lead to feelings of relief and achievement. Players have pushed themselves to the limits through tense and anxious states of play in these games, and to actually make it out the other side can be likened to Theseus' dramatic exit from the labyrinth, with or without their virtual Ariadne.

Notes

All websites were accessed November 4, 2013.

1 Zach Whalen, "Case Study: Film Music vs. Video Game Music: The Case of Silent Hill," in *Music, Sound and Multimedia: From the Live to the Virtual*, ed. J. Sexton (Edinburgh: Edinburgh University Press, 2007), 75.
2 Janet H. Murray, *Hamlet on the Holodeck: The Future of Narrative in Cyberspace* (Cambridge, MA: MIT Press, 1997), 129–130.
3 Gilles Deleuze and Félix Guttari, *A Thousand Plateaus: Capitalism and Schizophrenia*, trans. Brian Massumi (Minneapolis: University of Minnesota Press, 1987).
4 Murray, *Hamlet on the Holodeck: The Future of Narrative in Cyberspace*, 134–135.
5 Laurie Taylor, "When Seams Fall Apart—Video Game Space and the Player," *Game Studies* 3/2 (December 2003), available online at www.gamestudies.org/0302/taylor/.
6 Diane Carr, "Play Dead: Genre and Affect in Silent Hill and Planetscape Torment," *Game Studies* 3/1 (May 2003), available online at www.gamestudies.org/0301/carr/.
7 Isabella van Elferen, "¡Un Forastero! Issues of Virtuality and Diegesis in Videogame Music," *Music and the Moving Image* 4/2 (Summer 2011), 30–39.
8 Jacques Lacan, *Écrits: A Selection*, trans. Alan Sheridan (New York: Norton, 1977), 2. Full quotation: "We have only to understand the mirror stage *as an identification*, in the full sense that analysis gives the term: namely, the transformation that takes place in the subject when he assumes an image—whose predestination to this phase-effect is sufficiently indicated by the use, in analytic theory, of the ancient term *imago*."

9 Bob Rehak, "Playing at Being," in *The Video Game Theory Reader*, ed. Mark J.P. Wolf and Bernard Perron (New York: Routledge, 2003), 106.

10 Bernard Perron, *Horror Video Games: Essays on the Fusion of Fear and Play* (Jefferson, NC: McFarland, 2009), 123.

11 Rob Bridgett, "Dynamic Range: Subtlety and Silence in Video Game Sound," in *From Pac-Man to Pop Music: Interactive Audio in Games and New Media*, ed. Karen Collins (Aldershot, UK: Ashgate, 2008), 163.

12 Bridgett, "Dynamic Range: Subtlety and Silence in Video Game Sound," 163.

13 Joel Windels, "Scary Game Findings: A Study of Horror Games and Their Players," *Gamasutra* (September 2011). Other games in this study included *Alan Wake*, *Resident Evil 5*, and *Condemned*. It concluded that "actual combat is not as scary as the implied threat of combat" and that *Dead Space 2* was the scariest game among hardcore players and casual players, available online at www.gamasutro.com/view/feature/6480/scary_game_findings_a_study_of_.php?print=1/.

14 First-person shooters put the player directly in the eyes of the protagonist. Third-person shooters place the player slightly above the protagonist's shoulder or completely behind them so the in-game avatar is clearly visible.

15 Magy Saif El-Nasr, Simon Niedenthal, Igor Knez, Priya Almeida, and Joseph Zupko, "Dynamic Lighting for Tension in Games," *Game Studies* 7/1 (August 2007), available online at http://gamestudies.org/0701/articles/elnasr_niedenthal_knez_almeida_zupko.

16 At the date of publishing, *Resident Evil* is up to number six and *Silent Hill* continues to four, with two standalone titles, *Silent Hill: Homecoming* and *Silent Hill: Downpour*. This does not include spin-offs on handheld consoles and the *Resident Evil: Operation Raccoon City* shooter that was released as a standalone title.

17 Michael Thomsen, "How Limbo Came To Life," *IGN* (September 2010), available online at www.ign.com/articles/2010/09/14/how-limbo-came-to-life.

18 Martin Paré, Rebecca Richler, Martin ten Hove, and Kevin Munhall, "Gaze Behaviour in Audiovisual Speech Perception: The Influence of Occular Fixations of the McGurk Effect," *Attention, Perception & Psychophysics* 65/4 (2003), 553–567.

Lawn of the Dead

The Indifference of Musical Destiny in *Plants vs. Zombies*

K.J. Donnelly

Atavistic arcade game music has persisted into current video game culture, particularly in handheld games. Arcade-derived music engages distinctive aesthetics and psychology, and is evident in PopCap's tower defense game *Plants vs. Zombies*. In this game, the player must defend a house (screen left) from slowly moving zombies who, from screen right, traverse a lawn (sometimes with a swimming pool) and later a roof. Gameplay involves planting various vegetables, fungi, and flowers that counter the zombies through blocking, exploding, or showering them with projectiles. Rather than looking like many other horror games, it has a parodic quality, with comic zombies, a deranged neighbor (called Crazy Dave) with a saucepan on his head, and bizarre anthropomorphic varieties of plant. The game is part of a torrent of zombie products (films, games, television, books, comics, and other consumer goods) that have materialized since the millennium, making the shambling undead one of the dominant metaphors of the times. *Plants vs. Zombies* has horizontal lanes of movement and 25 different types of zombie, beginning each level slowly with isolated attacking zombies but concluding with a massive torrent of them. It is a "tower defense" game: a siege with the enemy's relentless forward movement toward the player's battlelines.[1] Although Atari's *Ramparts* in 1990 is considered the first game of this type, *Space Invaders* (1978) has an underlying structure that is precisely the same. Originally to be called *Lawn of the Dead, Plants vs. Zombies* was developed by PopCap Games and published in 2009 initially for PC and Mac, but has since been ported to Xbox 360, PlayStation 3, Nintendo DS, and mobile phones (iOS, Android, and BlackBerry).[2]

The music is pre-rendered, recorded as a selection of pieces of distinct music rather than being interactive and dynamic, and although it is not tied securely to gameplay, perhaps it is related to the game through a different logic, engaging with a primitive essence rather than functioning as the more modern process of interactive and dynamic video game music.[3] *Plants vs. Zombies* utilizes a cartoon graphic style, and follows a similar strategy in its music. The music is cartoonish in that it appears exaggerated and burlesque, employing broad brush strokes, simple structures, and working through metonymy, with symbolic characteristics dominating any mimetic value. It has something of film music composer Danny Elfman's cartoonish gothic style to it.[4] There are a number of dark comic pieces of music and a continuum of (musically derived) sound effects for shooting, impacts, and zombie biting. The music was composed and realized by Californian Laura Shigihara, a classically trained pianist who attended University of California, Berkeley, but to study International Relations rather than music. According to her website, she apparently already had secured a contract as a singer-songwriter in Japan but then went on to write game music.[5] *Plants vs. Zombies* won the VGChartz Game of the Year Awards 2009; it also won Best Music Score (and was released as an MP3 album).[6] More generally, *Plants vs. Zombies* proved highly successful, involving many tied-in products, the game's cultural status even being recognized through providing the theme to state lottery tickets in the state of Virginia.[7] With the success of this game and its music, perhaps one would have expected *Plants vs. Zombies* to have music that was intimately interwoven with the gameplay, forming a dynamic and developing relationship. Instead, the music simply progresses, almost in parallel to the unfolding of the game, as a homology to the relentless shambling movement of the zombies.

Figure 8.1 Daytime level in *Plants vs. Zombies*

Arcades and Beyond

In *Reading the Popular*, John Fiske called video arcades "the semiotic brothels of the machine age."[8] In the early years of video gaming, they certainly were exciting and unpredictable places.[9] Arcades began with pinball and one-armed bandits. In 1978, the release of Taito's *Space Invaders* began the halcyon era of game arcades. The most successful games included *Space Invaders, Pac-Man, Ms.Pac-Man,* and *Galaxian* (all Namco); *Asteroids* (Atari); *Donkey Kong* and *Donkey Kong Jr.* (both Nintendo); *Defender* (Williams); and *Mr. Do!* (Taito). However, according to Steven Kent, 1983 was the beginning of the coin-op arcade decline, although Karen Collins dates the decline as starting later, in 1988.[10] Yet, in the US in 1991, $8 billion was still being spent on coin-op games whereas only $1 billion was spent on home gaming.[11] The disappearance of video gaming arcades was caused directly by the rise of home gaming consoles. It was not, however, an overnight supplanting, and there was an early 1990s minor resurgence in arcades (especially in the UK) with kicking and driving games.[12] The move to home consoles initially made gaming less public and allowed more control of the sonic environment by the producers.

The music for arcade games appears not very interactive by more recent standards. It was just a presence, rather than being defined by gameplay. Indeed, arcade music functioned as ballyhoo—the tradition of loud and raucous music that beckoned, aiming to call in punters to bars or fairground tents.[13] Thus, it aimed at exciting sounds and music, as a promise of the game's qualities. Significantly, arcade games produced music when not being played, together creating a wonderful but random Ivesian arcade soundscape and making for general excitement.[14] Music regularly has a high degree of autonomy from the game, relating with indifference to events and gameplay. It can prevail independently, almost as "absolute music," standing on its own two feet rather than making sense only when accompanying its video game.

Such music has been described in recent years as chip music, chiptune music, or 8-bit music. It was defined by technological parameters and limitations. 8-bit CPU and architecture (of the late 1970s and early 1980s) used 8-bit integers and code that was 8-bits wide. The technological capabilities led to the dominance of thin textures and particular timbres (generated rather than sampled), few available channels of noise generator and synthesized waveforms. Indeed, arcade games commenced a certain novel tradition of music in association with images. This music was characterized by its decidedly restricted parameters, in early years often merely comprising unaccompanied single-voice melodies. The limitations on music were provided not only by the small speakers but also by a lack of software space for an extensive musical program, as well as dynamic and timbre limitations and restricted number of sound voices available.[15] The consequent genre of music is characterized by bright and simple musical melodies, basic and unelaborated accompaniment, utilizing harsh tones with basic waveforms and thin textures.[16] It would often include the use of rapid arpeggios that could give the aural impression of more dense-sounding chords, but cost less in software space. This particular style was evident in the vast majority of video games until developments in the early 1990s, and sometimes still is.[17] This musical mode, originating in arcade games, sustained into early home console games. The arrival of more complex processing allied to 16-bit sample capabilities (and the availability of more sound voice channels) opened computer games to the same sonic options as film, television and the music world more generally. Although available in 1987, it was the Super Famicom in 1990 and, more significantly, the Sony PlayStation in 1994 that revolutionized sound for video games. The latter's reliance upon a CD-ROM drive allowed for 24 channels of CD-quality sound (using a sample rate of up to 44.1 kHz). According to Rod Munday, this technological development marked an end to "video game music" as a distinctive genre of music.[18] While this is certainly arguable, it opened up radical new opportunities for video game music. The difference in amount of dedicated memory-program space, as well as processor capability and working memory, meant game music could be more clearly interactive, and music could be more integrated with screen action. It could also be more complex and embrace a wider range of timbres and dynamics.

Published scholarship on video game music has rather neglected arcade games and, even to a degree, 8-bit games, too.[19] Karen Collins's systematic *Game Sound* contains relatively little about arcade or 8-bit music and is happier concentrating on more recent games. Similarly, Roberto Dillon in *The Golden Age of Video Games* concentrates on home consoles to the detriment of arcade games.[20] Writing about video game music has tended to privilege music written for high-production-values console games, where music has a particular form. This form is dictated by the gameplay and involves the use of software programs (known as engines) that marshal fragmentary cues into a continuous fabric through a dynamic relationship with the game events controlled by the player.[21] Yet, a relatively common form of game music derives directly from video games' arcade origins: that of non-dynamic and non-interactive music. Its connection to the rest of the game is more complex and less composed or directed.

Video game studies should be careful not to overplay the ideal of interactive dynamic music as the center of game music, particularly as disconnected, non-dynamic music exemplifies a strong tradition in game music, tracing back to the arcade. The aesthetic remains. Indeed, it is more common than we might give credit: many real-time games use little more than fairly simple trigger and loop mechanisms for music accompanying active gameplay. According to Karen Collins, there are eight in-game functions of video game music: "kinetic functions," "anticipating action," "drawing attention," "structural functions," "reinforcement," "illusionary and spatial functions," "environmental functions," and "communication of emotional meaning."[22] *Plants vs. Zombies'* music engages only two of these functions clearly: structural functions and environmental functions. So, is the music unimportant for the game?

The fact that the game can be played without music augurs that it is not an essential part of playing the game (which seemingly differentiates it from dynamic, interactive music). Significantly, certain types of game have the capability to retain sound effects but remove music. We should never forget that there are many games where the musical soundtrack is not essential, such as EA's best-selling sports franchises such as *FIFA* (annually since 1993) and the *FIFA Manager* series (annually since 1997 and different ranges). In games such as these, or "jukebox" games such as the *Grand Theft Auto* titles (Rockstar, 1997–), the player can change the music library for their own selection of MP3 files of music. Similarly, the vast majority of mobile games do not require musical input for gameplay or immersion.[23] If the music is not integrated on an essential or functional level, then it is not missed. With games that are played on mobile phones, sound regularly is muted by the player. With *Plants vs. Zombies*, music and sound effects are lost when the sound is switched off, although this does not inhibit gameplay as much as it might in many games, as only a minimum of relevant information is communicated through the soundtrack.

"Lawn, Day": Non-Interactive, Non-Dynamic Music

So what connection is there between music and the rest of the game? The first levels, which take place during the day on the front lawn of the player's unseen house, are accompanied by a piece of music that lasts 2:20 (timed from the game rather than the MP3) and simply begins again as a loop once finished. The gameplay does not take a single standard time, and thus the music does not correspond with activities on the screen. It mechanically restarts at the point where it finishes, irrespective of the events in the game.[24] Thus, it is able to have a strong rhythmic impetus that is not going to be interrupted, and is, in fact, predominantly a tango or habanera with a regular pulse all the way through (see Example 8.1), superseded by a more conventional section with a regular 4/4 beat. The use of such a distinct dance rhythm as the basis of the music is remarkable. Dances, with their regular pulses, tend not to be effective accompaniment to moving images, unless there is a desire to unite disparate images in a montage sequence with strong rhythmic music holding it together.[25] The very regularity of dances means that, as an accompaniment to audiovisual culture, they tend to marshal the proceedings, to make the action feel as if it is moving to the beat of the dance rather than following any diegetic or narrative logic.

Example 8.1 Tango bassline

This piece of music ("Grasswalk," as the MP3 file is titled) is based on distinct tonal harmonic movement: the opening chord progression relies upon an alternation of A minor and F seventh chords. Derived from Aeolian harmony, this alternation of a minor chord and a major chord four semitones below it is a common harmonic progression in horror film music and dark rock songs. It is evident in Wagner's funeral march for Siegfried from *Götterdämmerung*, although the addition of the seventh here adds an air of irony not evident in Wagner's piece. This note also provides an unexpected turn to the melody. Across the whole piece, the structure is based strictly on four-bar units, with melody from particular instruments (oboe, an arch deep comic melody in the strings, pizzicato strings). Indeed, this is a heavily regulated structure, based on a sense of integrity for regular rhythmic structure, namely four-bar, eight-bar, and 16-bar units. It is never far from traditional song form and melodies develop along highly traditional lines (often following antecedent-consequent, and AABA formations, etc.). The uniform regularity is essential. The piece's structure is premised upon units of four bars, bearing a distinct resemblance to the AABA form of the standard 32-bar song. The opening tango part lasts for 16 bars, followed by eight bars of soaring oboe melody (the same four bars repeated), then an orphan four-bar drop out section (where almost all instruments recede), then pizzicato strings for eight bars followed by the same with added sustained strings for eight bars, leading to piano arpeggios of 16 bars (the same four bars repeated), after which the piece repeats all over again. Apart from one section, all are eight- or 16-bar, but the four-bar strophe is the fundamental structural unit, with regularity giving something of a mechanical character to proceedings. Just after the first eight bars, when the music begins repeating, an eerie sound, accompanied by a voice intoning "the zombies are coming," gives warning that a zombie is about to appear on the right of the screen. The harmony never strays too far from the key of A minor (despite the F seventh chord), and the slow tango rhythm is held in the bassline, which plays chord tones with a short chromatic run. Some of the music on later night levels adopts a tango rhythm, too. Perhaps the regularity of the musical structure is slightly hidden by the syncopated melody in the opening section of the tango, which then leads to a section dominated by an oboe melody with a more uniform downbeat rhythm. Successful negotiation of the level triggers a burst of jazz guitar to crudely blot out the existing music. There is a sense of irony instilled by the playful tango section, which, at least partially, is due to its occasional chromatic runs (downward in the melody and upward in the bass, tending toward the predictable) and slightly-out-of-kilter seventh chord on the m. 6 of the scale. Later, the four-bar drop out is of exaggerated tonic-chord-dominant-chord piano accompaniment, and an arch and overdone section of melody performed by pizzicato strings. There is a strong sense of notes being overstressed, given an inflated and incongruous rendering, which moves the piece away from being normal and toward being parodic (see Example 8.2).[26] In fact, the music has nothing to do with zombies and plenty to do with comedic notions of music, particularly in the form that they have been standardized by mass media such as radio and television. The sense of irony comes from overstatement, where the listener feels aware of the music being overly obvious for the purposes of effect. Each level of the game has a different piece of accompanying music. The general sonic palette is overwhelmingly electronic, although aping traditional instruments. It includes marimba-like tuned percussion sounds, as well as more traditional orchestral-style sounds. The synthetic strings and brass have an inactive and lazy character, wholly unlike the tradition of loud strident brass in horror films, but nevertheless deep and resonant.

The relation of music to action is almost negligible, with the regularity of the music furnishing something of a mechanical character to gameplay. However, on the later level set at night, there is a minor sense of action being matched by the music. The piece here is a long marimba melody, which

Example 8.2 "Lawn Theme" (excerpt)

Example 8.2 continued

consists of five similar melodies, each of which has slight variations. These make up a succession that is then looped *ad infinitum*. As the player waits for the zombies' appearance on screen left, an eerie wavy synth sound enters with a voice over whisper saying, "the zombies are coming." At 0:17, a string melody enters and a lone zombie appears shortly afterward. At 0:48, brass enters and another zombie appears. At 1:29, both strings and brass as two zombies appear simultaneously. Overall, the music is a loop of about 1:53

that fails to develop and simply halts abruptly when the level is finished with a crudely intruding burst of unconnected jazz guitar.[27] However, beyond this, there appears to be no notable connection apart from the concluding segment of the level, where a drum beat enters as an accompaniment to the existing music, appearing kinetically to choreograph movement through grabbing proceedings by the scruff of the neck as what is billed on screen as a "massive wave of zombies" approaches at the conclusion of each card. The assumption is that the beat matches the excitement of action (and chaotic simultaneity on screen). However, again, if we turn the sound off, it does not have a significant impact on the experience of the game, and arguably none at all on the gameplay. So perhaps I should reformulate my earlier question as: is the *game* unimportant for the music? Shigihara's music was made available as CD/download, and indeed is not functional music (*Gebrauchsmusik*) that derives its nature from its cultural partner (in this case, the game), but has its own integrity as music in its own right. The conclusion of each level breaks the music's regularity. Apart from the succession of jazz guitar that materializes if the player vanquishes the zombies, there is another possible conclusion precipitated again by a vulgar interruption. Four notes of ponderous sinister cartoon music materialize if the zombies break through and win (eating the player's brains). Overall, *Plants vs. Zombies'* music expresses a burlesque of horror, warding off the possibility of any actual terror. However, it conceivably could fit another game with a profoundly different character. Having noted this, it might be connected most directly with the game, but on a deeper level, where the music's regularity relates to the unceasing regularity of the gameplay.

Isomorphism and Psychology

So, how is the music connected to the images of the game? Is it connected to representations of zombies and plants? There appears to be nothing objective to connect the music with such traditions of representation. It also is not functional dramatic music, in that it has little synchronous connection with the images. Yet, while the music is not doing the same thing as the images in terms of dynamics and kinesis, perhaps there is a deeper level of unity. The principle of isomorphism suggests that objects, including cultural objects, might have a shared essential structure and matching character on a deep (below surface) level.[28] Perhaps we can illustrate this process with reference to the fast food chain McDonald's. There is an expectation that in each restaurant, the architecture, decor, food, service and even music all complement one another. Perhaps these elements are of the same essence. Rather than being radically different, these aspects are manifestations of the same cultural impetus, perhaps even the same cultural archetype, although concretized in different forms. We never hear any avant-garde music in McDonald's. The character of the music is carefully chosen to fit the corporate character, and match with everything else on some deeper level of unity. Nothing should stick out like a sore thumb. According to Rudolf Arnheim, such "homology" and "structural kinship" in cultural objects works on a psychological level as an essential part of its unity across forms. This likeness is central to the "psychophysical parallelism" of mental state and object perceived.[29]

The game's aesthetics contain some clear homologies or parallels. The relentless forward movement of zombies in Plants vs. Zombies homologizes the looped music. Such game music is, in effect, simply a countdown—and, on one level, potentially a more general metaphor for being overtaken by age and death. Furthermore, the music can often appear indifferent to developments in games such as Plants vs. Zombies (for instance, when the player is nearing death, it just carries on relentlessly). Such indifferent music is not anempathetic music, but something even more emotionally disengaged. Rather than redoubling emotional effect, the effect can often be a mental dislocation. Anempathetic implies that it is important to miss the appropriate emotion. Emotional effect can be redoubled, seeing as we expect emotional congruence but instead receive no emotional engagement, and realize the extreme poignancy of the overall situation.[30] On the other hand, the indifference of unemotional music is a fundamentally different situation, where music does not provide any emotional tone for its accompaniment. Perhaps it is a film music-based idea that music should be emotional. After all, we are increasingly used to music with little or no emotional tone in public spaces, such as environmental ambient muzak.[31] From the point of view of emotional music that is functional in an audiovisual scenario, this unemotional music embodies an unacceptable indifference. While Chion claimed that anempathetic music was at the essence of cinema as a medium,[32] such indifference in game music might tell us something about the nature of modern culture, and the desire to hide the lack of emotional engagement and empathy beneath the shiny surface of commercial culture.[33] Adverts aim to integrate us as consumers, but we remain only an ace away from the clear indifference of such culture.

Perhaps we should not expect explicit interaction or involvement between sound and image. Indeed, a lack of focus on functionality or emotion might change much in the way of current audiovisual analysis.[34] Claudia Gorbman points out that music in film always signifies emotion, if not evoking and directing emotion.[35] However, while anempathetic music redirects emotional vectors, redoubling effect through incongruent emotional tone, under discussion here is music that fails to have an emotional impact.[36] This lack of such effect is due to primary dislocation between sound (music) and image (game on screen), meaning that the effect of emotional congruence between the two is minimal and the lack of momentary dynamic matching retains a sense of uninvolved parallel, where the player's emotional reaction to gameplay is not directed or enhanced by the music. It seems that the only way music can be unemotional is through eschewing any direct involvement with other aspects of audiovisual culture.

There is a telling contrast between the hot emotional aspects of shooting things in many video games and the cold indifference of planting destructive flowers, like mines or IEDs, which are destructive later rather than sooner in *Plants vs. Zombies*. The game portrays a relentless attack by mindless but deadly drones, while the music embodies a similar process. Musical destiny is the already known and expected, through the music's repetitive structure.[37] So, the game relies upon the indifference of musical destiny to match its steady, violent threat of action. However, while these two channels (of sound and image) may involve similar logics, they are not, strictly speaking, matching. They are two separate and parallel paths of inevitability, and their lack of integration suggests a strange, aberrant psychology in play. Disconnection aesthetically dramatizes, embodies, or perhaps even causes disconnection emotionally. This appears to be a very current cultural malaise, one of the (constant) repositioning of human psychology through technology. This aesthetic setup has distinct ramifications for perception. Sometimes understanding may be forced into a déjà vu, splitting the signal in the brain with a delay in reception and processing, particularly as a discrepancy exists between the speeds of aural and visual perception and processing.[38] The lapse could be compounded by the physical makeup of the brain as a parallel processing device, which channels impulses to different regions and works upon them simultaneously. Indeed, on occasions, brains appear able to go out of synch, dividing and confusing broad cerebral functions. Perhaps on one level, this is like the brain-dead zombies, who appear only to have lower brain functions. Such basic brain activity is dominated by the cerebellum, which governs motor activity and rhythm-oriented activity. On the other hand, the game forces the player into an arhythmic upper brain activity of thinking ahead in an advanced manner to halt the zombie attack rather than simply reacting to their immediate threat. If the game arguably embodies, physically, something of a split in the brain, this is compounded by the music's relationship to the gameplay. For the purposes of analysis, it proved extremely difficult to listen to and analyze the music while playing the game. Indeed, trying to do so underlined the schizoid processing needed to deal with both, while it was far easier to achieve one or the other alone. This seemingly split-brain aspect of the game is also homologized by the game's central depiction of social division. The game's scenario adumbrates a clear metaphor: the zombies appear to be the social underclass invading the lawns of respectable suburbia. Here, garden plants—which are a seemingly useless sign of the cultivated middle class—prove effective against the great unwashed. Thus, cultivation destroys barbarism (and, in terms of human development, agricultural planters succeeded the more primitive hunter-gatherers). The player embodies the civilized and must play through prediction and forethought, while the zombies represent the mindless masses, who live (after a fashion) from hand to mouth.

Figure 8.2 Nightime level in *Plants vs. Zombies*. Note the *Thriller* zombie

While it is not explicit, it is tempting to impute the use of a tango/habanera as the basis for the first assault on the house as in some small way ascribing a Latin or Hispanic character to this underclass invasion of civilized suburbia. Perhaps reactionary sociocultural ideas are close to the surface, but further, perhaps the game embodies a social indifference, too. This, at least partly, is an effect of the indifference of both the gameplay and its musical mechanisms. Despite the seeming remoteness of the game's representations, connections between the cartoon zombies and the real world are tangible. One zombie character was clearly based on Michael Jackson, referencing his famous *Thriller* music video, while wearing one glove and moonwalking on the spot. The estate of the recently deceased Jackson objected, and the producers replaced him with a generic disco-dancing zombie.[39] One might wonder if Jackson's video was tempting fate.

Conclusion

While much culture has such social resonances once the analyst scratches its surface, the processes of music that do not work explicitly to enhance and dovetail with the game's narrative and gameplay are less apparent. Such simple production (messy rather than heavily directed interactive music and image) potentially creates a much more complex psychology of sound–image relations.

In isomorphic terms, the game and the music are both predicated upon relentless progress, irrespective of the gamer's actions, but this inevitability is more evident in the music, which loops and is unresponsive to the events of the game. Its lack of sympathy means that it persists with the indifference of musical destiny as a reminder of the cold logic of the game's progress.

To a degree, arcade origins have been retained as aesthetic tradition by some video games. The format has been determined by arcade games' loud, brash music with its own integrity, and the technological tradition of 8-bit, with the dominance of clear, minimal textures, simple tunes, and short pieces with regular structures looped. Such music appears more mechanical, deficient of the seeming empathy of music that transforms with gameplay and new situations. In games such as *Plants vs. Zombies*, in psychological terms, such indifferent music is not anempathetic, but perhaps something even more emotionally disengaged.[40] Indifference seems particularly fitting to the relentless forward movement of zombies in *Plants vs. Zombies*. This is not the sort of immersive experience that so much expensive and meticulously composed game music aims toward, but a more complex cross-rhythm of temporal activities. This music is not crafted to make a seamless unified experience, but instead at the heart of the game is a clash of musical integrity and often repetitive gameplay. Deep inside many contemporary games, the arcade heritage remains.

Notes

All websites were accessed November 4, 2013.

1 Carl Therrien lists a variety of horror games ("sidescrolling action games," shooting galleries, first-person shooters, fighting games, text adventures, point-and-click adventure games, role-playing games, racing/vehicular combat games, and strategy games) but does not include tower defense games. Carl Therrien, "Games of Fear: A Multi-Faceted Historical Account of the Horror Genre in Video Games" in *Horror Video Games: Essays on the Fusion of Fear and Play*, ed. Bernard Perron (Jefferson, NC: McFarland, 2009), 32.

2 "*Plants vs. Zombies* was Almost Named 'Lawn of the Dead'," N4G, available online at http://n4g.com/news/1052212/plants-vs-zombies-was-almost-named-lawn-of-the-dead. It has inspired similar mobile phone games such as *Animals vs. Zombies* and *Samurai vs. Zombies*.

3 However, from a different perspective, the "pre-rendered" music forms a backing track over which the player can "solo" through, causing different sound effects through interactive gameplay.

4 Jeriaska, "Interview: The Terrifying True Story of the Plants vs. Zombies Soundtrack," *Gamasutra* (2009), available online at www.gamasutra.com/news/originals/?story=23666. For further discussion of Elfman's parodic gothic style, see K.J. Donnelly, "The Classical Film Score Forever? Music in the *Batman* Films" in *Contemporary Hollywood Cinema*, ed. Steve Neale and Murray Smith (New York: Routledge, 1998), 142–155.

5 Composer's Blog, available online at http://shigi.wordpress.com/profile/ 14.

6   Matt Schnackenberg, "PC VGChartz Game of the Year Awards 2009," *Gamrfeed*, available online at http://gamrfeed.vgchartz.com/story/6350/Pc-vgchartz-game-of-the-year-awards-2009/.

7   Shigehara made the soundtrack album available as a download, including the song *Zombies on Your Lawn*, which also had a music video using images from the game. Later, a song recording called "Wabby Wabbo," credited to neighbor Crazy Dave, was released for Christmas 2011 as a charity record for Concern Worldwide. The music video included game icons of plants, zombies, and Dave, while the press release noted that it was "the first hip-hop single ever released to feature a yodeling solo by a yeti zombie." Games Blog, *The Guardian*, available online at www.guardian.co.uk/technology/gamesblog/2011/dec/19/plants-vs-zombies-charity.

8   John Fiske, *Reading the Popular* (London: Unwin Hyman, 1989), 93.

9   For example, Desmond Ellis, "Video Arcades, Youth and Trouble," *Youth and Society* 16/1 (1984), 47–65.

10 Steven L. Kent, *The Ultimate History of Video Games: From Pong to Pokemon* (New York: Three Rivers Press, 2001), 116; Karen Collins, *Game Sound: An Introduction to the History, Theory and Practice of Video Game Music and Sound Design* (Cambridge, MA: MIT Press, 2008), 63.

11 Marsha Kinder, *Playing With Power: From Muppet Babies to Teenage Mutant Ninja Turtles* (Berkeley: University of California Press, 1991), 88.

12 Such as *Sega Rally* (Sega, 1994) and *Mortal Kombat* (Midway, 1992).

13 See the highly informative discussion of the antecedents of video game music in Neil Lerner, "The Origins of Musical Style in Video Games, 1977–1983," in *The Oxford Handbook of Film Music Studies*, ed. David Neumeyer (Oxford: Oxford University Press, 2014), 319–347. *Plants vs. Zombies'* death music derives almost directly from silent film music clichés, discussed by Lerner.

14 There is a memorable arcade sequence in the John Hughes film *Ferris Bueller's Day Off* (1986), while arcade game sounds abound in The Clash's song "Ivan Meets GI Joe" (from the album *Sandinista!* [CBS-Epic, 1980]).

15 Although technological determinism is unfashionable in this case, it is hard not to see the role of software and hardware limitations as defining.

16 The character of some of this early game music was reminiscent of cartoon music. Zach Whalen notes that "early cartoon and horror film music established certain tropes that videogames rely on today." Zach Whalen, "Play Along: An Approach to Videogame Music" *Game Studies* 4/1 (November 2004), available online at www.gamestudies.org/0401/whalen. Similarly, some children's games of this time included similar alliances of sound and image, such as *Major Morgan – The Electric Organ* in the 1980s.

17 Identifiable 1980s 8-bit video game-style music appears in the video game and the film *Scott Pilgrim vs. the World* (game Ubisoft, 2012; film Universal, 2010) and popular songs such as Ke$ha's "Tik Tok" (2010) and Nelly Furtado and Timbaland's "Do It" (2006), which controversially appeared remarkably similar to an existing chiptune recording.

18 Rod Munday, "Music in Video Games" in *Music, Sound and Multimedia: From the Live to the Virtual*, ed. Jamie Sexton (Edinburgh: Edinburgh University Press, 2007), 51.

19 Bernard Perron and Mark Wolf, "Introduction" in *The Video Game Theory Reader*, ed. Mark Wolf and Bernard Perron (London: Routledge, 2003), 8–9.

20 Roberto Dillon, *The Golden Age of Video Games: The Birth of a Multibillion Dollar Industry* (Boca Raton, FL: P.K. Peters/CRC Press, 2011).

21 Such as the LucasArts iMUSE engine.

22 Karen Collins, "An Introduction to the Participatory and Non-Linear Aspects of Video Game Audio" in *Essays on Sound and Vision*, ed. Stan Hawkins and John Richardson (Helsinki: Helsinki University Press, 2007), 263–298.

23 Mobile games "should be playable without sound," according to the Nokia guide. Collins, *Game Sound: An Introduction to the History, Theory and Practice of Video Game Music and Sound Design*, 78.

24 Although, the player's actions trigger musically derived sounds, forming something of a random "solo" performed over the top of Shigehara's musical bed, it is not easy to conceive this as a coherent piece of music.

25 Isolated instances of dance forms in cinema include Bernard Herrmann's music for *North By Northwest* (1959), where the repetitive incidental music is based on another Latin dance: the fandango, and Stanley Kubrick's use of Strauss's *Beautiful Blue Danube* waltz in *2001: A Space Odyssey* (1968).

26 Leonard Bernstein points to incongruity as one of the key aspects of humorous music. Leonard Bernstein, "Young People's Concert: Humor in Music," available online at www.leonardbernstein.com/ypc_script_humor_in_music.htm.

27 These timings are derived from a recording I made of my own playing of the PC version of the game.

28 Arnheim, "The Gestalt Theory of Expression," 308.

29 Rudolf Arnheim, "The Gestalt Theory of Expression" in *Documents of Gestalt Psychology*, ed. Mary Henle (Los Angeles: University of California Press, 1961), 308.

30 Michel Chion notes that the seeming indifference can intensify emotion. Michael Chion, *Audio-Vision: Sound on Screen*, ed. and trans. Claudia Gorbman (New York: Columbia University Press, 1994), 8.

31 Cf. Anahid Kassabian, *Ubiquitous Listening: Affect, Attention and Disturbed Subjectivity* (Berkeley, CA: University of California Press, 2013).

32 Kassabian, *Ubiquitous Listening: Affect, Attention and Disturbed Subjectivity*, 8.

33 This is utterly unlike conventional mainstream film incidental music. Indeed, it is more like avant-garde film music—or, should I say, music in avant-garde film.

34 Although, of course, there is the phenomenon of pareidolia, the human propensity to find patterns where none was constructed or intended.

35 Claudia Gorbman, *Unheard Melodies: Narrative Film Music* (London: BFI, 1987), 73.

36 Chion, *Audio-Vision: Sound on Screen*, 8.

37 Robert Fink, *Repeating Ourselves: American Minimal Music as Cultural Practice* (Berkeley, CA: University of California Press, 2005), 5.

38 While individual responses vary, auditory information is processed faster. The brain commonly activates 30–50 milliseconds earlier for sound than for image. Rob L.J. van Eijk, Armin Kohlrausch, James F. Joula, and Steven van de Par, "Audiovisual Synchrony and Temporal Order Judgments: Effects of Experimental Method and Stimulus Type" *Perception and Psychophysics* 70/6 (2008), 955.

39 "Michael Jackson removed from Plants vs. Zombies," *Bitgamer*, available online at www.bit-tech.net/news/gaming/2010/07/28/michael-jackson-removed-from-plants-vs-zomb/1.

40 Gillian Skirrow suggested that video games constitute a "paranoiac environment." Gillian Skirrow, "Hellivision: An Analysis of Video Games" in *High Theory/Low Culture: Analyzing Popular Television and Film*, ed. Colin MacCabe (New York: St. Martin's Press, 1986), 130.

Chapter 9

Music, History, and Progress in Sid Meier's *Civilization IV*

Karen M. Cook

In 2005, Firaxis Games released Sid Meier's *Civilization IV*. The fifth installment in the popular *Civilization* series, the game (hereafter *Civ IV*) earned high critical acclaim, winning 12 "Best Game" awards that year alone.[1] Like its predecessors in the series, *Civ IV* is a 4X, turn-based strategy game in which the player develops an empire over 6,000 years.[2] During the game, the player's civilization will discover new technologies, build cities, improve its land, and interact with other civilizations (see Table 9.1).[3] As the player achieves certain goals, he or she progresses through a series of historical game eras (Ancient, Classical, Medieval, Renaissance, Industrial, Modern), each of which makes available new strategies for play. The game is won when the player has dominated his or her opponents through brute force, size of empire, cultural status, diplomatic savvy, or technological achievements—in other words, by successfully becoming more "civilized" faster or better than one's rivals.

The *Civilization* series has received a great deal of academic inquiry since its inception in 1991. Kurt Squire and Shree Durga, among others, have investigated its use as a pedagogical tool in the classroom, outlining the ways in which playing this game might motivate students toward a deeper understanding of history, geography, and international relations.[4] Other scholars have aimed their attentions more at the ideologies underlying the game's design; some, perhaps most harshly Kacper Pobłocki, have criticized the *Civilization* series for its reliance on the Western/American myths of benevolent colonialism or imperialism and capitalist democracy.[5] Pobłocki asserts that the game "proves that the history of the West is the only logical development of the humankind," turning Western culture into a synonym for civilization itself.[6] Diane Carr and David Myers counter that reading, stating that there is a difference between the game's rules, in which those ideologies may very well be present, and the game's reception, or the meaning(s) that each player deciphers upon each new play.[7]

In both types of study, the features analyzed are the game's rules and options (elements of gameplay, victory strategies, types of civilization, map, or military unit, and so forth) and its visual makeup (the look and feel of the map, the appearance of the leaders and units). But, thus far, the game's aural components

Table 9.1 Civilizations in *Civ IV*

Civilization	Leader Name	Diplomacy Theme and Composer(s)
American	George Washington	"Washington," based on "Washington's Artillery Retreat"—Jeff Briggs, Mark Cromer, Michael Curran
	Franklin Roosevelt	"The Marines' Hymn"—traditional
Arab	Saladin	"Saladin"—Mark Cromer
Aztec	Montezuma	"Tenochtitlan Revealed"—Unknown
Chinese	Qin Shi Huang	"Huang Shi Ti," based on an "ancient folk tune"—Jeff Briggs, Michael Curran
	Mao Zedong	"The Shining Path"—Jeff Briggs, Mark Cromer
Egyptian	Hatshepsut	"Harvest of the Nile"—Unknown
English	Elizabeth I	"Fanfare-Rondeau"—Jean-Joseph Mouret
	Victoria	"Rule Britannia"—Thomas Arne
French	Louis XIV	"Harpsichord Sonata K. 380 'The Hunt'"—Domenico Scarlatti
	Napoleon Bonaparte	"La Marseillaise"—Claude Joseph Rouget de Lisle
German	Frederick the Great	"Goldberg Variation No. 4"—Johann Sebastian Bach
	Otto von Bismarck	"Symphony No. 3, Movement 2"—Ludwig van Beethoven
Greek	Alexander the Great	"Alexander"—Jeff Briggs, Roger Briggs, Mark Cromer
Inca	Huayna Capac	"Huayna Capac"—Unknown
Indian	Asoka	"Asoka"—Jeff Briggs, Mark Cromer
	Mohandas Gandhi	"Gandhi"—Unknown
Japanese	Tokugawa	Based on "Sakura Sakura"—Jeff Briggs, Michael Cromer
Malian	Mansa Musa	"Mansa Musa"—Michael Curran
Mongol	Genghis Khan	"Mongol Internationale"—Magsarshawyn Durgarshaw, Jeff Briggs
	Kublai Khan	"Mongol Internationale"—Magsarshawyn Durgarshaw, Jeff Briggs
Persian	Cyrus	"Hammurabi's Code"—Unknown
Roman	Julius Caesar	"Augustus Rises"—Unknown
Russian	Peter I	"The Volga Boatmen's Song"—Mily Balakirev
	Catherine the Great	"Catherine"—Unknown
Spanish	Isabella	"Malagueña"—Ernesto Lecuona, Mark Cromer

have received little critical attention, either in analyses of *Civ IV* or in more general studies of video game music.[8] This article investigates the music in *Civ IV* and argues three conclusions: that the aural elements, specifically the soundtracks, signify to the game player the sense of chronological motion and technological progress on which *Civ IV* is based; that this role is unique in video game music; and that, on the one hand, the soundtracks support the observation of an American hegemonic ideology underlying the game, but, on the other, they show that the player's ability to interact with cultural products reveals a distinctly postmodern framework.

Video game music is a relatively new field in which theoretical foundations and terminologies are still being developed. Karen Collins, Rod Munday, Isabella van Elferen, and Axel Stockburger, among others, have approached the subject from the theoretical perspective, helping to form vocabularies and modes of investigation that enable discussion of the uses of sound within video games.[9] Scholars have applied these different perspectives both to individual games and to broader ideas of genre.[10] *Civ IV* is a turn-based strategy game; it makes use of the same kinds of sonic elements that characterize other turn-based strategy (TBS) and real-time strategy (RTS), as well as first-person action, games. These elements can thus be inventoried using Stockburger's categories of sound objects: Speech, Effect, Zone, Interface, and Score (see Table 9.2).[11]

The first sounds the *Civ IV* player hears are from the Interface category. The theme song, "Baba Yetu," plays during game setup, and another track plays as the game loads. When the map is revealed, the player immediately hears numerous Zone sound objects: sounds that locate the player in a particular place. Birds chirp, waves crash, tree branches rustle; the terrain itself creates

Table 9.2 Stockburger's sound objects

Sound Objects	Definition	Examples in Civilization IV
Interface	Sounds heard during set-up or menu options	• Theme song: "Baba Yetu" • Music playing while game loads
Speech	Any spoken text	• Narrative by Leonard Nimoy • Phrases spoken by military units
Zone	Sounds that reflect location	• Naturalistic sounds (ocean waves, tree branches falling) • Battle sounds
Effect	Sounds that reflect an action or event	• Sounds accompanying discovering treasure, religion, etc. • Sounds of declaring war or peace
Score	Soundtracks	• Diplomacy themes • Terrain soundtrack

the sound objects unique to that particular game. As units explore the surrounding area, they discover treasure, announced by the clinking of coins, or stumble upon a barbarian, triggering guttural shouts. These types of sounds, reflecting an on-screen event or action, are part of the Effect category. More of these short auditory signals play when a religion is founded, when nations go to war or make peace, and so forth. Speech objects are heard when a selected military unit speaks a short phrase, or when narrator Leonard Nimoy reads a quote upon the discovery of a new technology. The category of interest in the present study is what Stockburger calls the Score, the background music that plays throughout the game. There are two such soundtracks: one for terrain gameplay, or action taken on the main map, and one for diplomatic discourse.

While Stockburger uses his system to categorize the different sounds in a video game according to their immediate purpose, Rod Munday asks that we look at video game music from the perspective of how it engages the player with the game.[12] In *Civ IV*, the Zone and Effect sounds, and, to a lesser extent, those of Speech, are the most important both for the creation of and the immersion of the player into a 360-degree game environment in which sounds, as much as visual stimuli, provide the player with important information. The same can be said for games similar to *Civ IV*, such as *Age of Empires III* (hereafter *AOE III*) or *Heroes of Might and Magic IV* (hereafter *Heroes IV*). The units in these games make certain sounds as they work (axe blades thunk into trees, picks clink in gold mines) or move across the map (hooves drum across tundra, skeletons clatter, wheels of cannonry creak under their weight). The units in *AOE III* speak when selected. Zone sounds reinforce the visual appearance of the map, whether waves crashing on the shore or wind rustling through forests. Of the three, only *AOE III* requires instantaneous reaction to imminent danger, using Effect sounds (the call of a military horn) to alert the player to a threat.

How does the Score in these types of games engage the player? *Civ IV*, *Heroes IV*, and *AOE III* have soundtracks that accompany gameplay on the main map. Yet, unlike, for example, *The Legend of Zelda* or *Super Mario Bros.*, the music does not change in different regions of the game world.[13] Nor do the soundtracks signal nearby danger, as in *The Legend of Zelda: Ocarina of Time*. Rather than being an active and immediate source of game information, these three soundtracks fulfill Munday's narrative function, communicating the "particular setting and narrative genre," even if there is no overarching storyline.[14]

For example, *AOE III*, also released in 2005, involves the player in the European colonization of the Americas between 1492 and 1850. This game is an RTS in which the player must immediately respond to any number of on-screen needs, signaled by the aforementioned Effect sounds. Its soundtrack, which consists of a series of newly composed tracks that loop throughout the game, pauses intermittently, thereby allowing the player to listen for cues that his or her attention might be needed elsewhere on the map. These compositions pull on musical tropes from American history (fifes and drums, or music that is reminiscent of that in Western film genres), acting as a loose reminder of historical time period. In contrast, *Heroes IV* has the player manipulate mythical units (mages, wizards, skeletons, orcs) across imaginary lands; its soundtrack consists of newly composed ambient, New Age-inspired tracks that play continuously, reinforcing this fantasy setting.

What sets the *Civilization* series, and *Civ IV* in particular, apart from these and other contemporaneous strategy games is its chronological scope. The 2K games website states that the game "offers players the chance to lead their chosen nation from the dawn of man through the space age," rewriting history ad infinitum.[15] The soundtracks in *Civ IV* therefore reflect a different narrative than other games: the entirety of human history.

The terrain soundtrack is incessant from the time it begins in *Civ IV*'s Classical era through to the end of the game, and each successive era offers a new playlist of compositions. Because *Civ IV* is a TBS, each turn could last seconds, hours, or even days. Consequently, the tracks in each playlist are randomly generated and repeat for the duration of the era. As such, the terrain soundtrack is what Karen Collins calls adaptive, non-dynamic, non-diegetic music because, while it reacts to gameplay, it is not directly affected by the player.[16] The continuous, wall-to-wall nature of the soundtrack sets *Civ IV* apart from its RTS cousins, while the use of multiple, non-overlapping playlists is unique among TBS games. Furthermore, while soundtracks in video games tend to be comprised of either newly composed music, à la *AOE III* or *Heroes IV*, or popular music such as that found in *Grand Theft Auto* or *Bioshock*, the overwhelming majority of the music in *Civ IV*'s terrain soundtrack consists of compositions from the Western art music tradition, as shown in Table 9.3.[17]

In the game's Classical era (triggered by the discovery of Iron Working or Horseback Riding), early huts upgrade to tiled buildings, and the discovery of new technologies enables the construction of armored and horsed units, all of which resemble Western European archetypes. The terrain soundtrack also begins to play for the first time. Since, up to this point, the only background sounds to be heard were the aforementioned Zone sound objects, the commencement of the terrain soundtrack is noticeable; along with the improvements to structures and units, it aurally represents the first successful milestone in cultural progress. Moreover, its presence signifies that the player's civilization has become both technologically capable of, and culturally interested in, music-making itself. But the soundtrack does not reflect the same predisposition toward Western archetypes shown in the visual elements. Since no music from this time period is extant, the game designers have composed four new pieces for this era's soundtrack. Each is fairly lengthy, lasting several minutes. Some are based loosely around a pentatonic scale while others are more familiarly tonal. All feature a variety of percussion

Table 9.3 Terrain soundtrack

Composer	Track Title	Game Era
J. Briggs/R. Briggs/ M. Cromer	Ancient Soundtrack 1 (clapping, marimba, grunts, wooden flute)	*Classical*
J. Briggs/R. Briggs/ M. Cromer	Ancient Soundtrack 2 ("native" men's vocals, marimba, percussion)	*Classical*
J. Briggs/R. Briggs/ M. Cromer	Ancient Soundtrack 3 (drums, rattles, horn/shofar, wooden flute)	*Classical*
J. Briggs/R. Briggs/ M. Cromer	Ancient Soundtrack 4 (wooden flute, percussion, marimba)	*Classical*
Chant	*Deus Judex Justus*	*Medieval*
Chant	*Laudate*	*Medieval*
Chant	*Regem cui omnia vivunt*	*Medieval*
Anonymous	*La Gamba*	*Medieval*
Anonymous	*Ay Santa Maria*	*Medieval*
Johannes Ockeghem	*Intemerata*	*Medieval*
Johannes Ockeghem	*Missa pro defunctis:* Kyrie	*Medieval*
Francisco de la Torre	*La Spagna:* Danza alta	*Medieval*
Josquin Des Prez	*El Grillo*	*Medieval*
Antoine Brumel	*Missa Et ecce terrae motus:* Gloria	*Medieval*
Jheronimus Vinders	*O Mors Inevitabilis*	*Medieval*
Diego Ortiz	*Recercada terzera*	*Medieval*
Giovanni Pierluigi da Palestrina	*Missa Papae Marcelli:* Gloria, Credo	*Medieval*
John Sheppard	*Media Vita*	*Medieval*
Orlando de Lassus	*Alma Redemptoris Mater*	*Medieval*
Michael Praetorius	"Ballet"	*Medieval*
Michael Praetorius	"Bransle"	*Medieval*
Michael Praetorius	"Volte"	*Medieval*
Gregorio Allegri	*Miserere*	*Medieval*
Johann Sebastian Bach	*Movements from the Cello Suites* Nos. 1 & 4	*Renaissance*
Johann Sebastian Bach	*Movements from the Brandenburg Concertos*	*Renaissance*
Johann Sebastian Bach	*Violin Concerto in A Minor,* III. Allegro assai	*Renaissance*
Johann Sebastian Bach	*Movements from the Concerto for Two Violins*	*Renaissance*
Wolfgang Amadeus Mozart	*Serenade No. 10 in B-flat Major – "Gran Partita",* III. Adagio	*Renaissance*

Table 9.3 continued

Composer	Track Title	Game Era
Wolfgang Amadeus Mozart	*Piano Concerto No. 20 in D Minor*, II. Romance	*Renaissance*
Wolfgang Amadeus Mozart	*Symphony No. 41 in C – "Jupiter"*, II. Andante Cantabile	*Renaissance*
Ludwig van Beethoven	*Movements from Symphonies Nos. 1 & 8*	*Renaissance*
Ludwig van Beethoven	*Romance No. 1 for Violin and Orchestra*	*Renaissance*
Ludwig van Beethoven	*Movements from Symphonies Nos. 5 & 6*	*Industrial*
Johannes Brahms	*Movements from the Hungarian Dances*	*Industrial*
Johannes Brahms	*Symphony No. 3 in F Major*, II. Andante; III. Poco Allegretto	*Industrial*
Camille Saint-Saëns	*Cello Concerto No. 1*, II. Allegretto con motto	*Industrial*
Nikolai Rimsky-Korsakov	*Scheherazade*, III. The Young Prince and the Young Princess	*Industrial*
Antonín Dvořák	*Movements from the Slavonic Dances*	*Industrial*
Antonín Dvořák	*Symphony No. 9 in E Minor, "From the New World"*, II. Largo	*Industrial*
Antonín Dvořák	*Suite in A Major, "American"*, I. Andantecon moto	*Industrial*
John Adams	*Christian Zeal and Activity*	*Modern*
John Adams	*Common Tones in Simple Time*	*Modern*
John Adams	*Grand Pianola Music*, Part IA & Part IB	*Modern*
John Adams	*Movements from Shaker Loops*	*Modern*
John Adams	*Movements from Harmonielehre*	*Modern*
John Adams	*The Chairman Dances: Foxtrot for Orchestra*	*Modern*
John Adams	*Two Fanfares*, Tromba Lontana	*Modern*
John Adams	*Nixon in China*: "The People are the Heroes Now"	*Modern*
John Adams	*Violin Concerto*, II. Chaconne: "Body through which the Dream Flows"	*Modern*

instruments, from deep, low drums to clicking sticks, rattles, and hand claps. Wooden flutes and marimbas are heard in three of the four compositions and, in one instance, a horn or shofar-like instrument blasts. Human voices also play a role in two of the tracks. In one, there are wordless grunts and laughs, but in the other, two men sing a call-and-response melody, that eventually merges into harmony. Altogether, these four tracks draw on stereotypical sound-images of pan-African, Native American, or Aboriginal music, despite their contemporary North American origins.

The game's Medieval era (generated by the discovery of Theology, which founds Christianity as a game religion), introduces the pre-composed selections from the Western art music tradition. For the most part, the implied game chronology aligns with the time period in which each composition was written, but in this and the subsequent era, there is a good bit of anachronism at play. The Medieval era includes diverse tracks ranging from chant to *a cappella* vocal pieces to seventeenth-century secular music played by recorders or viols. The game's Renaissance era features a more uniform selection of works by later composers Bach, Beethoven, and Mozart. Here, despite the wide variety of compositions written by these three composers, only stringed chamber ensembles and longer orchestral pieces played on modern instruments are heard.

The Industrial Revolution occurred in the eighteenth and nineteenth centuries; the music of *Civ IV*'s Industrial era is more closely aligned with this time frame, featuring works by Beethoven, Saint-Saëns, Rimsky-Korsakov, Brahms, and Dvořák. Again, despite the fact that opera, art song, and chamber music reigned alongside orchestral music during this time period, and each of the featured composers wrote pieces in all of these genres, the soundtrack for this portion of the game contains only longer, louder compositions played by a large symphony orchestra. Lastly, the Modern era jumps almost 100 years later, using movements from nine compositions by contemporary American minimalist composer John Adams. While these works all use modern orchestral instruments, their dynamic range and ensemble size are more varied than in prior eras, and human voices are briefly heard for the first time since the Medieval game era. The repetition of rhythms, the static tonal harmonies, and the relatively quieter mood of the minimalist music in the Modern era are all drastically different from the music that came before it, perhaps signifying both the very technologies that the game values and the kind of empty, vast landscape of outer space that the rush to build a colonizing spaceship (one of the victory conditions) implies—or the emptiness created within players upon finishing play and returning to reality outside the computer screen.

Unlike other video games, *Civ IV* makes use of a second soundtrack—the compositions that play during diplomatic discourse. When engaging in diplomacy with another civilization, the terrain soundtrack stops and a theme unique to that civilization's leader plays in the background (see Table 9.1 for the full list).[18] Some of these themes are recognizable: "Rule Britannia," which plays for Queen Victoria, or "La Marseillaise" for Napoleon. Others use a traditional song as their basis, such as "Sakura Sakura" for Emperor Tokugawa of Japan. But the themes for almost half the represented civilizations were composed specifically for this game.[19] Dr. Jeffrey Briggs, the President and CEO of Firaxis Games and composer of several tracks from this and earlier versions of the game, says:

> Each leader gets his own music and where possible, it is based upon a traditional tune associated with the culture or nation the leader represents. Of course in many cases, there simply is not a well-known tune to represent a culture, so we make it up.[20]

Regardless of whether each theme was newly created or borrowed from a particular culture, the musical directors have created three arrangements of it; over the course of the game, the different versions signify that leader's progress. Briggs continues:

> We wanted the music for each leader to reflect how developed his culture is at the current time in the game. So, we created three different versions of each leader piece (early, middle, and late), to represent the selected culture's current progress. The more advanced the culture (in science, industry, and the arts), the more developed the arrangements of the leader's music . . . Early in the game these tunes are presented in primitive fashion, but later they become more sophisticated until by the late game modern, sometimes orchestral or marching band renditions are used. So, the diplomacy music represents not only the culture being portrayed, but also the historical era the leader's culture is in currently.[21]

A clear example of this evolution is heard in "The Marines' Hymn," the theme for U.S. President Franklin Delano Roosevelt. At first, the melody is presented slowly on a low wooden instrument, with loud drums punctuating the texture and a constant rattling or clicking in the background. In its second orchestration, though, the theme is played by a sprightly fife and snare drum, imitating Revolutionary War-era America, while a full military ensemble reminiscent of the United States Army Band plays the last version. Bach's "Goldberg Variation No. 4," which represents Frederick of Prussia, shows a similar development. At first, an oboe-like instrument plays the melody slowly over plucked strings. The strings are then superseded by brass and wind instruments, while the third version uses a full string orchestra.

In comparison, the theme for Tokugawa of Japan, "Sakura Sakura," begins with a variety of percussion instruments, including low drums, finger cymbals, and wood blocks, over which a stringed instrument plays the melody. The second version adds a flute to the melodic line. But the last version fleshes out the melody, which is now played polyphonically on a harp-like instrument and immediately accompanied by multiple winds. Saladin of Arabia's theme, newly composed for the game, begins with a wooden flute playing a modal melody over a plucked accompaniment. The second version is the same melody, now played by an oboe-like instrument against several plucked strings and the rattle of percussion, while the third version adds both a wind instrument and a bowed violin over the top of the plucked strings and a now-expanded complement of percussion.

The player perceives progress very clearly in gameplay. The discovery of new technologies triggers each successive game era and allows for new religions, systems of government, economic civics, cultural buildings, and military units. The player also sees progress visually: cities and terrain improvements update their appearances to reflect the current era, while each new military or religious unit is dressed in somewhat period-appropriate attire. Players can observe both their own progress and that of their rivals. Scouting the map reveals whether another civilization has upgraded to new terrain improvements or units, while the score bar on the right-hand side of the screen and routine textual updates inform the player of the amount of technological or cultural clout each civilization currently has. Like the visual and ludic elements, the soundtracks update over the course of the game. By updating to a new playlist with each new game era, the terrain soundtrack demonstrates the player's success in attaining game goals as well as the forward progress through game time. The diplomacy themes also upgrade with specific game eras, the second arrangement playing during the Medieval and Renaissance and the third during the Industrial and Modern periods. Regardless of the progress of rival civilizations, the soundtracks reflect only the cultural and technological development of the player's civilization. The musical narrative of *Civ IV* is thus uniquely tailored to the pace of each individual game; as a result, the soundtracks reinforce the player's immersion into the game by creating a player-centric sound world and alert the player to the passage of time, both in and out of the game.

The diplomacy themes, as per Briggs above, are intended to signify historical progress by becoming modernized, "more sophisticated" versions of themselves. Reviewing these themes, the main differences between the initial and later iterations are an increase in volume, faster tempi, and the inclusion of more contemporary instruments, especially as part of larger symphony orchestras or military marching bands. Yet, the oldest of the diplomacy themes were composed in the eighteenth century, the most recent being written specifically for the game. This already makes them modern, in a sense, and at least for the Western themes, their original compositions included these "sophisticated" features.

This observation clarifies that the variations for each theme were constructed in reverse—they were not, in actuality, made more sophisticated, but arranged to sound older, or, in Briggs's words, more "primitive." In addition to showing each civilization's game progress, then, they also signify the game's starting place in antiquity, as does the terrain soundtrack in the Classical era. With regard to the latter, Briggs says:

> In the early stages of the game, there is very little music in the "soundtrack" (music that plays while you are playing on the main map) and what is there reflects our idea of what stone age or very early music might have sounded like (lots of log drums, wood flutes, and other percussion sounds—even grunts and vocalizations of various sorts), but of course seen through the eyes (and ears) of modern day composers. When "Music" is discovered and researched by the player, he begins hearing great music from history—medieval, renaissance, classical, romantic, modern, and so on, as time goes by. You'll hear works from luminaries like Palestrina, Bach, Beethoven, Vivaldi [sic], as well as pieces from the celebrated living composer John Adams.[22]

Briggs's "early stages of the game," in which either naturalistic sounds or "stone age" music are heard, correlate to the Ancient and Classical eras. The four newly composed tracks that comprise the Classical era soundtrack were designed to imitate potential prehistoric musical conditions. The instruments, including the "grunts and vocalizations," were deliberately chosen to reflect the purported technological abilities (or lack thereof) of people in this time period. Antiquity is thus signified through the use of pre-technological instruments and, in some cases, pre- or non-lingual vocal signals.

The "early" diplomacy theme arrangements are used in these two game eras. Accordingly, the characteristics found in the Classical era terrain soundtrack are also found in those compositions: thin or sparse textures, slower tempi, and fewer and quieter instruments, especially traditional or non-Western ones such as wooden flutes, sitars, horns or shofars, modal plucked strings, and drones. There is also a much greater emphasis on percussion, especially low or hollow drums, finger cymbals, gongs, and rattles.

As the game progresses through the subsequent game eras, the number of composers in each era dwindles (from 16 in the Medieval to one in the Modern), as does the number of compositions (from 20 in the Medieval to nine in the Modern). The average length of each piece also grows from two or three minutes to well over five minutes over the course of the game. The diplomacy themes all also develop in similar ways, their instrumentation growing louder, larger, and more "modernized." This, to the game designers, is progress: cultural advancement through the continual homogenization of music.

But it is a particular kind of progress. Briggs's statements above reveal that there is a definite dichotomy between the music of the Classical era—the new compositions created by the game designers to reflect their ideas of prehistorical traditions—and all of the "great music from history" that follows subsequently. This "great music" has been chosen specifically and solely from the Western art music tradition. Regardless of which civilization the player has chosen to operate, the terrain soundtrack is always the same; the aural representation of progress is thus only ever that of Western progress. The evolution of diplomacy themes also reinforces that narrative. Whether a preexisting folk song, a Western composition, or a newly composed anthem, the theme progresses according to (presumed) Western standards of modernization, growing louder, more fully textured, and more rhythmically or polyphonically intricate.

Conversely, the music of the Classical era and the retroactively designed early versions of the diplomacy themes rely completely on stereotypes of non-Western or pre-Western music. Instruments made of wood, an abundance of percussion, and musical sounds made with the human body (hand claps as well as the aforementioned "grunts and vocalizations") are featured in the terrain soundtrack, signifying the presumably lower level of technological innovation that "stone age" peoples would have had. The diplomacy themes feature some specific instruments traditional in particular cultures, such as the sitar for the Indian civilizations, but the newly composed themes rely on general stereotypes of non-Western music revolving around percussion and modal melodic patterns. The early arrangements of all diplomacy themes, Western or not, also use the same stereotypes: Western themes are slowed down, made more modal or percussive, played with earlier or wooden instruments, and so forth.

It is important to recognize that the characteristics that are supposed to signify this early period are universal in their genericness, in that neither those tropes at work in the Classical era soundtrack nor the earliest diplomacy themes are unique to any of the cultures available for gameplay, nor are they drawn from any one specific real-world culture. The soundtracks in the game thus equate Western(ized) music with cultural advancement, leaving stereotypes of non-Western music to represent only prehistoric sound and actual non-Western music out of the narrative of the game entirely. They also demonstrate that certain types of Western art music—the symphony orchestra or, to a slightly lesser extent, the military marching band—are considered to be the teleological pinnacle of musical civilization, ignoring developments in popular and non-art music and even in vocal art music. As Lawrence Levine discusses, this concept of "highbrow" culture, represented musically by the symphonic hall, the opera house, and to a certain extent the works of John Philip Sousa, developed in the late nineteenth-century United States.[23] The soundtracks thus narrate a particularly American concept of elitist culture: they begin by introducing "great music from [Western] history" (thereby ousting the prehistoric music of the Classical era), adapt using technological developments in Western instrumentation, and culminate in the minimalist, almost futuristic, music of John Adams.

This reading of the soundtracks thus supports Pobłocki's opinion of *Civilization* as a game encoded with Western imperialist and cultural ideologies, which he believes could be internalized by the player on a subconscious level. However, as David Myers has shown, once players of the *Civilization* series have become familiar with the game's rules and elements, they do not correlate those variables to their real-world counterparts.[24] Diane Carr builds on Myers's work, stating:

> It is not difficult to find examples of Western texts that feature cultural or political bias. Yet it is one thing to identify such patterns within the structure of a text—and another to conclude that this is what that text means to its audience.[25]

In other words, players experience *Civ IV* in many different ways and their interpretations can and will differ not only between players, but also between a single player's experiences. Western ideologies being a fundamental part of the game's rules does not necessitate that the player will either take umbrage with them or internalize them, if indeed he or she is even aware of them.

Carr and Myers use as an example the barbarians that are also at the heart of Myers's study. In the *Civilization* series, barbarians are nomadic military units that can attack others and steal cities but cannot grow their own civilizations. Myers notices that *Civilization* players focus on the ludic significance of these units, ignoring their possibly troubling or patronizing representation of extinct world cultures. Carr uses that observation in support of her own reading of *Civilization*, in which she states that "as soon as play enters the equation, the assertion that barbarians, for instance, necessarily mean anything specific begins to disintegrate—not least because a player loading a new game can simply choose to omit barbarians from the scenario."[26]

Just as a player can choose to play a game of *Civ IV* with no barbarians, so too can he or she choose to manipulate the sound objects in the game. The player can adjust the volume of, or even mute, any or all of the sound objects in the game. If desired, the player can then substitute his or her own musical accompaniment. In fact, that has been a popular topic on fan forums for the game; players debate the relative merits of the compositions in the soundtrack and discuss what kinds of music they prefer instead.[27] The soundtracks therefore both complement and undermine Pobłocki's interpretation, since while they point to the centrality of Western culture in the game, they can also be completely ignored by the player. Pobłocki believes the game draws too deeply on modernist ideas of civilization, yet the ability of each player to reject the soundtracks and substitute his or her own individualized canon is a fundamentally postmodern concept that destabilizes the primacy of Western culture in *Civ IV*.

It is also important to recognize that designers make musical choices for their games based on a number of important factors, only some of which have to do with maintaining narrative consistency. Soren Johnson, lead designer for *Civ IV*, recently discussed his rationale for some of those decisions on his game design journal.[28] One of the prime motivators or rewards for using preexisting music was cost of production; funding an entirely new score (and likely licensing current popular music) would have been extremely expensive, while using music from the Western art tradition was much less so. He based the musical selections largely on his own tastes, aiming to choose pieces that complemented each other in terms of dynamic range, timbre, style, and so forth. The aforementioned anachronism between the Medieval and Renaissance game eras and its representative soundtracks was, he says, due to his own personal desire to highlight Bach, Beethoven, and Mozart, while, at the same time, reflective of his own lack of knowledge of earlier musics. From this interview, it is clear that immersion into the sound world of the game was a priority; it was important that the music in each era be stylistically, dynamically, and instrumentally similar in order to maintain a sense of continuity and to enhance the player's immersive interaction with *Civ IV*. But, again, Johnson and the other game designers encoded into the game the ability for players to reject his musical preferences and insert their own sounds, or even silence. In that light, Pobłocki's fear that the game player will, by default, internalize Western ideologies is largely unfounded, at least with regard to *Civ IV*'s aural components.

As I have shown, the game designers signify progress in *Civ IV* through specific ludic, visual, and aural cues. The use of different playlists for each game era, and the multiple arrangements of diplomatic themes, indicate to the player his or her current level in the game and act as a reminder of the passage of time both inside and outside the game. This particular use of musical soundtracks is unique among video games. But the soundtracks reveal that cultural and technological modernization is based on a Western worldview—more specifically, a North American worldview—despite its wide release.[29] The music is, in all circumstances, completely Western, whether by origin or creative license. The approach of the game designers to the soundtracks discloses their assumption that they and the game's players will interpret aural signifiers in the same fashion, recognizing the tropes chosen to connote the adjectives "early," "primitive," "traditional," and/or "non-Western," as well as the equation of progress with Western art music. This reading of the soundtracks supports scholarly criticism of the Western imperialist, colonial, and culturally hegemonic ideologies embedded in the *Civilization* series. Yet, the soundtracks were chosen not just to support a particular narrative, but also to promote the game player's immersion into the game world. In that vein, the fact that the soundtracks, and indeed all sounds, can be completely removed from the game without changing the player's ability to successfully play it highlights a postmodern approach to culture in which the player is given control both over the game itself and how he or she chooses to interact with it. Perhaps, in this way, the game offers the player not only the opportunity to rewrite history, but to (re)write the present as well.

Notes

All websites were accessed November 4, 2013.

1 Available online at www.2kgames.com/civ4/awards.htm.
2 4X is an abbreviation for the words "explore, expand, exploit, exterminate," and refers to strategy games such as *Civilization* in which the player is in charge of developing an empire. Alan Emrich coined the term in a 1993 review of the game *Master of Orion*. Turn-based strategy (TBS) games allow the player to take action only during his or her turn, and rival civilizations during theirs; this is opposed to real-time strategy (RTS) games, in which all players may act simultaneously.
3 In *Civ IV*, game players have the option of competing against computer-generated opponents (single player), or against players via the Internet (multiplayer). This article only discusses single-player games.
4 See Kurt Squire, "Video Games in Education," *International Journal of Intelligent Simulations and Gaming* 2 (2003), 49–62; Kurt Squire and Shree Durga, "Productive Gaming: The Case for Historiographic Play," in *The Handbook of Research on Effective Electronic Gaming*, ed. Richard E. Ferdig (Hershey, PA: Information Science Reference, 2009), 1124–1141.
5 Kacpar Pobłocki, "Becoming-State: The Bio-Cultural Imperialism of Sid Meier's Civilization," *Focaal—European Journal of Anthropology* 39 (2002), 163–177. See also Ted Friedman, "Civilization and its Discontents: Simulation, Subjectivity, and Space," in *On a Silver Platter: CD-ROMs and the Promises of a New Technology*, ed. Greg M. Smith (New York: New York University Press, 1999), 132–150; and Matthew Kapell, "Civilization and its Discontents: American Monomythic Structure as Historical Simulacrum," *Popular Culture Review* 13/2 (Summer, 2002), 129–136.
6 Pobłocki, "Becoming-State: The Bio-Cultural Imperialism of Sid Meier's Civilization," 168.
7 Diane Carr, "The Trouble with Civilization," in *Videogame/Text/Player/Play*, ed. Tanya Krzywinska and Barry Atkins (Manchester: Manchester University Press, 2007), 222–236; David Myers, "Bombs, Barbarians, And Backstories: Meaning-Making Within Sid Meier's Civilization," in *Civilization Storie Virtuali, Fantasie Reali*, Videoludica, Game Culture series, ed. Matteo Bittanti (Milan: Costa and Nolan, 2005), available online at www.loyno.edu/~dmyers/F99%20classes/Myers_BombsBarbarians_DRAFT.rtf.
8 An unpublished exception is the recent reading by Kyle Roderick of the soundtrack as an interpretation of music history. See Kyle Roderick, "Mass Historia: Rewriting (Music) History in *Civilization IV*," Ludomusicology Ludo2013 Easter Conference (Liverpool, UK), unpublished conference paper.
9 Karen Collins, "An Introduction to the Participatory and Non-Linear Aspects of Video Games Audio," in *Essays on Sound and Vision*, ed. Stan Hawkins and John Richardson (Helsinki: Helsinki University Press, 2007), 263–298; Karen Collins, *Game Sound: An Introduction to the History, Theory, and Practice of Video Game Music and Sound Design* (Cambridge, MA: MIT Press, 2008); Karen Collins, "Grand Theft Auto? Popular Music and Intellectual Property in Video Games," *Music and the Moving Image* 1 (2008), 423–441; Isabella van Elferen, "¡Un Forastero! Issues of Virtuality and Diegesis in Videogame Music," *Music and the Moving Image* 4/2 (2011), 30–39; Rod Munday, "Music in Video games," in *Music, Sound and Multimedia: From the Live to the Virtual*, ed. Jamie Sexton (Edinburgh: Edinburgh University Press, 2007), 51–67; Axel Stockburger, "The Game Environment from an Auditive Perspective," in *Level Up: Proceedings from DiGRA* (2003), available online at www.audiogames.net/pics/upload/gameenvironment.htm.

10 See William Gibbons, "Wrap Your Troubles in Dreams: Popular Music, Narrative, and Dystopia in Bioshock," *Game Studies: The International Journal of Computer Game Research* 11/3 (December 2011), available online at http://gamestudies.org/1103/articles/gibbons; Kristine Jørgensen, "Left in the Dark: Playing Computer Games with the Sound Turned Off," in *From Pac-Man to Pop Music: Interactive Audio in Games and New Media*, ed. Karen Collins (Burlington, VT: Ashgate, 2008), 163–176; Kiri Miller, "Jacking the Dial: Radio, Race, and Place in *Grand Theft Auto*," *Ethnomusicology* 51/3 (Fall 2007), 402–438; Zach Whalen, "Play Along: An Approach to Video Game Music," *Game Studies: The International Journal of Computer Game Research* 4/1 (November 2004), available online at www.gamestudies.org/0401/whalen/; Zach Whalen, "Case Study: Film Music vs. Video Game Music: The Case of *Silent Hill*," in *Music, Sound and Multimedia: From the Live to the Virtual*, ed. Jamie Sexton (Edinburgh: Edinburgh University Press, 2007), 68–81.

11 Stockburger, "The Game Environment from an Auditive Perspective," 5.

12 Rod Munday, "Music in Video games," in *Music, Sound and Multimedia: From the Live to the Virtual*, ed. Jamie Sexton (Edinburgh: Edinburgh University Press, 2007), 51–67.

13 It does, however, change depending on the level of magnification of the map. The further out a player zooms, the quieter the music gets, until the moment in which the map becomes the sphere of Earth as seen from space and the only sound is of wind. Zooming in, on the other hand, increases the volume of the terrain soundtrack. At the closest level of magnification, the terrain soundtrack disappears and the diplomatic theme for the leader of the player's civilization plays in its place, further reinforcing the cultural identity of the player's empire.

14 Munday, "Music in Video games," 62.

15 Available online at www.2kgames.com/civ4/complete/.

16 Collins, "An Introduction to the Participatory and Non-Linear Aspects of Video Games Audio," 263–298

17 Steven Poole, *Trigger Happy: The Inner Life of Videogames* (London: Fourth Estate, 2000); Kiri Miller, *Playing Along: Digital Games, YouTube, and Virtual Performance* (New York: Oxford University Press, 2012); see also Miller, "Jacking the Dial: Radio, Race, and Place in *Grand Theft Auto*," 402–438; Whalen, "Play Along: An Approach to Video Game Music"; and Gibbons, "Wrap Your Troubles in Dreams: Popular Music, Narrative, and Dystopia in Bioshock."

18 Note that while the preexisting compositions for the terrain soundtrack are all actual recordings, the Classical era tracks and diplomacy soundtrack appear to be entirely MIDI-generated. Many of the diplomacy themes and other sounds from the game can be heard at www.2kgames.com/civ4/home.htm – Media – Music.

19 According to the official *Civ IV* soundtrack, the theme for Qin Shih Huang is based on a Chinese folk tune, but no name is given. Composing credit for the theme is given to Jeff Briggs and Mark Cromer, lead audio designer for the game, available online at http://vgmdb.net/album/3207.

20 Jeffrey Briggs, "Music," *Sid Meier's Civilization IV* (2005), available online at www.2kgames.com/civ4/home.htm – Media – Music.

21 Briggs, "Music."

22 Briggs, "Music."

23 Lawrence W. Levine, *Highbrow/Lowbrow: The Emergence of Cultural Hierarchy in America* (Cambridge, MA: Harvard University Press, 1988).

24 Myers, "Bombs, Barbarians, And Backstories: Meaning-Making Within Sid Meier's Civilization."

25 Carr, "The Trouble with Civilization," 232.

26 Carr, "The Trouble with Civilization," 230.

27 As one example, see the forum discussion at http://forums.civfanatics.com/showthread.php?t=130740.
28 Soren Johnson, "Choosing the Soundtrack for Civ 4," *Designer Notes: Soren Johnson's Game Design Journal* (October 29, 2012), available online at www.designer-notes.com/?p=449.
29 While full sales information is not available, the game was released in North America, Europe, and Australia in 2005.

Chapter 10

"The Place I'll Return to Someday"

Musical Nostalgia in *Final Fantasy IX*

Jessica Kizzire

Most of us have experienced the feeling of nostalgia at some point in our lives; an image, smell, or sound took us back to fond memories of childhood, home, or some other past event we recalled with pleasure. Nostalgia's conflation of past and present experience in a single moment can revive intense emotions, making it a powerful motivator.[1] Not surprisingly, many industries recognize the profitability inherent in the nostalgic response, leading them to capitalize on nostalgia as a prime marketing tool.[2] This practice is not uncommon in the video game industry, which simultaneously works to attract new audiences and to allow longtime fans to revisit the games of their youth through downloadable emulators. In some instances, game designers strive to merge old and new elements in the same game, as in Square's *Final Fantasy IX* (2000), which unites technical innovation with elements designed to trigger a nostalgic response in players.

The nostalgic response results from the complex interaction of present experience and past memory, coexisting in the same temporal moment. Although the idea of nostalgia has roots in the seventeenth-century medical profession as a severe form of homesickness, today it has taken on a broader set of meanings, expanding to include things and places we have neither experienced nor seen.[3] Regardless of whether the nostalgic past embodies lived memory or antiquarian fantasy, it necessarily idealizes the past; both types of nostalgic experience are equally imagined.[4] Industry has become adept at playing on the imaginative powers of consumers, utilizing what literary scholar Aaron Santesso calls "standardized nostalgic rhetoric" to "create an appealing vision of time."[5] A present stimulus containing nostalgic rhetoric invokes an idealized past (personal or cultural), thus creating a nostalgic experience in the consumer.

As a part of one of the most recognizable and longest-running video game franchises to date, *Final Fantasy* games possess the unique ability to create a sense of nostalgia for games more than two decades old. The original game, *Final Fantasy*, was released in 1987 for the Nintendo Entertainment System. Its creator, Hironobu Sakaguchi, intended to leave the field of video game programming, making this his final (and only) fantasy-based game—hence the title. However, the enthusiastic reception of the game in Japan, and later the United States, spawned a series of games and films spanning five generations of home consoles and more than 25 years (see Table 10.1).[6] When creating *Final Fantasy IX*, designers decided that the game's aesthetic goal should be a nostalgic return to the early games of the blockbuster series. In order to accomplish this goal, they used nostalgic rhetoric to draw on both lived memory and antiquarian fantasy. Series-specific cues, meant to appeal to the lived memory of existing fans, and signifiers of an idealized historical past, intended to appeal to antiquarian fantasy, pervade the visual, narrative, and auditory elements of the game.

The Nintendo-era games of the series were stylistically quite different from their PlayStation successors, and they served as a touchstone for *Final Fantasy IX*'s nostalgic rhetoric. The early games appeared on the Nintendo Entertainment System (NES) and the Super Nintendo Entertainment System (SNES)—8-bit and 16-bit machines, respectively. At that time, console technology was still in its youth, and both the NES and SNES were constrained by technical limitations; sound capabilities restricted both the available instrument sounds and the number of voices that could sound simultaneously, while limitations on graphics resulted in two-dimensional pixilated characters and environments (see Figure 10.1).[7] True to the series' title, the games featured fantasy-oriented plots, many involving the collection of mystical crystals to restore balance and avoid world-ending catastrophe.

In 1997, Square Soft, the parent production company of the *Final Fantasy* series, altered the technological and narrative direction of future games by

Table 10.1 Original release dates for the main games of the *Final Fantasy* series in Japan and North America

Game Title	Japanese Release Date	North American Release Date	Game Console
Final Fantasy	1987	1990	Nintendo Entertainment System
Final Fantasy II	1988	Not released	Nintendo Entertainment System
Final Fantasy III	1990	Not released	Nintendo Entertainment System
Final Fantasy IV	1991	1991	Super Nintendo Entertainment System
Final Fantasy V	1992	Not released	Super Nintendo Entertainment System
Final Fantasy VI	1994	1994	Super Nintendo Entertainment System
Final Fantasy VII	1997	1997	PlayStation 1
Final Fantasy VIII	1999	1999	PlayStation 1
Final Fantasy IX	2000	2000	PlayStation 1
Final Fantasy X	2001	2001	PlayStation 2
Final Fantasy XI	2002	2003	Windows (PC)
Final Fantasy XII	2006	2006	PlayStation 2
Final Fantasy XIII	2009	2010	PlayStation 3
Final Fantasy XIV	2010	2010	Windows (PC)

Figure 10.1 Screenshot, *Final Fantasy IV* (SNES)

breaking its tie with Nintendo and producing games exclusively for Sony's next-generation console, the PlayStation (1994).[8] With the dramatically increased technological capabilities of the PlayStation, game designers sought to update the series, replacing traditional fantasy scenarios with science fiction-influenced plots. For the first time, characters could move within a simulated three-dimensional environment. In addition, designers modernized the verbal language used within the game world through the incorporation of adult language and a less formal linguistic tone.[9] *Final Fantasy VII* (1997) was the first game to employ these changes, which *Final Fantasy VIII* (1999) took to even greater extremes; the hyperrealistic style of *Final Fantasy VIII* featured some of the most lifelike character graphics that had ever been achieved on a home console. This push for realism and complexity brought many new fans to the series (*Final Fantasy VII* sold 6 million copies worldwide in 1997 alone, for example), but also alienated fans who had grown up with the high-fantasy games that formed the series' roots.[10]

Nintendo-era fans' sense of alienation created fertile ground for the production of a nostalgic product meant to lure them back to the series. Santesso argues that modernization and technological advancement are often "particular spur[s] to nostalgic reflection,"[11] and the changes to the series brought about through technological innovation and the shift to science fiction themes elicited comparison with the high-fantasy NES and SNES games. This act of comparison created the foundation of nostalgic experience,[12] and its production laid the necessary groundwork for an olive branch that would merge old and new in a single game: *Final Fantasy IX*.[13] Designers carefully balanced progressive technology and a complex narrative with recognizable elements from earlier games; for example, *Final Fantasy IX* updates the black mage, a familiar icon from the early games, by giving him a deeply philosophical and human character (see Figure 10.2, which offers an update of the black mage depicted in Figure 10.1).

This reimagining of the Nintendo-era games' beloved character types, cartoonish design styles, and gameplay systems forms a significant portion of the nostalgic rhetoric in the game, which draws on series-specific cues to appeal to fans' sense of nostalgia. As another example, *Final Fantasy IX* employs a fairly simple combat system that hearkens back to the early games —a significant departure from the complex systems developed in *Final Fantasy VII* and *Final Fantasy VIII*. In this class system style of gameplay, characters have a specific job class (warrior, mage, etc.) that limits the abilities they can learn or the special skills they can use. The first five games of the

Figure 10.2 Black Mage Vivi Ornitier, *Final Fantasy IX*

Final Fantasy series relied on some form of this system, resulting in the close association of specific character models with particular job classes. *Final Fantasy VI–VIII* abandoned the class system for more versatile combat systems; its return in *Final Fantasy IX*, along with the associated character models, was another obvious vehicle for recreating the experience of playing the earlier games.

Still other prominent elicitors of nostalgia are the return of fantasy elements to the environments and the overall design style of the game. *Final Fantasy IX* reduces the number of technologically advanced elements within the game world, returning to common symbols of the fantasy genre, including princesses, knights, and castles.[14] In addition, the slightly cartoonish quality of the character designs stands in strong contrast to the hyperrealistic graphics of *Final Fantasy VIII* (see Figure 10.3). The cartoonish designs are also reminiscent of the two-dimensional characters from the NES and SNES eras of the series. Critic Andrew Vestal summarizes the atmosphere of the game succinctly: "Nearly every element of *Final Fantasy IX* seems designed to trigger a nostalgic response in series fans."[15]

"The Place I'll Return to Someday"

The nostalgic rhetoric that pervades the visual, interactive, and narrative aspects of *Final Fantasy IX* extends quite clearly to the musical soundtrack as well; like his colleagues, composer Nobuo Uematsu draws simultaneously on series-specific cues and signifiers of an idealized historical past. Through allusion and quotation, Uematsu incorporates nostalgic musical themes from Nintendo-era games that are immediately recognizable to series' fans. For example, the "prelude," the "chocobo" theme, and the "moogle" theme appear in nearly every game of the series and are regarded as classics in the *Final Fantasy* repertoire. [16] He also manipulates players' nostalgic responses through musical signifiers of an idealized past. In an interview with *Weekly Famitsu*, a Japanese

a) Squall Leonhart, lead male role *Final Fantasy VIII*   b) Zidane Tribal, lead male role *Final Fantasy IX*

Figure 10.3 Character design comparison, *Final Fantasy VIII* and *Final Fantasy IX*

video game magazine, Uematsu described his source of inspiration for these signifiers:

> This time the theme for me was [European] medieval music . . . So I was given a break and went to Europe. Looking at old castles in Germany and so on. And so I was thinking of getting the elements of medieval music this time. If I made all the tracks medieval-style, it would be unbalanced, so, no, not all the pieces are in that mode, but, for example, in the opening demo track, it has that feeling.[17]

From this interview, it is clear that Uematsu closely links medieval-style music with the imagery of old castles and a romanticized past. In actuality, Baroque and Renaissance styles heavily influence the soundtrack, rather than medieval musical styles as Uematsu claims.[18] Regardless of the accuracy of his terminology, what is most significant is that Uematsu intentionally mixes a variety of Renaissance and Baroque styles to create the musical nostalgic rhetoric of the game.

On *Gamefaqs*—an online repository of game walkthroughs, cheat codes, reviews, forums, and other game-related information written by gamers—comments by user "Psycho Penguin" recounting his first experiences of the game illustrate the efficacy of Uematsu's stylistic choices:

> At first glance, the game seemed perfect. I had not really enjoyed *Final Fantasy VIII* too much, especially once I had beaten it. So, I expected *Final Fantasy IX* to be a lot better than *Final Fantasy VIII*. And from the moment I turned the game on, I knew it was going to be better.[19]

Psycho Penguin's response immediately raises a question: what could evoke such a strong reaction before actual gameplay had even begun? In the case of *Final Fantasy IX*, the visual and aural combination presented in the game's introductory video has been crafted to trigger a nostalgic response in players. Regardless of prior experiences with the series, the cartoonish quality of the design style emphasizes associations with childhood and fairy tales, rather than evoking an adult science fiction atmosphere. For gamers familiar with the series, this design style has the potential to raise a *Final Fantasy*-specific sense of nostalgia, while gamers new to the series may experience a nostalgic response in relation to their own childhood memories of fantasy-oriented stories.

While the visual content of the introductory video and subsequent title screen plays strongly on the nostalgia of lived memory, the music that accompanies these scenes primarily appeals to nostalgia that idealizes the distant past. This musical accompaniment, a piece titled "The Place I'll Return to Someday," enters before any images are shown, making the musical establishment of the environment the first sensory experience of the intended game world. By drawing on musical signifiers of the Western Renaissance tradition, Uematsu creates the perception of a Renaissance-like environment. Imagination and cultural coding from popular media drive the construction of this perception, effectively evoking a past that is necessarily unknowable for both composer and listener.[20] This invocation of a distant idealized past also defines the impending game world in contrast to the musical world created for its predecessor, *Final Fantasy VIII*. To players familiar with the franchise's previous games, the music immediately informs them that this game will not be like its futuristic predecessors, but will provide an experience that pays homage to the early games of the series.

The instrumentation and texture of "The Place I'll Return to Someday" firmly contribute to the signification of an idealized Renaissance past; Uematsu creates a transparent texture, orchestrating "The Place I'll Return to Someday" with a simple recorder trio. For most players, the hollow sound of the recorder will be something reserved for quasi-historical movie scenes of medieval minstrels or something heard in the context of a medieval or Renaissance fair. Open spacing between the individual lines contributes to the hollow sound, and the texture recalls the independent lines and contrapuntal textures of Renaissance polyphony.[21] The tendency for one or more parts to cadence late fundamentally shapes the perception of counterpoint; for example, delayed cadences occur in the alto and bass parts in m. 8 and in the alto part in m. 16 (see Example 10.1).[22] Modern popular music genres typically lack this type of contrapuntal activity, so these staggered cadences reinforce the generically Renaissance quality of the piece.

The treble-bass polarity the counterpoint creates implies some form of Renaissance dance, and, stylistically, "The Place I'll Return to Someday" strongly resembles a sixteenth-century pavan.[23] The slow duple meter and two repeated metrically regular phrases are indicative of its dance form (see Figure 10.4). The pavan was also typically accompanied by a perpetual half-quarter-quarter-note drum rhythm. In "The Place I'll Return to Someday," this rhythmic pattern becomes a quarter-eighth-eighth pattern. Although there is no percussion in this piece, the rhythm frequently appears in the supportive bass recorder part (see mm. 5–7 in Example 10.2). In addition, the homophonic style of "The Place I'll Return to Someday" bears similarities to ensemble settings from sixteenth-century France. Although the A section has relatively

Example 10.1 Delayed cadencing in "The Place I'll Return to Someday"

independent parts, they do not carry equal importance as would be expected in a true polyphonic arrangement; a clear melody remains in the descant throughout the piece. Associations with French ensemble settings of the pavan become still more evident in the presentation of the B section. Aside from brief elements of syncopation and decorative figuration in the descant, all three parts of the trio participate in an essentially homophonic phrase (see Example 10.3).

Throughout the piece, Uematsu uses these and other signifiers as nostalgic rhetoric, presenting uncommon instruments and compositional techniques to depict an idealized Renaissance past. Like the hollow sound of the recorder and the delayed cadences, the modal nature of the melodic line carries culturally coded meanings that identify it with a medieval or Renaissance past. Modality, especially in conjunction with the style of counterpoint found in "The Place I'll Return to Someday," rarely occurs in contemporary popular music. Its presence strikingly contrasts with modern culture, eliciting the comparison of past and present central to nostalgic experience.

A		B	
a	a′	b	b
m. 1	m. 9	m. 17	m. 25

Figure 10.4 Phrase structure, "The Place I'll Return to Someday"

Example 10.2 "The Place I'll Return to Someday," mm. 1–8

Example 10.3 "The Place I'll Return to Someday," B Section, mm. 17–24

Other Occurrences: "A Transient Past" and "Ipsen's Heritage"

As the first sensory experience of *Final Fantasy IX*, "The Place I'll Return to Someday" immediately sets the tone for the game world and establishes the nostalgic rhetoric used throughout the remainder of the game. As is typical in the *Final Fantasy* games, musical elements from one part of the game will return in another capacity, usually modified in some form. The melody of "The Place I'll Return to Someday" returns several times throughout the game, each time reinforcing the nostalgic rhetoric players experience in the introductory sequence. The most notable recurrences of "The Place I'll Return to Someday" occur in "A Transient Past" and "Ipsen's Heritage." The Renaissance qualities of these two transformations of "The Place I'll Return to Someday" not only appeal to an idealized past, but do so in conjunction with nostalgic events that occur diegetically.

"A Transient Past," for example, uses the melody of "The Place I'll Return to Someday" to create an association between a distant historical past and an ancient society within the game world. At this point in the game, the characters are in an ancient edifice, filled with lost technology; "A Transient Past" plays while the characters receive an account of the history of a lost civilization.[24] The addition of an eight-measure chant-like phrase extends the existing melody, which is now performed by synthesized voices, rather than the introduction's recorder trio. This new chant element highlights the modality of the original tune and emphasizes associations with early church music of the Western musical tradition. Inserted before each section of the original binary form of "The Place I'll Return to Someday," its texture and location resemble the alternatim style used in the organum of the early Christian church (see Figure 10.5). The chant is sung by all three voices, with the alto, tenor, and bass performing in octaves (see Example 10.4). This chant section also gives the impression of being unmeasured because all eighth notes receive equal emphasis, negating any clear sense of pulse. The unmeasured, modal, and unison nature of this chant-like element draws close parallels with the plainchant portion of the alternatim style.[25]

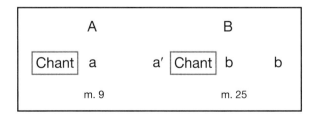

Figure 10.5 Insertion of chant element in "A Transient Past"

Example 10.4 "A Transient Past," chant element, mm. 1–8

This chant phrase gives way to "The Place I'll Return to Someday" melody A, presented as a metrically regular, polyphonic verse in contrast to the unison chant (see Example 10.5). The contrapuntal textures of the original recorder trio are simplified, with all voices presenting the melody in a predominantly homorhythmic texture. The alto performs the melody in its original form from the recorder trio, while the tenor moves in strict parallel motion with the alto, a feature that once again emphasizes the modal nature of the piece. The bass doubles the alto melody at the octave in a simplified form, resting during sixteenth-note decorative motion, such as that found in m. 10.

Only in the final four measures of the A section does the homorhythmic texture break down into independent melodic and rhythmic ideas (see Example 10.6). The alto continues with the expected melodic material from "The Place I'll Return to Someday," while the bass moves in contrary motion (m. 21) or reflects the general intent of the alto (mm. 22–23). Most striking is the abrupt change in rhythmic values that occurs in the tenor as it shifts to a steady quarter-note pulse. The sudden rhythmic augmentation of the tenor is audible, and this shift foreshadows the treatment of the tenor in the B section.

In keeping with alternatim style, the chant element returns (in this case, the chant is a direct repetition of mm. 1–8) before the presentation of the second verse: the B section of "The Place I'll Return to Someday." Once again, the texture of the original recorder trio is modified, with the homophonic texture of the original reversing to contrapuntal activity (see Example 10.7). The alto continues to present the melody as it appears in "The Place I'll

Example 10.5 "A Transient Past," mm. 9–16

Example 10.6 "A Transient Past," mm. 18–24

Example 10.7 "A Transient Past," mm. 33–40

Return to Someday," doubled by the bass in octaves. As foreshadowed in the final four measures of section A, the tenor moves at a slower pace than the alto and bass, sustaining tones with longer durational values and a strongly independent melodic line. This texture further references the polyphony of the early Christian church, since it is reminiscent of the early use of the tenor *cantus firmus* in that musical tradition.

The music of "The Place I'll Return to Someday" returns yet again in "Ipsen's Heritage," another example of the association between Renaissance-based musical elements and an archaic and long-lost past.[26] Ipsen's Castle, where players hear "Ipsen's Heritage," is an ancient, abandoned castle containing mystical weapons and necessary quest medallions (a common feature of NES- and SNES-era games). Like "A Transient Past," "Ipsen's Heritage" combines nostalgic rhetoric of an idealized past (via the music) with a nostalgic diegetic environment.

"Ipsen's Heritage" combines several of the musical signifiers previously heard in other iterations of "The Place I'll Return to Someday." In "Ipsen's Heritage," Uematsu layers the hollow recorder of "The Place I'll Return to Someday" with vocal cues from "A Transient Past" in one of the most complicated treatments of the melody in the game. "Ipsen's Heritage" fully realizes the contrapuntal activity implied in "The Place I'll Return to Someday," with clear contrapuntal relationships between the recorder duo and strongly independent and equally important melodic relationships between the duet and the voices. The A section melody is performed in hocket, a contrapuntal technique in which two parts alternate between sound and silence to construct a unified melodic idea, with the descant and alto recorders sounding their respective portions of the melody an octave apart (see Example 10.8). The B section is then treated as a canon at the octave, with the descant recorder leading (see Example 10.9). The vocal part recites the *Dies irae* beneath the recorder duet, moving in a restricted range and doubled at the octave, creating a very low drone effect. One unique feature of "Ipsen's Heritage" is the addition of percussion instruments, yet even this addition reinforces the established sense of historical nostalgia: the tambourine participates in a perpetual quarter-eighth-eighth-note pattern throughout the piece—the same percussion rhythm characteristic of the pavan found in "The Place I'll Return to Someday."

Conclusion

The nostalgic rhetoric of the *Final Fantasy IX* soundtrack goes beyond the Renaissance-inspired "The Place I'll Return to Someday," and its variations "A Transient Past" and "Ipsen's Heritage." Often hearkening back to Western music's Baroque period in their search for signifiers of the past, several pieces prominently feature the harpsichord as a solo instrument. In addition, these Baroque-influenced pieces often display a sense of perpetual motion characteristic of the period. To maintain a balanced soundtrack overall, Uematsu uses a variety of styles, contrasting tracks that utilize nostalgic rhetoric with tracks featuring more contemporary characteristics; however, Renaissance- and Baroque-influenced pieces dominate throughout. This juxtaposition of

Example 10.8 "Ipsen's Heritage," A section, mm. 1–10

Example 10.9 "Ipsen's Heritage," B section, mm. 19–34

past and present styles within the overall soundtrack bears the hallmark comparison of nostalgic experience, further contributing to the nostalgic rhetoric of the game.

Uematsu's musical rhetoric fundamentally shapes the nostalgic experience that the designers of *Final Fantasy IX* sought to attain. Since its days as a malady of the imagination, nostalgia and music have been closely associated; nostalgia scholar Svetlana Boym calls music the "permanent accompaniment of nostalgia."[27] Nonetheless, musical signifiers alone could not create an effective nostalgic product. The success of *Final Fantasy IX* depended on its combination of aural, visual, and narrative nostalgic rhetoric—a fact clear to Uematsu, who observed, "What we are looking to create is not the perfect musical composition but a superb video game as a whole."[28]

The legacy of *Final Fantasy IX* continues to influence games both within and outside of the franchise. The game was meant to be an epic return to the glory days of the series' youth, and this stylistic decision turned the game into a historical monument within the series. It was not only the last *Final Fantasy* installment released for the PlayStation, but it also possessed the last soundtrack composed solely by Nobuo Uematsu. Since its release, console-based *Final Fantasy* installments have continued to straddle the line between old and new, often alternating between science fiction- and fantasy-based narratives, but never again engaging with nostalgic rhetoric in the same way.[29] With the continued rereleasing of PlayStation and Nintendo-era games of the series as downloadable packages (a trend common to other franchises as well), the market for nostalgia remains alive and well, continuing to bring our past into our present.

Notes

All websites were accessed November 4, 2013.

1 Linda Hutcheon, "Irony, Nostalgia, and the Postmodern," in *Methods for the Study of Literature as Cultural Memory*, ed. Raymond Vervliet and Annemarie Estor (Amsterdam: Rodopi, 2000), 199.
2 Janelle L. Wilson, *Nostalgia: Sanctuary of Meaning* (Cranbury: Rosemount Publishing & Printing Corp., 2005), 158.
3 Sociologist Fred Davis offers a thorough discussion of the medical roots of nostalgia in seventeenth-century Swiss physician Johannes Hofer's dissertation. Fred Davis, *Yearning for Yesterday: A Sociology of Nostalgia* (New York: The Free Press, 1979), especially Chapter 1. Later scholars, such as Aaron Santesso, have expanded the definition of nostalgia well beyond its original pathological meaning: "Nostalgia today is no longer simply a synonym for homesickness: we can be 'nostalgic' for hula hoops and ancient Greece; we can be 'nostalgic' for homes we never had and states we never experienced." Aaron Santesso, *A Careful Longing: The Poetics and Problems of Nostalgia* (Cranbury, NJ: Rosemount Publishing & Printing Corp., 2006), 14.
4 "It is the very pastness of the past, its inaccessibility, that likely accounts for a large part of nostalgia's power—for both conservatives and radicals alike. This is rarely the past as actually experienced, of course; it is the past as imagined, as idealized through memory and desire." Hutcheon, "Irony, Nostalgia, and the Postmodern," 195. I use lived memory to mean personally experienced past, while antiquarian fantasy encompasses a past that is unable to be experienced, such as nostalgia for ancient Rome.
5 Santesso, *A Careful Longing: The Poetics and Problems of Nostalgia*, 187.
6 Steven L. Kent, *The Ultimate History of Video Games: From Pong to Pokémon and Beyond—The Story Behind the Craze that Touched our Lives and Changed the World* (California: Prima Publishing, 2001), 540–541. Only the main games of the series are included in Table 10.1; it does not include spin-off or sequel games. The numbering system is based on the Japanese titles, rather than the North American releases. *Final Fantasy II*, *Final Fantasy III*, and *Final Fantasy V* were not originally released in North America, but have since been rereleased in nostalgia-oriented packages such as *Final Fantasy Chronicles* for PlayStation and PSP consoles.
7 For a detailed discussion of the sound capabilities on 8- and 16-bit console systems, see Chapters 2 and 3 in Karen Collins, *Game Sound: An Introduction to the History, Theory, and Practice of Video Game Music and Sound Design*, (Cambridge, MA: MIT Press, 2008).
8 Kent, *The Ultimate History of Video Games: From Pong to Pokémon and Beyond—The Story Behind the Craze that Touched our Lives and Changed the World*, 542.
9 These changes, particularly the change in linguistic tone, are evident in the American translations of the games and may or may not be reflected in the original Japanese.
10 Kent, *The Ultimate History of Video Games: From Pong to Pokémon and Beyond—The Story Behind the Craze that Touched our Lives and Changed the World*, 543. These sentiments are reflected in comments by gamers reviewing *Final Fantasy IX* on online repositories such as *Gamefaqs*. Reviewer "Denouement" remarks:

"Not to say that *Final Fantasy VII* and *Final Fantasy VIII* were bad—each was a well-executed combination of old and new material—but the trend of these new elements seemed to point to future installments becoming more generic and more bland. Fortunately, *Final Fantasy IX* halts this so-called progress and revives many of the elements from earlier titles in the series, particularly the successful Super Nintendo releases." Denouement, "Let Me Take You Back in Time, Rewind to '89," *Gamefaqs*, available online at www.gamefaqs.com/ps/197338-final-fantasy-ix/reviews/review-55734. This quote has been edited for minor typographical errors.

11   "Many of the nostalgic poems of the eighteenth century can be seen as a general response to the modernizing world; advances in industrial technology . . . were a particular spur to nostalgic reflection." Santesso, *A Careful Longing: The Poetics and Problems of Nostalgia*, 17.

12   "The ability to feel nostalgia for events in our past has less (although clearly something) to do with how recent or distant these events are than with the way they contrast—or, more accurately, the way we *make* them contrast—with the events, moods, and dispositions of our present circumstances." Davis, *Yearning for Yesterday: A Sociology of Nostalgia*, 10–11.

13   "*Final Fantasy IX* was supposed to be the bridge between the old and the new. It was advertised as a pre-*FFVII* style of *Final Fantasy*—something that would please old-school gamers while still maintaining Square's reputation as one of the chief blockbuster-makers in the industry." Erin Bell, "Final Fantasy IX," *GameCritics*, available online at www.gamecritics.com/review/ff9/main.php.

14   Player reviews on *Gamefaqs*, such as that offered by user "Halron2," have made note of the return of fantasy elements to the environment of *Final Fantasy IX*: "The setting of the game recovers the more classic fantasy feeling of older games in the series. Not only because there are less hi-tech elements in the game, but also for the return of emblematic symbols of this tradition, like kings, queens, princesses, castles and so on, that were absent from the last two games." Halron2, "Now, Can Anyone Tell Me What is a Qu?," *Gamefaqs*, available online at www.gamefaqs.com/ps/197338-final-fantasy-ix/reviews/review-37603.

15   Andrew Vestal, "Final Fantasy IX Review," *GameSpot*, available online at www.gamespot.com/ps/rpg/finalfantasy9/review.html.

16   A chocobo is an ostrich-sized bird used for transportation around the game world. When riding a chocobo, players avoid random battle encounters and increase travel speed. These creatures first appeared in *Final Fantasy II*. A moogle is a white mole-like creature with pink, bat-like wings. They have a characteristic red pom-pom on an antenna at the tops of their heads. Moogles first appeared in *Final Fantasy III* and function in several capacities throughout the series. These characters are unique creations for the *Final Fantasy* series, and, like their musical accompaniments, they have become hallmarks of the series. The melodic content remains the same across various games, but the title and style of these themes varies.

17   Sachi Coxon, "Nobuo Uematsu Interview," *RPGamer*, available online at www.rpgamer.com/new/Q3-2000/070800b.html. This interview was originally with Japanese video game magazine *Weekly Famitsu*, but was translated by *RPGamer* for English-speaking audiences.

18   The inaccuracy of Uematsu's statement is most likely a result of his lack of formal musical training. He taught himself to play keyboard and guitar at the age of 12, aspiring to be like his idol, Elton John. Following college and participation in several amateur bands, Uematsu turned his attention to composition, eventually gaining a full-time position with Square. Chris Greening "Nobuo Uematsu," *Square Enix Music Online*, available online at www.squareenixmusic.com/composers/Uematsu/biography.shtml.

19 Psycho Penguin, "Legendary. That's What I Expected. Oh So Close. That's What I Got.," *GameSpot*, available online at www. gamespot.com/ps/197338-final-fantasy-ix/reviews/review-17506.

20 For a discussion of culturally coded musical cues in film music, see Claudia Gorbman, *Unheard Melodies* (Bloomington: Indiana University Press, 1987).

21 The independence of each part gives the impression of a horizontal conception of individual lines as melodic entities, rather than a vertical conception of harmonic progressions. Jessie Ann Owens describes this lack of compositional verticality as one of the fundamental elements of the Renaissance compositional process: "There is no single 'compositional process' in music of this period, but there are certain overriding principles and approaches that in turn reveal basic attitudes about the construction of music and the relationship among the voices. The most fundamental is the fact that the composers of vocal music did not use scores for composing, but instead worked in separate parts or quasi-score." Owens goes on to state: "I believe that composing in separate parts reflects the basic character of the music: lines woven together to form harmonies, and not a series of sonorities. Composers heard harmonies, but did not see them arrayed in columns on the page." Jessie Ann Owens, *Composers at Work: The Craft of Musical Composition 1450–1600* (Oxford: Oxford University Press, 1997), 7.

22 "The Place I'll Return to Someday" was downloaded from David Lawrence, "Video Game Music Archive," available online at http://vgm usic.com. The transcription and instrumental designations (descant, alto, and bass recorder) are my own.

23 For more information on the pavan, see Alan Brown, "Pavan," in *Grove Dictionary of Music and Musicians Online*, ed. Deane Root, available online at www. oxfordmusiconline.com.

24 Nobuo Uematsu, *Final Fantasy IX*, downloaded from Zophar's Domain, available online at www.zophar.net/music.html. The transcription and vocal part distinctions (altus, tenor, bassus) are my own.

25 For more information on alternatim style, see Edward Higginbottom, "Alternatim" in *Grove Dictionary of Music and Musicians Online*, ed. Deane Root, available online at www.oxfordmusiconline.com.

26 Transcription, vocal, and instrumental designations are my own.

27 "The music of home, whether a rustic cantilena or a pop song, is the permanent accompaniment of nostalgia—its ineffable charm that makes the nostalgic teary-eyed and tongue-tied and often clouds critical reflection on the subject." Svetlana Boym, *The Future of Nostalgia* (New York: Basic Books, 2001), 4. For an extensive discussion of the relationship between music and nostalgia in film, see Caryl Flinn, *Strains of Utopia: Gender, Nostalgia, and Hollywood Film Music* (Princeton, NJ: Princeton University Press, 1992).

28 Christopher John Farley, "In Fantasy's Loop," *Time*, available online at www. time.com/time/innovators_v2/music/profile_uematsu.html.

29 This observation is made particularly in regards to *Final Fantasy X*, *Final Fantasy XII*, and *Final Fantasy XIII*. Even though *Final Fantasy XII* does incorporate fantasy elements into the narrative, the music does not participate in this process as it does in *Final Fantasy IX*. No other *Final Fantasy* game has employed nostalgic rhetoric so completely and effectively. These observations do not include the MMO games, *Final Fantasy XI* and *Final Fantasy XIV*.

Chapter 11

From *Parsifal* to the PlayStation
Wagner and Video Game Music

Tim Summers

Richard Wagner looms large in the history, practice, and criticism of film music, a spectral presence evident in the frequency with which his name is invoked in scholarly and casual literature on the subject. The history of Wagnerian discussion of film music is extensive, controversial, and varied;[1] however, little attention has been paid to Wagner and video game music. This chapter considers how Wagnerian musical thought, and its surrounding discourse, can be used as a way of understanding aspects of video game music. I am not concerned specifically with the representation of opera in video games here; instead, I wish to use Wagner and Wagnerism as an investigative framework for exploring game music.[2] I will address three main intersections between Wagner and game music: (1) games that are Wagnerian in musical content; (2) games that are Wagnerian in the way that the scores deploy musical material; and (3) games that show affinity with Wagnerism in other aspects of musical aesthetics. In each of these topics, attention will not only be on the particular "case study" game texts under discussion, but how the analysis of such games might inform the understanding of game music more generally.

Wagner's Music in Games

The most obvious starting point for a Wagnerian investigation of game music is a consideration of games that deploy Wagner's music in significant ways—that is, more substantially than a brief inclusion of "The Ride of the Valkyries" for comedic effect (*Full Throttle* [LucasArts, 1995]) or a citation of *Lohengrin*'s "Bridal Chorus" during a wedding (*King's Quest VI: Heir Today, Gone Tomorrow* [Sierra, 1992]).[3] Games that use Wagner's music extensively may be found in several different genres: *The Dig* (LucasArts, 1993) is a graphic adventure game, *Ring Cycle* (Maelstrom/Psygnosis, 1995) is a first-person role-playing game, and *Ring: The Legend of the Nibelungen* (Arxel Tribe/Cryo Interactive, 1998), like its sequel *Ring II: Twilight of the Gods* (Arxel Tribe/ Mindscape and Global Star, 2003), is a puzzle game. All of these games are for the PC platform.

Der Ring des Nibelungen Games

Three games have been explicitly based upon Wagner's *Ring* operas. In *Ring Cycle*, a role-playing game, the player controls Siegmund from the first-person perspective and engages in generic quest gameplay (collecting items, slaying enemies, conversing with non-playable characters) in a large open-world environment, similar to the *Might and Magic* series (New World Computing, 1986–2002) or the *Elder Scrolls* series (Bethesda, 1994–2012). The games relate to Wagner's *Ring* primarily by using the opera to furnish the gameworld with characters and a background mythology, rather than any sense of "acting out" the opera. The player's journey is accompanied by a looped playlist of MIDI orchestral versions of musical episodes from the cycle (such as the prelude to *Das Rheingold*, Loge and Wotan's descent into Nibelheim, "The Ride of the Valkyries," and so on). Despite the fact that the game's narrative bears little resemblance to the *Ring*'s, the manual includes a detailed plain-language synopsis of all four *Ring* operas, presumably to provide players with an appreciation of the intertextual dimension of the game. By importing the music and icons from the opera, *Ring Cycle* attempts to bestow a sense of significance on the otherwise unremarkable gameplay. Wagner's cultural reception is used to assert the game's own importance; the game's packaging explains that "*Ring Cycle* . . . draws from Wagner's classic opera to provide the most powerful and evocative soundtrack ever heard as part of a gaming experience." The assumed power of Wagner's music is deployed with the goal of creating an aesthetically substantial game, even if the central play activity is generically derivative.[4]

Like *Ring Cycle*, the *Ring* games, produced by Arxel Tribe, also use musical excerpts from Wagner's *Ring* to accompany the gameplay. In these games, however, rather than synthesized recreations of the score, the audio is sampled from Georg Solti's recordings of the *Ring* operas. In these games, players solve puzzles in the 3-D environment. These challenging tasks are interpolated into the opera plots—when playing as Alberich, for example, one must solve nonverbal puzzles to repair the mines and steal from the Rhinemaidens. Unlike *Ring Cycle*, the *Ring* games follow the plot of the operas, which the games set in a futuristic science fiction universe; *Ring: Legend of the Nibelungen* traces *Das Rheingold* and *Die Walküre*, while *Ring II: Twilight of the Gods* completes the cycle. The puzzles are accompanied by looped samples from the Solti recordings—the excerpts are taken from sections of the opera that vaguely relate to the plot as traced in the game (for example, Alberich's mine puzzle is accompanied by a passage from Wotan and Loge's journey to visit Alberich in *Das Rheingold*).

Even though the Arxel Tribe games adhere more specifically to the plots of the operas than *Ring Cycle*, the motivation for using Wagner's work is similar. The discrete puzzles that form the core of the *Ring* games' gameplay, like the questing in *Ring Cycle*, have little to do with the specifics of the

Wagnerian operas—the puzzles might be replicated in any other 3-D puzzle game, such as *Myst* (Cyan, 1993). In the Arxel Tribe *Ring* games and *Ring Cycle*, the Wagnerian source and the accompanying music is used as framing for the core gameplay mechanics in order to impart a sense of meaning and monumentality to the activity. Using a famous musical work of indisputable artistic merit lends an air of worthiness to what otherwise might be understood as mere window-dressing to games that would be, in other circumstances, largely unremarkable.

Not all games that include Wagner's music use it for this contextualizing purpose. While most of the games that include Wagner's music do so as part of an explicit link to the composer's operatic works, *The Dig* is fascinating because, at first glance, there is no direct connection between Wagner and the game's subject matter.

Graphic Adventure Games and *The Dig*

The Dig belongs to the category of games known as graphic adventure games, a genre that enjoyed widespread popularity during the late 1980s and early 1990s. The financial success of such games prompted producers to invest significant resources in developing game technologies for use in adventure games, spurred on by an industrial rivalry that existed between the two premier producers of graphic adventure games: LucasArts and Sierra On-Line. One of the most significant game music innovations of the 1990s, the iMUSE MIDI engine (discussed further below), was created for adventure games in this industrial context.

Graphic adventure games include gameplay components of exploration, problem-solving, item collection, player adoption of a character/role, and a motivating plot, but without significant emphasis on action (shooting, fighting, jumping, etc.).[5] The player controls a diegetic character by instructional commands. In a typical graphic adventure game interface, such as that of *Monkey Island 2: LeChuck's Revenge* (LucasArts, 1991), the player clicks on the verb word, and then on an appropriate object within the game world to command the avatar character. Adventure games that include mouse support are also known as "point-and-click" (adventure) games. Most adventure games are viewed side-on and draw upon film genres such as medieval fantasy, pirate, science fiction, etc. The adventure game is typically segmented into discrete screens/areas. Faced with puzzle challenges, players spend long periods of time in the same game state, which, in turn, prompt programmers and composers to create lengthy looped cues. *The Dig*, a "point-and-click" graphic adventure, follows human scientists as they explore a strange alien world to which they have been unexpectedly transported. In the mysterious and apparently long-abandoned environment, the humans encounter advanced quasi-magical technology integrated into the landscape. Music in *The Dig* plays nearly continuously, primarily cued as loops of music that are selected according to the player's avatar location in the game world. These cues are sometimes interrupted or changed depending on particular gameplay events.

The Dig's score is partially created from instrumental chords isolated from recordings of Wagner operas. The game's composer, Michael Z. Land, describes:

> I went through two hours of Wagner orchestral music and isolated about 300 little segments, ranging from 2 to 10 seconds, where a nicely orchestrated chord is played without too much melodic activity on top. I then took these chord snippets, adjusting their pitch as needed, and added them one measure at a time to compositions that I had performed on a MIDI keyboard.[6]

Added to this sonic mix are synthesized sound and newly recorded solo instruments.[7] Why might Land undertake such a complex and time-consuming process? It is particularly curious that he should invest such effort into the score when, if it were not for the highlighted credit to Wagner on the game's packaging, the atomized samples are not immediately identifiable as definitively Wagnerian.

One reason for this approach may be sound quality: the audio from the Wagner recordings is of greater sonic depth and orchestrational complexity than that easily achievable by basic PC sound cards, although the impression is not one of attempting to simply simulate an orchestral soundtrack: Land creates a Wagnerian soundscape made, in effect, alien through the addition of the synthesizers and solo instruments. The score forms a swirling mass of sound that oscillates between pure synthesizer tones and Wagner's orchestral textures. Wagner's prowess as an orchestrator makes his work an attractive choice for sampling, while his expansive compositional style features sustained moments of little, or repeated, melodic musical material, which facilitates easy fragmentation.

The cultural capital granted Wagner as a philosophically charged, indisputably canonic composer makes his music well-suited for a game with clear high-art aspirations of its own: the Wagnerian score was emphasized in promotional material for the game, which advertises *The Dig* as featuring an "Alluring Wagnerian musical score [that] sets the epic tone." The word "allure" resonates with Nietzsche's later anti-Wagner arguments in *The Case of Wagner*, in which the composer is characterized as a superficial and dishonest conjurer.[8] That the game describes the music this way might indicate the use of another aspect of Wagner's critical reception on the part of the game producers—the perhaps more dangerous, deceptive, and manipulative dimension of the music in question might be part and parcel of its appeal and function in relation to the beautiful, captivating, but dangerous, alien world in *The Dig*.

A rather more substantial explanation of the motivations behind Land's Wagnerian orchestral soundscape may lie in how the composer understands

this sonic medium as appropriate for the expressive aims of the score in relation to the metaphorical and metaphysical elements of the video game text.
This game is primarily character-driven; as the box blurb describes, the
scientists "must dig for answers, both on the planet's surface and deep within
themselves." Wagner's later composition was steered by the concept of making heard the Schopenhauerian "Will," the hidden undercurrent of existence,
in music. Land's use of Wagner's orchestral sound world—developed to express
the Will in the action of the operas—similarly aims to voice the psychological and dramatic undercurrent of the characters and plot in *The Dig*.
In an interview, Land repeatedly refers to how his music aims to express
notions of the "subliminal" and "psychological themes" that exist "under the
surface" of the game.[9] With this function in mind, it makes sense that Wagner
is here heard vertically, atomized in the moment, as a representation of an
existential present, rather than horizontally, alongside narrative trajectories
and leitmotif development that would be concerned with teleological progress.

Land's discussion of the score reveals his intentions. Schopenhauerian/
Wagnerian philosophy emphasizes the inherent sadness, emptiness, and futility
of life that is only alleviated by being "taken out of oneself"; redemption, a
perennial theme in Wagner, comes (according to Schopenhauer) from the
denial of the personal self's drive to continued individual existence.[10] As well
as the sentiments of interiority and excavation that apparently aim to sound
the "Will," Land's comments even come strikingly close to invoking the
Schopenhauerian/Wagnerian notion of *Wahn*, which can be described as a
sadness that proceeds from the deluded folly of existence. He says:

> I always felt that with this score I was reaching inside of myself and
> expressing what I really feel . . . I think that for me, the score expresses
> a vaguely religious feeling I have about the spirituality of life, perhaps
> the sadness of its temporariness, as well as the hope and redemption that
> comes from connecting to forces larger than oneself. For me, there's a
> certain way in which sadness and beauty come together in a particular
> feeling, and that's what I was trying to express.[11]

Land's language makes obvious how a version of Schopenhauerian thought
informs his use of Wagner in *The Dig*—from its operatic use, Wagner's sound
world is the traditional, established mode for dealing with such ideas and
sentiments, and is thus appropriate for the expression that Land seeks. A
straightforwardly Wagnerian score of the kind observed in *Ring Cycle* would
be inappropriately earthbound, and loaded with unwelcome specific ties to
the particular operatic moments from which the samples were drawn, but a
highly fragmented, alienated reincarnation of Wagner serves Land's expressive
goals perfectly. Furthermore, in using Wagner's music in this way, *The Dig*'s
metaphor of excavation is mirrored by the embedded history in the soundtrack
formed from the fragmented and buried Wagnerian samples. In the course of

The Dig, a human character dies, and is resurrected in an alien form: is Wagner likewise resurrected and reconfigured in the score?

The Dig's score changes smoothly as the player's character moves through the mysterious environment. Musical contrasts occur when the player's character moves from one location to another: a new instrument may be introduced or the texture may change with the environment. For example, the alien museum location cue uses a solo cello-like mellow-timbred synthesizer voice, which plays a melodic line with distinct arpeggio gestures, while moving to the adjacent library prompts a sonorous soundscape with sustained ringing sounds and little identifiable melodic material. In addition to its connection to location, the music also reacts to certain dramatic events. Some moments of surface drama are musically silent (such as a main character's death), while soliloquies and moments of psychological drama are musically accentuated alongside the visual action and recorded dialogue. This game seeks to use music to unite environment, narrative, philosophical ideas, and psychological undercurrents in a way that remains implicit and unspoken: instead, it is expressed auditorially.

Land sought to create a score for *The Dig* that engages with both the "surface" narrative and more "thematic" elements of the text, in the process relating the two together. Wagner's music similarly aimed to voice the dramatic and psychological undercurrents of the operatic onstage activity; in the score for *The Dig*, the Wagnerian moments are reanimated on an interactive model.

Wagnerian Musical Processes: Leitmotifs in Games

A Wagnerian Musical Interface: Loom

While *The Dig* and games based on the *Ring* may be Wagnerian in the sense that they borrow musical content from Wagner's works, other games may be understood as Wagnerian because of the motivic processes evident in the game scores. *Loom* (LucasArts, 1990), like many of the games in this chapter, is a graphic adventure game. While the player's character may manipulate objects in the "diegetic" world just as in any other adventure game hero, the player also interacts with the fictional universe through musical motifs.

In *Loom*, the playable character wields a distaff—a magical weaving tool, which acts as a kind of musically powered wand. The player assembles four-note melodic fragments that are played on the distaff by clicking pitch on the interface or pressing particular keyboard commands. It is the melodic properties of the motifs that define their identities—the rhythm with which the player selects the notes does not alter the motif's power. The melodies ("drafts," as the game terms them) are spells that then affect elements in the diegetic world. Using these spells is similar to the way that the user of *Monkey Island 2* will click on the verbs on the interface, but the spells are seen to be more powerful than the hero character's regular agency. As the players progress through the game, they learn new drafts, and a larger number of pitches become available, widening the distaff's repertoire.

In an appropriately Wagnerian fashion, the melodic fragments in *Loom* are not explicitly defined in the game,[12] but rather, in reminiscence motif style, the player observes an event, accompanied by a short motif that sounds from the ether. The player then may repeat this melody in a new context with the hope of musically prompting a similar effect. Some drafts contain word painting: the "reflection" draft is palindromic, and by similar logic, players can retrograde drafts to invoke the inverse effect (open to close, sharpen to blunt, etc.). The game creates a Wagnerian wonderland, where diegetic events find musical expression. In this construct, music can be utilized as an active agent. This power may be appropriated by players through the hero's magical musical performance.

The Dig and *Loom*, through Wagnerian aesthetics, aptly reveal the way that game music can deal with interaction and perception. *Loom* seeks to apply Wagnerian motivic policy to the interactive nature of the game. As a result of this interactive format, players come to understand and perceive the world and its effects in terms of musical fragments. In *The Dig*, Land aims for the score to reveal to the player's perception a dimension that would normally remain hidden, voicing of the Will-like undercurrent to the game's action. This topic of perception will be developed further below, but first, *Loom* prompts the consideration of a particular dimension of Wagner's association with scoring for visual media, one that is readily engaged with by musicians and critics.

Leitmotifs in Cinema and Video Games: Halo and Final Fantasy VI

One of Wagner's most obvious effects on film music has been his indissoluble association with the concept of the leitmotif. This association has permeated common musical discourse to the degree that thematic film scores are readily branded "Wagnerian," even if the film composer's motivic practice holds only superficial similarity to that of Wagner. While game scores are less routinely described as "Wagnerian," thematic processes in game music are nevertheless worth careful consideration in the context of Wagnerian criticism.

Martin O'Donnell, composer for the *Halo* first-person shooter games (Bungie/Microsoft, 2001, and sequels), has explicitly voiced his dislike for using a basic leitmotivic method for scoring games, what he describes as a "'Peter and the Wolf' approach to [game] music."[13] Aside from the problem of repetition between cues in a musical format that routinely relies on loops, O'Donnell is concerned about the banalities that simplistic thematic association can easily end up producing. O'Donnell's own composition deploys recurring melodic material in a complex fashion that is more similar to Wagnerian motif technique. O'Donnell's discussion of recurring thematic material in games echoes the famous critique of leitmotifs in film scoring by Adorno and Eisler in *Composing for the Films*. Adorno and Eisler argue that the leitmotif is unsuitable for a film score for two interrelated reasons:

1   The "limited dimension" of a film "does not permit of adequate expansion of the leitmotif."
2   Film "has no need of leitmotifs to serve as signposts." The "metaphysical significance," the symbolic signification, of the motif is lost "in the motion picture, which seeks to depict reality."[14]

Games such as *Halo*, and even game scores with more straightforward leitmotif processes such as *Final Fantasy VI* (Square, 1994), can challenge Adorno and Eisler's criticism. The total time, on average, that a player spends with any one game is significantly longer than the running time of most mainstream films, and even longer than most individual Wagner operas. A reviewer of *Ring: Legend of the Nibelungen*, for example, complained that the game required less than 10 hours to complete.[15] Games are able to include a significant duration of musical material, and game scores are often produced in the form of short clips of music that are assembled to create the cues as they sound in the game. In the chronological span and flexible assembly of musical output afforded by this context, the "musical canvas" is very much available for the "expansion of the leitmotif."

Halo's cues are made up from small segments of music that are sequenced to make up the cues. Thus, in *Halo*, to use Adorno and Eisler's words for describing Wagnerian music dramas, "the atomization of the musical element is paralleled by the heroic dimension of the composition as a whole."[16] As these small clips and longer leitmotifs are used and reused by the score throughout the extensive duration of the game, they accumulate a complexity of meaning from the diversity and multiplicity of situations and contexts in which the material is (re)used. Thus, the leitmotif gains a more expansive domain of meaning than the situations that Adorno and Eisler have in mind. Musical recurrence is not simply in the form of a specific theme that remains anchored to one signified property. Instead, in a fashion more similar to Wagnerian practice, the huge musical canvas employs musical repetition in a fluid and dynamic manner that forges links between entities and evokes recurring, evolving concepts through the music. The *Halo* games' main "Halo Theme," which takes the form of a Dorian mode faux Gregorian chant motif sung by male voices, serves to refer to an artificial world (the titular "Halo"), the overarching plot that is bound up with the Halo world, the immediate on-world location, the link between the world and the player's character, and the game's identity itself (when it is heard accompanying a menu screen). The musical recurrence creates links between the referents and imbues the music with more metaphysical capital as a creative entity than in the case of a simple theme/character relationship.

Partly because of the graphical limitations of game technology, and partly because of restrictions that proceed from regimented modes of player interaction, games frequently use musical signs for their ability to signify their referent's presence without that element being visually (or otherwise) observably present in the text (part of the effect that I have elsewhere described as "musical texturing").[17] The musical sign is therefore routinely more powerful in games than in the film situation that Adorno and Eisler describe. Even overlooking Adorno and Eisler's problematic claim that the motion picture "seeks to depict reality," the restrictive parameters of interactive gameplay and the limitations of graphical realism often mean that the constructed artificiality of the video game is foregrounded by the game text. In this context, the "metaphysical significance" of the motif is retained.

Leitmotivic scoring in games regularly uses music as a creative, rather than simply descriptive, force. Thus, musical agency can be more powerful in games than in film, because music in games often has a greater aesthetic weight than in films. To take just one example, in *Final Fantasy VI*, music plays nearly constantly throughout the game, and while it is often combined with the (admittedly quasi-musical) sound effects, its audio dominance is unchallenged—no recorded voices are heard, and the music is programmed to sound at a high volume.

Final Fantasy VI creates a referential musical vocabulary through leitmotifs that contribute to the depiction of each of the game's main characters, subsequently standing as referential symbols of those characters. A character's musical identity is introduced before it is named or described by the on-screen text (sometimes even prior to the character's on-screen appearance). Given the small size of the pixelated avatars, more than any other single element of the game text, it is the music that most distinctly provides the character with an identity. The musical identity is more concrete even than the names of the characters: while the character themes cannot be changed, the player has the opportunity to give a name to the playable characters in a screen accompanied by the character's theme, which creates the impression of music defining the character.

Since character cues accompany dramatic events that involve the character in question, a character's narrative journey is bound up with his or her musical identity. The valiant Locke, for example, has a theme that includes standard signifiers of heroism (secure major harmony, rising fourth gestures, military percussion and topic, etc.), communicating and asserting his role in the game's story. Terra's mournful theme, by contrast, mirrors the tragic life events she experiences (minor mode, slow tempo, sustained pitches, ornamented melody, bittersweet excursion to relative major). The theme for the secretive assassin-for-hire, Shadow, clearly references Ennio Morricone's music for the Sergio Leone films featuring the "Man with No Name." The music signifies the role that the character plays in the game's narrative. Classical Hollywood practice prioritizes character themes that semiotically communicate elements of the character's identity and role in the plot. *Final Fantasy VI* uses character themes in the same way, though because of the limited means of characterization, music makes a proportionally greater contribution to character identities, just as the leitmotif for the giants in Wagner's *Ring* connote the physical weightiness of the characters, even if the singers playing *Fasolt* and *Fafner* cannot capture the promise of the term "giant" corporeally.

Beyond the repetition of musical material in looped cues and the long duration of gameplay, music in games is a significant and substantial part of the text, particularly in games of the 8-bit and 16-bit eras, which had little foley sound, nearly continuous music, musical sound effects, and little or no recorded speech. Game music may make a greater contribution to the player's understanding and interpretation of the game than the same situation for the average film score, not least because of the technological limitations on the visual component of the game, the aesthetic dominance of the music, and the degree to which gamers have been taught to actively interpret game music in order to seek information and advantage in play.[18]

Games that feature music as one of the most impactful components of the text evoke another art form in which music has a similarly privileged status: opera. Wagner's operas are notable for the musical emphasis on the instrumental component of the works, particularly in the pieces written after his discovery of Schopenhauer.[19] Thus, it is appropriate that the empowered leitmotif in games should come hand in hand with a musical aesthetic that recalls the works that first expounded the metaphysical significance of the leitmotif.

While nothing suggests that the leitmotif always harbors greater metaphysical capital in games than in cinema, the examples of *Loom*, *Halo*, and *Final Fantasy VI* prompt consideration of the possibilities afforded music in video games, and how this might be conducive to significant and quasi-Wagnerian deployment of the leitmotif. This situation arises first because of the prioritization of music in the aesthetic makeup of most games, and second because the duration of play and the size of the potential musical canvas of a game provide the opportunity for a more than basic object-accompanying theme relationship. Music can serve as an important part of the player's game experience. The interactive dimension of musical metaphysics in games bears further investigation, particularly when player-directed changes in music represent a distinct component of the way that players perceive a virtual game world.

Wagner, Voodoo, and Metaphysics

The close correspondence between music, words, and on-stage action in Wagner's music dramas make the seamless musical fabric of these operas appear similar to the closely synchronized dynamic music systems sought by some game composers. The aesthetics of dynamic music systems may be fruitfully investigated through the lens of Wagnerian discourse, particularly with respect to notions of perception and interaction.

LucasArts, the company that produced *Loom* and *The Dig*, developed a music engine known as iMUSE.[20] This groundbreaking dynamic music system was first deployed in *Monkey Island 2*, a graphical adventure game. iMUSE, developed by Michael Land and Peter McConnell, uses MIDI data with programmed information in the musical score to control the parts and sequence of the music.[21] iMUSE facilitated gameplay-directed musical changes, such as adding or removing musical parts, transposition, looping, branching, and deploying transition sequences. Since MIDI does not deal with sounds directly, the transitions are seamless and sonically coherent.

The *Monkey Island* series features compelling characters and irreverent humour in a story concerning the would-be pirate Guybrush Threepwood and his archenemy, the ghost pirate LeChuck. Set on fictional Caribbean islands, the game injects a "golden age of piracy" environment with modern day elements, such as vending machines, printed T-shirts, and rubber chickens. The music of *Monkey Island 2* contributes substantially to the player's experience and understanding of the game's plot, characters, and environments. As such, it is a central part of the player's perceptual apparatus. The musical score in *Monkey Island 2* helps construct the gameworld; for example, the score features rhythms and instruments from reggae and calypso music as a way of giving geographic specificity (and exoticism) to a quasi-legendary environment. The hornpipe melodies securely reference seafaring activity. The main theme uses steel drums, wooden-timbred flutes, and percussion, but also includes anachronistic instruments prominently (electric organ, bass guitar). Such juxtapositions describe the universe of *Monkey Island*, while the andante reggae rhythms signify the jolly attitude of the game.

Musical themes in *Money Island 2* round out the depiction of characters beyond the fairly simple graphics, their musical identities making the eccentric populace all the more memorable and significant to the player.[22] LeChuck's chromatically slippery motif in low brass tones immediately encapsulates his dastardly character, so players understand the threat he poses without the need for dialogue to establish the character. Music helps to characterize secondary characters for whom there is no room for lengthy textual fleshing out, as exemplified by the drinking song theme for the alcoholic pirate Rum Roger. More than simple accompaniment, the themes are part of how the characters are perceived by the player. The leitmotifs are so central to the characters (and the player's perception of the characters) that the motifs always accompany their referent, to an almost pantomime-like extent. This link is ostentatiously demonstrated: when Threepwood is scared by a LeChuck imitator in a costume, a shrill, vibrato-heavy sounding of a fragment of LeChuck's theme is heard, only to dissolve into descending glissandi when the mistake is revealed. This moment anchors the musical narration to

Threepwood (his response) and yet utilizes more objective knowledge (the thematic statement is not "genuine").

Monkey Island 2 also shapes player understanding of the fictional environment by providing a kind of musical geography. Rather than using a single cue for each environment, the variation capabilities of iMUSE provide continuity and variation over several sub-locations. The Woodtick town location, for example, has a variety of areas accessible from the main street, which is accompanied by the main Woodtick theme. Depending on the door and sub-area the player enters, iMUSE segues into one of several variations on the Woodtick theme—without stopping the cue—at the next musical junction. The result is a rondo form of sorts, since the player has to return to the main street to access different sub-locations. These (musical) geographies are defined in terms of their character relevance: in one instance, entering a character's hotel room prompts his theme to be added to the hotel variation, even though he is absent. In another sub-location of Woodtick, an accordion part is introduced to the score if the player directs Threepwood to awaken some sleeping pirates. When they fall asleep again, the part fades out. The music thus demonstrates its close connection with, and attention to, the action in the diegetic world.

The iMUSE transitions illustrate that Woodtick's sub-areas are not separate, but a continuation of one another (even if the visual track "cuts"), creating a musical-virtual geography tied directly to Threepwood's exploration of the environment. In contrast to the musically related sub-areas of Woodtick, each of the discrete islands in the game is given a distinctly different central theme. This musical accompaniment individualizes the locations and helps the player keep track of each island's geography and inhabitants. The musical geography creates a virtual model of the game world and allows players to orient themselves in the environment. These musical techniques form yet another way in which the player perceives the game world, as geographic distance is equated with the degree of musical similarity.

Both the character and location themes make it obvious how music serves as a channel of communication for the player to perceive the game world. The Voodoo Lady's hut offers a particularly clear example. To reach this destination, Guybrush must row to the middle of a swamp, a distance of several continuous screens. MIDI elements are introduced into the musical underscore, based on the player's proximity to the hut, reaching completion when the player enters the cabin. At this point, a gamer who has played the first *Monkey Island* (LucasArts, 1990) will recognize the music as the Voodoo Lady's theme from that game. The Voodoo Lady appears to "emit" this music; her identity coalesces out of the musical elements as Threepwood approaches and disintegrates as he moves away. Thus, the player is able to sense the Voodoo Lady's presence through the aggregating musical material. (Perhaps this musical sphere of influence is one way in which the power of voodoo is embodied.) With the music linked to Guybrush's diegetic position, the score is shown to be closely dynamically reactive as part of the interactive media. Furthermore, in being anchored to Threepwood and his experience of the virtual world, the music almost seems to represent a sort of sixth sense for him, made audible and communicated to the player through music.[23]

Music synchronizes with Threepwood's actions and those of others that affect him. In doing so, it emphasizes the interactive dimension of the game, monumentalizes and dynamizes in-game events, and accentuates the player's perception of the diegetic events to which the musical material relates. The most overt of such examples are humorous, such as the Mickey-Mousing glissandi that punctuate slapstick moments, the *Indiana Jones* theme fragment that is heard when Threepwood swings from a rope, or the way the musical ensemble disintegrates in dismal disappointment when Guybrush fails at a spitting contest. Diegetic music in *Monkey Island 2* provides a sonic portal into the world, through Guybrush's ears. With music synchronized to the actions and reactions of Guybrush, players also have a sense of perceiving the world through the frame of the character. An interactive score notices the player's involvement with the text, and rewards this with reciprocal reaction. In an attempt to create a malleable universe, the sense of immersion and realism is heightened by both diegetically and non-diegetically demonstrating the repercussions of the player's actions. The link between music and diegetic universe is thus strengthened and the player is advised to interpret the cues as meaningfully relevant to the game. The seamless dynamic the iMUSE engine invites parallels with Wagner's own dynamic composition. The adaptability of iMUSE means that play does not expose the cracks (hard cuts, unmusical changes) that reveal the game's constructedness: the universe remains stable, interactive, and immersive. Dynamic music can relate the player to the diegetic world, while affirming the power of the player through its responsiveness.

In the discussion of *Monkey Island 2*, music was described as a channel of perception of the game world that runs alongside the visual (and non-musical, sonic) elements of the game. But perhaps this is not the full story. Returning to the Wagner/Schopenhauer musical nexus, a particular aspect of Kant's philosophy underpins the Wagnerian/Schopenhauerian thought. This area of Kantian thought, "transcendental idealism," is based upon the distinction between the "appearances" (visual et al.) of objects, and "things in themselves," because of the apparatus used to perceive these "things."[24] In philosopher Bryan Magee's concise explanation:

> Kant made the observation . . . that what we can apprehend or experience must necessarily depend not only on what there is to apprehend or experience but also on the apparatus we have for apprehending and experiencing . . . The sum total of everything we can conceivably apprehend in any

way at all is the sum total of what the apparatus at our disposal can do or mediate . . . total reality is comprised of a part which can be experienced by us and a part which can not [sic]. Kant's term for the part of reality that we can experience, the world of actual or possible phenomena, is simply "the phenomenal," while his expression for the part which we cannot experience is "the noumenal."[25]

Thus, as Kant writes, "all objects that are given to us can be interpreted in two ways: on the one hand, as appearances; on the other hand, as things in themselves."[26]

There is no reason to suggest that the real-world human's limit of knowledge and perception should match that of the player's interaction mode (whether through an avatar or otherwise) in the game construct. The player does not have real eyes, ears, or other perceptual apparatus in the game world, so why should real-world perceptual limits hold? While players only have two sensory channels to use when interacting with the game (audio and visual), within this perceptual frame the game may present players with information that would be inaccessible to them in the real world. Thus, players' perception of the game world's (Kantian) objects is possibly more extensive than the perception of objects in the real world. Music in *Monkey Island 2* contributes significantly to the player's perception of the game world and construct. In providing greater understanding (informational or emotional) of in-game elements—be they characters, objects, puzzles, events, environments, dramatic undercurrents, etc.—or even by adding aesthetic weight to these things (in the Kantian sense), the score extends human perceptual apparatus in a simulated way beyond the ability to perceive mere appearances. The normally noumenal is made sensual.

In this reframing, this transcendence of the everyday human, players are taken out of themselves. The musical score does not give access to the entire noumenal world, but the reframed perceptual boundaries, through the musical score, place the player in a superhuman perceptual point of view (or point of experience): the distinction between the phenomenal and the noumenal is redrawn. Even if, at a third-person viewpoint, the player is linked to a particular avatar in *Monkey Island 2*, while receiving information and knowledge assumed to be unavailable to that same avatar. Since the avatar character is a simulation, however, and any understanding that the avatar character has is actually supplied by the player, a recursive loop is formed by which unknowable information *is* knowable by the character, as filtered through the player.[27] This sixth sense role of the score is easily observed in many games. In games focalized through one character, such as the adventure game examples discussed here, the game is generally concerned with that character's particular experience of the diegetic world. Perhaps it is the combination of avatar-focalization with the player's distanced viewpoint that allows the redrawing of perceptual boundaries.

The score for *Monkey Island 2* illuminates, describes, and intensifies the world of the game (including its inhabitants, events, etc.), a heightened perception of the game universe that affords the player more power and privilege than any diegetic character. The smooth transitions of iMUSE and adaptive music systems minimize the disjunctive breaks in the perceptual fabric that might potentially disturb the seal of fictionality. Similarly, dynamic, interactive music must be immediate, lest the artificiality of the musical sense become untrustworthy, unnatural, or distanced from the diegetic goings-on to which it is closely tied. Schopenhauer, Wagner's idol, founded his thought upon Kant, and concepts such as the metaphysical Will are derived from the work of the earlier Königsberger. Wagner was familiar with Kant, and his goal in the later music dramas to represent the Will approach a similar role for music as with some of the game scores discussed here: providing access to the realm of the otherwise imperceptible. It is thus perhaps unsurprising that games sometimes adopt Wagnerian aesthetics of one kind or another.

*   *   *

In the preceding discussion, I have examined both particular instances of the use of Wagner's music in video games, and some of the discourse surrounding Wagner(ism) to instigate questions concerning music and the video game medium. The games of Wagner's *Ring* showed how music was used to provide contextual meanings to the gameplay activity through invoking the well-established touchstone of the *Ring* operas. Music, particularly from a great work by a great composer, serves as demonstration of a game's artistic credentials, as the game seeks to be understood as a genuine artwork. *The Dig*, by contrast, prompted consideration of more conceptual and philosophical ideas concerning a game score. Here, the use of Wagner's music was not an end in itself—unaltered passages of Wagner's music would be a more effective way to achieve this goal. Instead, the result of *The Dig* is music that is one degree away from direct citation, drawing on the sensual and cultural reception properties of the composer's work for expressive ends (as Land's comments reveal) in an attempt to unite different levels of the game text: the conceptual, the narrative, and the perceptual.

While *Loom*'s use of the leitmotif as part of the player's interface with a game is unusual, the game highlights the potentially privileged role that the leitmotif can adopt in the game construct. Using the criticism of the leitmotif in cinema as a starting point, a consideration of the possibilities of the leit-motif in the video game were seen to be bound up with the aesthetic position of music in the medium more generally. In particular, *Loom*, *Halo*, and *Final Fantasy VI* showed how the metaphysical properties of the motif may be exploited through the use of music as a constitutive, constructive agent, and one that can be part of the perceptual apparatus of the player. My discussion of *Monkey Island 2* further developed this connection of game music as perception, arguing that the use of music for the perception of the game is part of how the player is constructed by the game. Players are positioned as superhuman through the reframing and/or removal of real-world perceptual boundaries.

Investigating the relationship between Wagner and game music sheds new light on how players interact with, perceive, and experience games. Yet, beyond the specifics of these examples, even enacting this discussion serves a broader purpose. This chapter has sought to be a critical examination of game music using materials—such as metaphysics and aspects of Wagnerian thought—that have usually been seen as the exclusive domain of art music scholarship. The preceding text demonstrates that the criticism and appreciation of popular culture texts need not avoid conceptual frameworks forged for application to high-art music. Such activity is part of a larger project of developing a critical discourse surrounding game music, which makes the argument for game music to be appreciated in terms of an art. This is not to say that such criticism necessarily entails demands for an elite high-art status for the music under consideration, only that such concepts create a space for the appreciation and rigorous academic investigation of game music, arguing for game music's place in the artistic-academic pantheon. As we develop and encourage a critical appreciation of game music as an artistic entity, we may find that there may not be quite so much difference as we might expect between a hero that wields Nothung and one that wields a weaving tool.

Notes

All websites were accessed November 4, 2013.

1 For more on the history of Wagner and cinema, please consult Jeongwon Joe and Sander L. Gilman, eds., *Wagner and Cinema* (Bloomington: University of Indiana Press, 2010).
2 Intersections between opera and games include the well-known example of the "Draco and Maria" opera in *Final Fantasy VI* and the short film *Salome in Low Land* (dir. Christian Zagler, 2006), which provides an animated staging of Strauss's *Salome* in the style of 1980s video games.
3 "The Ride of the Valkyries" is used to accompany an army of marching toy rabbits in *Full Throttle* (LucasArts, 1995), and variations on *Lohengrin*'s "Bridal Chorus" are heard during the wedding scenes in *King's Quest VI: Heir Today, Gone Tomorrow* (Sierra, 1992).
4 William Gibbons has also observed similar cases of preexisting classical music in games that attempt to use the general cultural cachet of art music to imply similar qualities of the video game. While the cases described above are not as arbitrary as some of the situations that Gibbons describes, nevertheless, a similarity in using music to borrow elements of the reception afforded "high art." William Gibbons, "Blip, Bloop, Bach? Some Uses of Classical Music on the Nintendo Entertainment System," *Music and the Moving Image* 2/1 (2009), 40–52.
5 Ernest Adams and Andrew Rollings, *Fundamentals of Game Design* (Upper Saddle River, NJ: Prentice Hall, 2007), 619.

6   Michael Land quoted in Santiago Mendez, "Music in the Air: Exclusive Interview with Michael Land," available online at http://dig.mixnmojo.com/museum/interview_land.html.

7   *The Dig*'s credits list additional instrumental performers alongside the copyright information for the Wagner recordings utilized in the score. The instruments include "violin," "viola," "guitar," and "digeridoo" [*sic*].

8   Friedrich Nietzsche, *The Case of Wagner*, trans. Walter Kaufmann (New York: Vintage, 1967), §5 and §7.

9   Land in Mendes.

10 There is continued debate as to what extent Wagner's own rendering of "redemption" in his operas entirely concords with Schopenhauer's understanding of the same. Nevertheless, redemption is significant to both Wagner and Schopenhauer, and finds echo in Land's words in his description of *The Dig*'s score.

11 Land in Mendes.

12 The drafts are defined in the game's accompanying manual. This is similar to Hans von Wolzogen's pamphlet guides to Wagner's operas, which were written and produced for the audiences at the first Bayreuth festivals. These documents included the explicit identification and naming of the major leitmotifs in the works. A more modern analog is Rudolph Sabor's five-volume guidebook for the *Ring*, which also includes the illustration and naming of the *Ring*'s motifs. Rudolph Sabor, *Richard Wagner: Der Ring des Nibelungen Translation and Commentary* (London: Phaidon, 1997).

13 Music4games.net [Anonymous], "Interview with Halo 2 Composer Marty O'Donnell," available online at http://web.archive.org/web/20080408192713/www.music4games.net/Features_Display.aspx?id=25.

14 Theodor W. Adorno and Hanns Eisler, *Composing for the Films* (London: Athlone Press, [1947] 1994), 5.

15 IGN Staff [Anonymous], "Ring: The Legend of the Nibelungen," *IGN*, available online at http://uk.ign.com/articles/1999/07/21/ring-the-legend-of-the-nibelungen.

16 Adorno and Eisler, *Composing for the Films*, 5.

17 Tim Summers, "The Aesthetics of Video Game Music: Epic Texturing in the First-Person Shooter," *The Soundtrack* 5/1 (forthcoming).

18 See Isabella van Elferen, "¡Un Forastero! Issues of Virtuality and Diegesis in Videogame Music," *Music and the Moving Image* 4/2 (2011), 30–39.

19 See Carl Dahlhaus's chapters "The Music" and "Wagner's Musical Influence," in *Wagner Handbook*, ed. Ulrich Müller and Peter Wapnewski, trans. Alfred Clayton (London and Cambridge, MA: Harvard University Press, 1992), 297–314 and 547–562.

20 Michael Z. Land and Peter N. McConnell, "Method and Apparatus for Dynamically Composing Music and Sound Effects Using a Computer," US Patent 5,315,057, filed November 25, 1991, and issued May 24, 1994.

21 For further technical detail, see Land and McConnell, "Method and Apparatus for Dynamically Composing Music and Sound Effects Using a Computer"; Karen Collins, *Game Sound: An Introduction to the History, Theory and Practice of Video Game Music and Sound Design* (Cambridge, MA and London: MIT Press, 2008), 51–57; and Willem Strank, "The Legacy of iMuse: Interactive Music in the 1990s," in *Music and Game: Perspectives on a Popular Alliance*, ed. Peter Moormann (Wiesbaden: Springer VS, 2013), 81–92.

22 In this chapter, I discuss the original version of *Monkey Island 2*, rather than the "special edition" remake of the same title (LucasArts, 2010).

23 This sixth sense is similar to the effect that van Elferen describes as "half-diegetic music": music that is music that does not acoustically exist within the virtual

environment, but is nevertheless anchored to events and the player's actions within the gameworld. van Elferen, "¡Un Forastero! Issues of Virtuality and Diegesis in Videogame Music," 35.

24 Immanuel Kant, *Critique of Pure Reason*, trans. J.M.D. Meiklejohn (London: Bohn, 1855), 178–189.

25 Bryan Magee, *The Tristan Chord: Wagner and Philosophy* (New York: Owl Books, 2000), 152–154.

26 Immanuel Kant, *Philosophical Correspondence: 1759–99*, trans. and ed. Arnulf Zweig (Chicago and London: University of Chicago Press, 1967), 103. Also quoted, with subtly different translation, in Roger Scruton, *Kant: A Very Short Introduction* (Oxford: Oxford University Press, 2001), 55.

27 While my argument is framed in terms of knowledge, Isabella van Elferen relies upon a similar notion of recursion in her problematization of diegetic music—she describes how players who control avatars are able to hear non-diegetic music that is not supposedly audible to the in-game characters. van Elferen, "¡Un Forastero! Issues of Virtuality and Diegesis in Videogame Music," 34.

Contributors

Karen M. Cook is Assistant Professor of Music History at the Hartt School of the University of Hartford. Her primary research interests are in medieval and Renaissance music theory, notation, and performance, liturgical studies, neo-medievalism, and music in contemporary culture. She is currently working on several articles and a book on fourteenth- and fifteenth-century mensural notation and an article on the musical soundtracks in *Civilization V*.

K.J. Donnelly is Reader in Film at the University of Southampton, where he convenes the Film Studies masters program. He is author of *Occult Aesthetics: Synchronization in Sound Film* (Oxford University Press, 2013), *British Film Music and Film Musicals* (Palgrave, 2008), *The Spectre of Sound* (BFI, 2006), and *Pop Music in British Cinema* (BFI, 2001). He edited *Film Music: Critical Approaches* (Edinburgh University Press, 2001) and co-edited *Music in Science Fiction Television: Tuned to the Future* (Routledge, 2012) with Philip Hayward.

William Gibbons is Assistant Professor of Musicology at Texas Christian University. His primary areas of research interest are opera studies and music in video games. He is the author of *Building the Operatic Museum: Eighteenth-Century Opera in Fin-de-Siècle Paris* (University of Rochester Press, 2013) as well as a number of articles in journals including *Music and the Moving Image, Game Studies, Opera Quarterly*, and *19th Century Music*. He is currently at work on a monograph on classical music in video games.

Jessica Kizzire is a Ph.D. candidate in musicology at the University of Iowa. She is currently completing her dissertation on musical adaptations of Lewis Carroll's *Alice's Adventures in Wonderland* and *Through the Looking Glass*. Her research interests include the relationship between music and narrative, particularly within film, video games, and other popular media.

Neil Lerner is Professor of Music at Davidson College, where he is co-coordinator of the concentration in film and media studies. In addition to serving as Editor of the journal *American Music*, Lerner edited *Music in the*

Horror Film: Listening to Fear (Routledge, 2010), co-edited *Sounding Off: Theorizing Disability in Music* (Routledge, 2006), and is presently co-editing *The Oxford Handbook of Music and Disability Studies.*

Elizabeth Medina-Gray is a Ph.D. candidate in music theory at Yale University. She holds a B.A. in music and chemistry from Swarthmore College and M.A. and M.Phil. degrees in music theory from Yale. Her dissertation-in-progress, "Modular Structure and Function in Early 21st-Century Video Game Music," focuses on analyzing the mobile, dynamic music of recent video games. Her wider academic interests include music in modern multimedia, twentieth-century tonal music, and mathematical musical models.

Roger Moseley is Assistant Professor in the Department of Music at Cornell University; his current research reflects his interest in the combination of play, musical performance, and digital media. His publications address topics including the music of Brahms, eighteenth-century keyboard improvisation, and relationships between music and visual culture in digital games. He is currently working on a book, tentatively titled *States of Play: Music as Ludic Medium from Mozart to Nintendo.*

Steven Beverburg Reale joined the faculty of Youngstown State University in 2009 as Assistant Professor of Music after earning his Ph.D. in Music Theory at the University of Michigan. His research focuses on intersections of music and narrative and he has published and presented research on video game music, Wagner's *Ring* cycle, vocal timbre in *The Rocky Horror Picture Show*, and an application of discrete calculus used to model metric dissonance.

Rebecca Roberts holds an M.Mus. in musicology from the University of Southampton, where she focused her studies on music in video games, particularly from the survival horror genre. She now works in the games industry in PR and Marketing and commissions freelance indie game audio projects on the side.

Aya Saiki is a graduate student in musicology at Cornell University. Ranging from Haydn to Hatsune Miku, her research explores musical culture in eighteenth- and nineteenth-century London and twentieth- and twenty-first-century Japan.

Tim Summers is the Stipendiary Lecturer in Music at St. Catherine's College, Oxford. His research focuses primarily on music for new media, and he is currently writing a monograph on music in video games. As well as contributing to essay collections, he has written for *Music, Sound, and the Moving Image* on music in multimedia franchises and for *The Soundtrack* and *Act* on video game music. He is a co-founder of the "UK Ludomusicology" game music research group.

Chris Tonelli completed his doctoral work in the Critical Studies and Experimental Practices in Music program at the University of California, San Diego. After this, he was Visiting Lecturer in Contemporary Music and Culture at the New Zealand School of Music, Visiting Assistant Professor of Ethnomusicology and Popular Music Studies at Memorial University of Newfoundland, and a postdoctoral fellow with the Improvisation, Community, and Social Practice project at the University of Guelph, undertaking a multi-sited ethnography of vocal improvisation. His research interests include transnational musical exchanges in and from Japan, imitation in popular music, and theories of vocality. He has chapters forthcoming on chiptune music and improvisational soundsinging, respectively, in the volumes *The Oxford Handbook of Mobile Music Studies* (Oxford University Press) and *Intensities: The Intersensory Affect of Sound* (in progress).

Index

Note: Page numbers in *italics* indicate tables, figures, and musical examples; numbers in parentheses preceded by *n* refer to endnotes.